'The "Blue Labour" movement has [...] influential and controversial innov[...] generation. Rooted in a deep reading [...] offers a compelling critique of the Bl[...] a potential route to renewal – revisiting the past so as better to face the challenges of the future.'

– RAFAEL BEHR, Political Columnist, *The Guardian*

'Something went horribly wrong with British politics in the 1990s. The modernisers drained the meaning out of political engagement by focusing on strategy and presentation rather than substance. As a result all British political parties are now facing mortal crisis. This book on "Blue Labour" is the most thoughtful attempt yet to help devise an answer to a conundrum which no twenty-first-century politician has yet been able to solve.'

– PETER OBORNE, formerly Chief Political Commentator,
Daily Telegraph

'Anyone looking for an antidote to the stale and stultifying brand of liberalism which has dominated British political discourse for far too long will find a refreshing and thought-provoking alternative in the contributions to this timely volume.'

– MARK GARNETT, Senior Lecturer in British Politics,
Lancaster University

'*Blue Labour* ably exposes the deficiencies of neo-liberalism and offers an inviting political agenda based on a "moral economy of mutual obligations". With neo-liberalism discredited by predatory banking, and socialism by the collapse of the planned economies, the paths back to a "moral economy" are well worth exploring. They are not the property of any political party, but will be of special interest to Labour supporters trying to develop an alternative narrative to that of the free market and the centralized state.'

– ROBERT SKIDELSKY, FBA, Emeritus Professor of Political
Economy, University of Warwick

In memoriam
John Hughes (1978–2014)

Contents

Foreword   ix
Acknowledgements   xiii
Contributors   xv
Preface to the New Edition   xix

Introduction: Blue Labour and the Politics of the Common
Good   1
Adrian Pabst

PART ONE: NARRATIVE AND PROGRAMME

1.   The Good Society, Catholic Social Thought and the
     Politics of the Common Good   13
     Maurice Glasman
2.   The Blue Labour Dream   27
     John Milbank
3.   A Blue Labour Vision of the Common Good   51
     Frank Field

PART TWO: LABOUR – PARTY AND POLITICS

4.   Blue Labour: A Politics Centred on Relationships   63
     David Lammy
5.   Community Organising and Blue Labour   71
     Arnie Graf
6.   Blue Labour and the Trade Unions: Pro-Business and
     Pro-Worker   79
     Tom Watson

PART THREE: POLITICAL ECONOMY

7. The Common Good in an Age of Austerity   87
   Jon Cruddas
8. 'Civil Economy': Blue Labour's Alternative to Capitalism   97
   Adrian Pabst
9. Globalisation, Nation States and the Economics of
   Migration   121
   David Goodhart

PART FOUR: ALTERNATIVE MODERNITY – ON NATURE,
PROGRESS AND WORK

10. Nature, Science and the Politics of the Common Good   143
    Ruth Davis
11. The Problem with Progress   155
    Dave Landrum
12. Meaningful Work: A Philosophy of Work and a Politics
    of Meaningfulness   179
    Ruth Yeoman

PART FIVE: LABOUR'S RADICAL 'CONSERVATISM'

13. Labour's 'Conservative' Tradition   195
    Rowenna Davis
14. The Gentle Society: What Blue Labour Can Offer
    Conservatives   203
    Ed West

PART SIX: FAITH AND FAMILY

15. Vision, Virtue and Vocation: Notes on Blue Labour as
    a Practice of Politics   217
    Luke Bretherton
16. The Labour Family   235
    Michael Merrick

Conclusion: Blue Labour – Principles, Policy Ideas and
Prospects   253
Adrian Pabst

Postscript to the New Edition   265
Index of Key Names   271
Index of Key Subjects   273

Foreword

Rowan Williams

At the heart of our current cultural muddle lies a paradox that far too few people seem to have noticed. All sorts of intellectual disciplines, from neuroscience to literary theory, have in recent decades questioned the idea that the 'starting position' for human identity is a solitary, speechless individual who moves out from primitive isolation to negotiate cautiously with other similar creatures, and learns to use language as a tool for labelling objects that can be variously managed and utilised. This powerful myth cannot credibly survive the analysis of how language and consciousness actually work: we ought to be more than ever alert to the fact that our self-awareness is shaped by the inseparable awareness of other subjects, that projection into the life of the other is there from the start, that how others speak to us, imagine us, nurture or fail to nurture us, is not an 'extra' to our sense of who or what we are but completely woven into the very idea of being a 'self'.

Yet so much of our public rhetoric and popular imagination is still clinging to the myth. Self and other is a zero-sum game for many; it shows up in attitudes to foreigners and migrants, in the world of finance, in demands for more explicit teaching about a single dominant national history to be defined over against others. The language of human rights – an essential moment in the development of a critical and humane politics – has encouraged some to speak as though the self-evident needs I identify for myself have an intrinsic authority. We are fast losing, as many commentators have pointed out, a solid idea of public service and public good – the idea of universally shared responsibility for shared well-being, and the idea that there are some goods for human beings that are necessarily held in common and achieved by collaboration. And that is to say that we are losing the sense that there are other kinds of relationship between people than the exchange of commodities.

There is nothing new in this reading of our situation; what needs to be brought out a bit more clearly is that there is a contradiction between this powerful cultural myth and the way in which sciences and humanities alike are describing us. In other words, we need to wake up to the fact that a lot of our politics assumes various things about our humanity that are not true; that we are being actively encouraged to lead lives at odds with what we actually are, with how our minds and feelings actually work. The challenge to conventional politics at the moment is the question of what the political world might look like if it tried to work with rather than against the grain of our humanity. This collection of essays seeks to meet that challenge.

These essays do not represent a simple argument for the priority of 'community' over 'individualism'. That can too easily become another zero-sum exercise. The difficult and necessary job is to do with rethinking what we mean by an individual – not lobbying for some sort of subjection of person to collective. Can we build a realistic political platform from the vision of persons always in relation, not just 'entering into' relation? A political platform from which our dependence and indebtedness to one another and to the entire material environment we inhabit can be acknowledged in a way that lets us live within our limits and attend to one another's well-being with a measure of grace and generosity? In short, can we make politics a 'humanist' affair, in the proper and wide sense of the word that has to do both with the thick fabric of civic solidarity and with the opening up of imaginative and intellectual horizons to all citizens?

Any political agenda that reflects this 'humanism' needs to think hard about the state and its task. As several contributors stress, we cannot be content with views of the state that see it either as the sole and all-powerful provider of values and solutions or as a residual guarantor of legal stability and not much more. We need to think through what a moral state looks like: not an authority that imposes values but one that gives due weight to supporting what is already supportive, nourishing what is already nourishing, in the primary communities that make up society. Such a state will be robustly capable of challenging localism when it becomes defensive and exclusive, but not afraid of building local capacity and trusting local perception. And, as we know all too well, it is not good enough to express aspirations about this without doing what is needed for that building work. The state as 'community of communities' is a frequently quoted formula, as relevant now as it has ever been: it takes for granted that the state will be holding the ring in serious and demanding discussion about resources and plans and relative needs among the diverse communities and localities of a society. And it takes for granted that participation at local and wider levels can happen and is effective.

Again and again since the financial crisis of 2008 onwards, people have said that we cannot go 'back to normal', if 'normal' is a world dominated by the artificial manipulation of financial exchange, the massive inflation of uncontrolled credit and the assumption that a virtual economy is more important than the business of making things and maintaining public well-being. Thus far, relatively few political voices have offered a persuasive way of turning our backs on the seductions of this bizarre 'normality' in the name of what I earlier called political humanism. Now, if ever, is the time for more voices to be raised. I hope that these essays will speak effectively to those on all parts of the political map who want to see a programme that has something more to do with the real processes of human growing, maturing and flourishing. We cannot indefinitely go on planning against our own nature – not to mention the nature of what lies around us.

Acknowledgements

The idea for this book originated during a car journey from the Cotswolds to south-east London on a beautiful summer's evening in June 2010 when Paul Bickley encouraged Ian Geary to compile an essay collection on Blue Labour as a vital component for the renewal of the wider Labour movement. Ian began to assemble a group of contributors, and after a dinner at the home of John Milbank in November 2011 he invited Adrian Pabst to join him as co-editor.

In addition to Paul, many friends and colleagues have helped us with advice and encouragement, notably Maurice Glasman, Dave Landrum, John Milbank and all the other contributors to this volume: Luke Bretherton, Jon Cruddas, Rowenna Davis, Ruth Davis, Frank Field, David Goodhart, Arnie Graf, David Lammy, Michael Merrick, Tom Watson, Ed West, Rowan Williams and Ruth Yeoman. We thank them for their generosity and patience.

We are also enormously grateful to John Clarke, Andy Flannagan, Dan Leighton, Patrick Macfarlane, Jonathan Moules, James Mumford, Matthew Rhodes, Martin Robinson, Richard Robinson, Jonathan Rutherford and Nick Spencer.

Our warmest thanks go to all those who have supported the Blue Labour Midlands seminars since 2012. We received much encouragement and stimulus from the conversations and debates. A special word of gratitude to Simon Oliver of the University of Nottingham for his extraordinary efforts in hosting the seminars on campus.

Our great thanks also go to Alex Wright and his colleagues at I.B.Tauris for their enthusiastic backing and superb work in publishing this book. We owe a debt of gratitude to the School of Politics and International Relations and the Faculty of Social Sciences at the University of Kent for the award of two grants without which this collection could not have progressed to completion. In particular, we would like to place on record our appreciation to Feargal Cochrane, Richard Sakwa and Richard Whitman at Kent for their support and wise counsel.

Finally, we express gratitude and love to our wives, Susan Geary and Elena Lileeva, and our children, Joshua, Samuel and Martha Geary, and Alexander Pabst.

We immensely enjoyed working together. The regular conversations over coffee in Portcullis House were always a great source of inspiration and delight. This book has been a long time coming, and it would not have been possible without our collegiate cooperation and friendship.

We dedicate the book to Reverend Dr John Hughes who was killed in a car accident on 29 June 2014, aged 35. John was a dear friend, trusted colleague and a fine Christian socialist. His earthly life was short, but his legacy is a grace that will endure and help sustain us.

Ian Geary and Adrian Pabst

Contributors

LUKE BRETHERTON is Professor of Theological Ethics and Senior Fellow at the Kenan Institute for Ethics, Duke University. His most recent book is *Resurrecting Democracy: Faith, Citizenship, and the Politics of a Common Life* (2015).

JON CRUDDAS has been Member of Parliament for Dagenham since 2001 and for Dagenham and Rainham since 2010. In May 2012, he was appointed as Policy Review Coordinator for the Labour Party.

ROWENNA DAVIS is the Labour parliamentary candidate for Southampton Itchen in the 2015 General Election and a former Labour Councillor in Southwark. She is the author of *Tangled Up in Blue: Blue Labour and the Struggle for Labour's Soul* (2012).

RUTH DAVIS is Political Director of Greenpeace UK.

FRANK FIELD has been Member of Parliament for Birkenhead since 1979 and is a former Minister of Welfare Reform (1997–8).

IAN GEARY is an executive member of Christians on the Left and Co-Convenor of the Blue Labour Midlands Seminar. He was a Labour parliamentary candidate and has worked in public affairs.

MAURICE GLASMAN, Baron Glasman of Stoke Newington and Stamford Hill, is a Life Peer (Labour), and author of *Unnecessary Suffering: Managing Market Utopia* (1996).

DAVID GOODHART is Chairman of the Advisory Board of the think-tank Demos, and author of *The British Dream: Successes and Failures of Post-war Immigration* (2013).

ARNIE GRAF is an American community organiser. He is currently working as an independent consultant for the Industrial Areas Foundation and for the Labour Party.

DAVID LAMMY has been Member of Parliament for Tottenham since 2000 and is a former Minister for Higher Education. He is the author of *Out of the Ashes: Britain After the Riots* (2012).

DAVE LANDRUM is Director of Advocacy of the Evangelical Alliance.

MICHAEL MERRICK is a teacher and commentator. He blogs at http://michaeltmerrick.blogspot.co.uk

JOHN MILBANK is Professor of Religion, Politics and Ethics at the University of Nottingham and Director of the Centre of Theology and Philosophy. His most recent book is *Beyond Secular Order: The Representation of Being and the Representation of the People* (2013). Currently he is writing (together with Adrian Pabst) *The Politics of Virtue: Post-liberalism and the Human Future* (2015).

ADRIAN PABST is Senior Lecturer in Politics at the University of Kent. He is the author of *Metaphysics: The Creation of Hierarchy* (2012). Currently he is writing (together with John Milbank) *The Politics of Virtue: Post-liberalism and the Human Future* (2015).

TOM WATSON has been Member of Parliament for West Bromwich East since 2001 and is a former Minister in the Cabinet Office. He is the co-author (together with Martin Hickman) of *Dial M for Murdoch: News Corporation and the Corruption of Britain* (2012).

ED WEST is Deputy Editor of the *Catholic Herald* and a blogger for *The Spectator*. He is the author of *The Diversity Illusion: What We Got Wrong About Immigration & How to Set It Right* (2013).

ROWAN WILLIAMS, Baron Williams of Oystermouth, is the Master of Magdalene College in the University of Cambridge. From 2002 until 2012, he was the 104th Archbishop of Canterbury. His most recent books include *Being Christian* (2014) and *Faith in the Public Square* (2012).

RUTH YEOMAN is Research Fellow, Mutuality in Business, at the Saïd Business School at the University of Oxford. She is the author of *Meaningful Work and Workplace Democracy* (2014).

And the Lord said:

Stand at the crossroads and look; ask for the ancient paths,
ask where the good way is, and walk in it, and you will find rest for
your souls.

Jeremiah 6:16

Smile at us, pay us, pass us; but do not quite forget, For we are the
people of England, that never has spoken yet.

G. K. Chesterton

PREFACE TO THE NEW EDITION

Why Labour Lost and How It Can Win Again

Adrian Pabst

WHERE LABOUR IS

After its crushing defeat in the 2015 General Election, Labour faces an existential crisis. Wiped out in Scotland, pushed back in Wales and dismissed in England, the party is staring at the prospect of years in the political wilderness. Once the Conservatives redraw constituency boundaries and extend the franchise to around 3.3 million long-term expatriates (many of whom belong to the over-55s who are the single largest voting cohort), they stand to gain an additional 30–40 seats in England, which could lock Labour out of power for a decade. Then there is UKIP, which has replaced the Lib Dems as the third party. It received nearly four million votes and came second in 118 constituencies – many in the north where it is attracting the Labour Party's traditional supporters. Ed Miliband's ill-timed resignation plunged Labour into a premature leadership campaign, depriving it of space and time to express grief for losing the country and remorse for not listening to its people. The contest has highlighted Labour's deep divisions and the risk of permanent irrelevance. Whoever will become leader, Labour could split and die.

At the heart of the party's present predicament is not so much an ideological confusion (too left-wing in England, too right-wing in Scotland) as a moral void: the absence of an overarching common purpose that can bind together the party and the country. Labour seems incapable of speaking at the same time to the middle classes who are unconvinced by the Tories and the working classes who now have UKIP or the SNP. Instead, it increasingly stands for the more affluent, secular, metropolitan elites as well as public sector workers and minorities – a protest march made up of sectional interests and vocal pressure groups. That is why the Labour Party did well in London but had little appeal across the rest of Britain. Labour abandoned the people of Britain, and now they are abandoning Labour.

The party's woes go much deeper than the lack of leadership, little economic credibility or the core-voter strategy that neither mobilised its traditional core nor even held on to its 2010 voters. What Labour lacks most of all is relating to people as they are, with their fears, beliefs, desires and hopes. In northern Labour strongholds that are political wastelands, there are widespread fears about debt, dispossession and despair. At the same time, some core belief in family life, the country and its traditions endure. A belief in fundamental fairness – that duties beget rights and that privileges have to be earned. Most people have a desire for mutual recognition more than wealth and power, for just reward, and for a society that honours hard work and contribution. There are also hopes that past sacrifice will be remembered and that future generations will be better off. That is now less certain than at any point since 1945 and worries a growing majority. Labour has so little popular support because it neither speaks to the specific concerns of its former core supporters, nor reaches out to the growing middle classes, nor defends universal principles across class and creed: work, family, community, care, loyalty, shared prosperity, pride of place – locality and country.

More than any other force within the wider Labour movement, Blue Labour has owned the scale of Labour's crisis and urged the party to abandon its comfort zones – a position articulated in this book. From the outset, Blue Labour was always a source of debate and renewal for the party and the wider Labour movement rather than a campaign group with a fixed agenda. It seeks to reconcile the country's estranged interests – young and old, owners and workers, Celts and Saxons, immigrants and natives, city and countryside, Christians and Muslims, faithful and secular – around the common good.[1] An appeal to the common good brings to life Labour's forgotten founding principles of free association, mutual self-help and fair play between all based upon work and contribution rather than welfare and entitlement. Instead of disowning the party's post-war past or being wedded to Old or New Labour, Blue Labour suggests that Labour's original traditions provide a source of imagination and practical wisdom for a common good politics.[2]

The best response to Labour's current crisis is therefore not a fudge of 'something New and something Blue'.[3] For that would be to wallow in nostalgia for the 1990s and pretend that New Labour was more on the side of society than the central state and the global market. Perhaps this applied to the communitarian and Christian socialist thinking of Blair in opposition, but it was crowded out during his premiership. Change and progress were elevated into absolutes regardless of whether they served the needs and interests of people – not to mention the loss involved in the 'permanent revolution' against the 'forces of conservatism', as Blair was rather too fond of saying.

In just a few years New Labour lost the people it had taken for granted and its popularity began to fade well before Iraq. Outside London and metropolitan Manchester, middle-class support for New Labour owed something to the absence of a credible Tory alternative under unelectable leaders such as Hague or Howard. By the time of the 2005 General Election, New Labour's 35.2 per cent share of the vote – a mere 21.6 per cent of the entire electorate – was the lowest of any majority government in British political history, and the popular vote in England went to the Conservatives. Blair had won and then lost England, and now New Labour, like Thatcherism, had run its course.

To win again and govern better, Labour needs to recapture its place in the life of the country and regain people's trust. Where New Labour defended the old politics of global finance backed by the managerial state, Blue Labour forges new coalitions around mutual interests such as devolving power to people and sharing wealth more widely through civic and community institutions. And where New Labour was defined by the stale social democracy of the Third Way, Blue Labour combines a political philosophy of the common good with a politics that transforms rather than perpetuates Thatcher's settlement. It seeks to embed states and markets into local, decentralised and democratic institutions, which can hold the forces of power and money to account. Such a politics of the common good is built between people, restores their dignity and agency, and it can once again command majority support in England and across Britain.

WHY LABOUR LOST

In 2010, Labour suffered the worst defeat in the party's history since 1931. It was worse than 1983 not in terms of votes or seats, but because between 1997 and 2010, the Labour Party lost five million supporters and was routed in its heartland. The 2010 election result was dire: not only did the south-west, south-east and eastern regions turn into virtual no-go areas, but when measured against historical performance and seat size, Labour's collapse was actually higher in the traditional strongholds of London, the East, the Midlands and Yorkshire. Even though Labour regained a handful of seats in those regions on 7 May, the 2015 outcome was much, much worse. It was the easiest election to win for a generation and the biggest rout since 1918: destroyed in Scotland, threatened in Wales and beaten in England, Labour lost everywhere to everyone – the SNP, UKIP and the Tories.

The party not only failed to regain the five million working-class voters who had left Labour between 1997 and 2010 but also lost lifelong Labour voters: in 2015 more than a million who had backed Labour in 2010 (and before) voted Conservative for the first time, and they are unlikely to return unless there is a profound rethink.[4] Along with floating voters and a majority of the population, they view Labour as weak on the economy and out of step with the country on the deficit, welfare and immigration. Crucially, Labour could not be trusted on spending public money sensibly, controlling the UK's borders and standing up for England. Compounding its lack of competence and connection with the concerns of ordinary folk was the constant rebranding and new messages based on focus groups, which confused voters and reinforced the deep distrust in the party.[5] Once a great force of national renewal, Labour 'lost its place in the life of the people'.[6]

Ed Miliband's claim that Labour lost the election but not the argument and that it was defeated only because two million Labour supporters failed to turn out is fanciful and deluded. Labour lost the election *and* the argument precisely because it had not earned the trust of the people whose views it ignored. Except for One Nation Labour, there was no genuine attempt by the leadership between 2010 and 2015 to reach out to people, listen to their concerns and build a broad coalition of estranged interests – starting with a proper social partnership between employers, trade unions and government. With the exception of Arnie Graf's work on community organising to rebuild the party from the grassroots up, Labour was run from London by a tiny clique of ex-special advisers drawn from ever-narrower backgrounds. A party that embodies the Westminster establishment and represents metropolitan centres was never going to get popular support across the country.

And so it proved. In Scotland and Wales, Labour was hammered on its association with the arrogance of the Westminster elites. In the north of England and in the Midlands, it haemorrhaged support to UKIP, which gained 17 per cent of the vote and came second in 44 constituencies. That is because UKIP's brand of politics speaks to the concerns of traditional Labour supporters, especially older white working-class voters who have been left behind by the collapse of industry and the impact of globalisation – in terms of immigration, welfare and Europe. In the south, Labour offered nothing to people who are prosperous, patriotic and feel that English identity is under threat from Scottish nationalism and a remote, technocratic EU. The election was not decided by a combination of 'lazy Labour' and 'shy Tory' voters. Rather, the people of Britain trusted a Conservative government far more than the Labour opposition.

The party's strength in inner cities cannot hide the fact that the places where it needed to win but lost are culturally the furthest away from Labour's metropolitan mentality. According to a comprehensive post-election analysis by the Smith Institute, 'Labour failed in struggling seaside towns, in suburbia, in new towns, in rural areas and in general in "small town Britain"'.[7] Nor could Labour's gains in its new London stronghold ever compensate for the disastrous losses in its former heartlands where people voted UKIP or the SNP.

The trouble for Labour is that the rest of Britain is not going London's way.[8] Never mind the wealth gap, it is the deepening divide along cultural lines – between a more liberal-cosmopolitan and a more conservative-communitarian outlook – that the party has ignored for far too long.

Of course, growing numbers of Britons are socially liberal in certain respects (against massive inequality of wealth or power and in favour of equal rights). They prefer a fair and open-minded mentality to an insular and bigoted attitude (in terms of ethnic diversity, Europe and immigration).

However, a sizeable majority is much more small 'c' conservative and communitarian than Labour and the London commentariat think: most people (including ethnic minorities) choose a fairly traditional family life, want to live in safe, stable places, and are generally sceptical about change. They think that the welfare state wrongly privileges rights over responsibilities and that claims to entitlement by immigrants should not take precedence over the rewards for the contribution by nationals. Therefore they want EU citizens to work for a few years before qualifying for benefits and immigration to return to lower levels. In short, many voters are socially liberal on some issues and kind of conservative on many others.

For decades Labour has been on the wrong side of history. By embracing a purely progressive politics that idealises change and mobility over tradition and belonging, the party now speaks predominantly to university graduates and mobile professionals who tend to be liberal-cosmopolitan. And even then many of them settle down and become culturally more conservative and communitarian. They worry less about high mobility and more about buying their own house, finding their children a place in a good school and living in relatively stable communities with low levels of crime and a moderate degree of trust and neighbourliness.

Labour's metro-liberal identity has alienated not just its own traditional working-class supporters for whom globalisation has generated new forms of cultural insecurity in addition to economic anxiety.[9] Labour's lack of cultural connection extends to 'new affluent workers' and 'emergent service workers' (bar staff, carers, call centre workers) who want to start their own business or learn a new trade but feel ignored by 'Big Government' and 'Big Business' alike. They all view Labour as the party of the liberal elites plus public sector workers and minorities – not the millions of people doing ordinary private sector jobs. The recovery may not benefit them much, which is why they are not enthusiastic about the Tories. If they vote for them rather than for Labour, it is with the head and a heavy heart. They think Labour just doesn't get it: it bangs on about inequality and the 'cost of living crisis', but it has no liking or sympathy for people whose way of life is threatened by ever-faster change, nor does it help people who want to get on and provide for their families.

The cultural divide between the metropolitan areas and the rest of the country is hurting Labour far more than any other party, as Frank Field shows in his essay. Between 1997 and 2010 Labour support fell by five million votes at a time when the electorate grew by 1.8 million.

Of those five millions, some are semi- and unskilled workers as well as the poorest who have abandoned the party in droves. But it is the skilled working and lower middle class who see Labour as the 'party of welfare' and the liberal establishment. Little wonder that they have left and aren't coming back. By contrast, the decline in Labour's share of upper-middle-class voters has been much lower than the total decline in the party's vote. Wooing business and more affluent voters will be necessary but not sufficient to win a majority in England and elsewhere. The low- and middle-income voters have deserted Labour, and the party cannot win without them.

Crucially, culture – more than class – is the key issue for Labour. What puts people off Labour is its liberal-cosmopolitan disdain for patriotism and its endorsement of a social allocation system which, as Field puts it, 'favours the newcomer and the social misfit' over the vast majority who contribute and play by the rules.[10] Thus the culture gap cannot be mapped onto the old class divide whose significance is declining as the class system has fragmented. With the old ideological clash of left vs right fading, rival conceptions of contribution and belonging will increasingly define politics.

In the 2015 election the combined vote for the Conservatives, UKIP and the DUP outstripped the total number of votes for left liberal parties (Labour, Liberal Democrats, SNP, Plaid Cymru, and Greens). Thus the idea that there is a clear and growing progressive majority is just as misguided as the idea that Labour can win by turning its back on the country's culturally conservative core.

In addition to geography, culture and class, age plays a significant role. Labour has banked its electoral strategy on young people who are far less likely to vote than middle-aged people or the over-55s who do not trust Labour with the economy or their pensions. In the 2015 election, the Conservatives finished almost 25 points ahead among pensioners, 78 per cent of whom turned out at the election. As John Curtice has argued, 'never before has Ipsos MORI recorded anything like as much as the 20 point difference in Labour support between older and younger voters that was in evidence in 2015. Labour may not have lost the middle-class vote, but it certainly lost the grey vote'.[11]

In summary: Labour was crushed because it is not where most people are on family, place, work, community, loyalty, prosperity and nationhood.[12] As long as it is associated with the metro-liberal self-righteousness of London that is loathed outside the M25, it will not be able to reach out beyond its more cosmopolitan voters and reconnect with the more conservative communitarian population across Britain. Nor is this a right-wing as opposed to a left-wing point. As John Harris has written,

> the party should lose its cringe about whether there might be strong communitarian ideas inherent in modern conceptions of all the UK's constituent nations, including England [...]. Reflecting that, as well as what it might change, Labour should finally think seriously about what needs to be conserved and protected: the town centre, the green-belt fields, the bus route, the pub. For much of the past 20 years, the party has failed to speak that language. It has tended to reduce equality and fairness to a mess of tax policies and financial enticements. Now its vision ought to be much, much richer.[13]

HOW LABOUR CAN WIN AGAIN

In the aftermath of defeat, Labour is tempted by two equally misguided paths that would lead the party down the road to perdition. The first is to embrace the anti-austerity politics of the hard left and form an alliance with 'progressive partners', including the SNP, the Greens and Respect. Quite apart from the need for fiscal discipline and paying down the national debt, this ignores the growing popular backlash against the large institutions of 'Big Business' *and* 'Big Government', and the desire for greater accountability through local control and civic participation. It also forgets that Labour's electoral base is fast eroding. The old industrial working class is no more. Its remnants have split and largely vote for UKIP or the Conservatives. Moreover, Tory policy will continue to reduce the number of public sector workers and those on welfare who are Labour's new core voters. As Jason Cowley has remarked, 'by 2018, for instance, there will be more self-employed than public service workers. Gordon Brown's "client state" is being dismantled, and little will be left of it by 2020'.[14] A purely progressive strategy will permanently deprive the party of a popular majority.

The second road to nowhere is a reinvention of New Labour. Leaving aside its toxic reputation, New Labour's brand of politics will fail to connect with people who have a more conservative-communitarian outlook. Whatever Blair's and Brown's professed principles, New Labour created a cold, transactional, utilitarian type of politics that represented liberal London and lost the majority vote in England. Today it would offer nothing to the people of Scotland and Wales who are patriotic and united in their dislike of London metropolitan liberalism. It would further antagonise ex-Labour voters in northern England who are voting for UKIP. And it would be like a pale imitation of the Tories in the south, and people always prefer the original to the copy. Cameron is the true heir to Blair, and Labour cannot win by imitating the liberal Conservatives.

In any case, appealing to New Labour is like fighting yesterday's war. Assuming that Cameron will step down before the next election, the Tories are already repositioning themselves in a more communitarian way, passing a budget with a national 'living wage' (rising to over £9 by 2020), city devolution and a more vocational, social-market economy (with an apprenticeship levy on large businesses). Michael Gove and the new deputy party chairman Robert Halfon MP invoke Disraeli's One-Nation Tory vision with a renewed emphasis on blue-collar conservatism aimed at both skilled and unskilled workers[15] – something on which the Scottish Conservative leader Ruth Davidson has led the way. In this they all follow George Osborne's maxim that 'in opposition, you move to the centre. In government, you move the centre' – towards a much smaller public sector as well as more power in the hands of individuals and cities. While Labour is waging past battles, the Conservatives are mapping the future, though one fraught with deep divisions over Europe, the fallout from excessively punitive welfare cuts and an attack on institutions such as the BBC. Without the Lib Dems, the Tories have arguably shifted the centre-ground left – not right – and are trying to push Labour further to the hard left.

If Labour wants to stand a chance of winning again, it needs to offer a new politics that combines individual fulfilment with mutual flourishing – how to live the good life in common. The task is to move the emphasis of politics away from individual entitlements and socio-economic utility to a politics of virtue that promotes personal agency and responsibility to fulfil oneself and ensure that others flourish too. Work, rather than welfare, is central to this as it affords us not just an income for our own needs but also a sense of dignity and the ability to provide for those we love most. Love is vital because it is people's close relationships, from the family and the local street to the national web of fraternal bonds, that makes society resilient. As Cruddas argues, 'strengthening community and relationships is the great purpose of our politics. [. . .] the social freedom which is the basis of a settled life. Edmund Burke describes this as "that state of things in which liberty is secured by equality of restraint". In the past, we called it fraternity'.[16]

In the old politics of left vs right, the emphasis on liberty and equality squeezed out fraternity, which binds together people and society around shared traditions of the good life in common.[17] Those, like the *Times* columnist and former Blair speechwriter Philip Collins, who implore Labour to embrace once again New Labour's 'permanent revolution', have not understood that the people of Britain are much closer to Burke than to Blair in opposing revolutionary politics and supporting a politics of virtue. In a review of a book on Burke by Jesse Norman MP, Cruddas praised Norman as one of the few true Conservatives for recovering the notion that '[p]olitics is about the nurturing of virtue: honour, loyalty, duty and wisdom. It is not about atomised exchange'.[18]

Labour has much to learn from such Burkean themes. Burke's tradition of 'radical conservatism' (as developed by William Cobbett and then socialists in the pluralist tradition such as J. N. Figgis, G. D. H. Cole and R. H. Tawney) provides the party with ideas on how to link individual rights to mutual obligations. This tradition defends private property as a driving force for stable investment, production, and trade against both market monopoly and state control. It views property not merely in terms of economic status but as a stake in society that fosters greater civic participation. In this manner, love and work can be complemented by an emphasis on shared ownership and stewardship in relation to business, housing, technology, our natural environment and the global commons. Such ideas are conservative and radical, and this paradox is a source of inspiration and practical action. It can help Labour recover a sense of moral purpose and tell a story of renewal for both party and country.

However, in one key respect Blair remains a reference for Labour and British politics, as Cruddas and Rutherford rightly remark: 'He had an intellectual project which was the Third Way, a political project which was New Labour, and an organisational project which was the Clinton campaign machine'.[19] Going forward, the only winning formula for Labour is to fuse the Blue Labour narrative with a common good politics and the model of community organising.

To regain its place in the life of the country, Labour needs to reflect the people whose trust it seeks, and this involves listening to them where they are – in their communities, localities, and professions. Labour has to combine a genuine compassion for the dispossessed who feel abandoned by the still predominantly liberal Conservatives with an authentic focus on new groups whom the party does not as yet represent. This includes those trapped in low-skill occupations or the over five million in higher-skilled jobs such as sole traders, small businesses, and family-owned firms. Moving beyond its new core in liberal London also means speaking to the increasing number of middle-class people across the UK who fear for the future of their children and resent the growing gap with certain elites who do not play by the same rules that they demand of everyone else.

One way to bridge the culture divide is for Labour to appeal to people in new ways that favour local community and civic solutions over the impersonal mechanisms of state bureaucracy and commodity exchange. In both the public and the private sector, this involves addressing the crisis in the professions by fostering greater participation of professionals and more accountability to users. In turn, this requires a rebalancing of power from institutional shareholders to managers and employees and from legislators, regulators and administrators to front-line professionals and users. Labour also has to find novel means of reducing the psychological pressures of excessive inner competition within firms or organisations in favour of the energies of collaboration that facilitate innovation and a more family-friendly workplace. To sustain work and love, Britain needs the new settlement around relationships and responsibility that Blue Labour is developing.

The politics of the common good is a response to the limits of liberalism and the desire for a polity in which everyone has a place and a voice. Liberalism's focus on freedom has far too little to say about the goods we enjoy in common: love, family, friendship, collegiate workplaces and safe communities, as John Milbank's essay suggests. The liberal emphasis on equality forgets the quality of life – employing one's vocation and talent to useful, beautiful and meaningful ends, especially work that has meaning, creates value and forms character. But equally important are goods of real worth such as a sufficient stock of affordable and good-quality homes, enough schools with a strong ethos, many more British-trained nurses and doctors, better food at work and in schools... In short, equality is not about making everyone the same (in the mould of metro-liberals on the left and right) but rather about creating equal access to the good life in common.

It is the neglect of the good and of virtue that leads to a culture of rewarding vice in the form of greed, selfishness, deception and dishonesty. Too often the worst human instincts prevail and corrode both the common sense and common decency on which a vibrant democracy and market economy depend. Thus Blue Labour argues for a new set of incentives and rewards that promote more individual virtue and a greater sense of public honour. For example, British company law gives too much power to shareholders and thus helps to bring about corporate short-termism, depressing investment, innovation, productivity and workers' pay – as the Bank of England's chief economist Andy Haldane has argued.[20] A rewriting of company law by the social partners is needed to encourage productive activities and shared prosperity over short-term speculative gain.[21] Similarly, more work and less welfare dependency requires proper pay and better working conditions by linking wages to productivity growth and rewarding employers who pay the 'family wage' and provide apprenticeships (e.g. tax breaks, public tender and procurement). A moral economy of mutual obligations rather than a culture of abstract claims to individual entitlement has to value contribution and broaden it to include care for relatives, services to the community and many more informal activities.

To transform the party and make common good politics the new centre ground, community organising is vital because it enables Labour to do politics with people rather than to them. That involves strengthening self-association at the workplace, in neighbourhoods and indeed in the party itself – from local branches and constituencies all the way to the National Policy Forum. Organisationally, it means reviving and extending Arnie Graf's project, which is to transform the party into a popular movement around work, family and pride of place. To stop another shutdown of this vital work by the party machine, Labour needs to turn into a federation of independent parties, starting with a new English Labour Party where members meet, debate and decide on an English Labour manifesto aimed at winning a majority in England. Such a party federation would also enable a more independent Scottish Labour Party and a stronger Welsh Labour Party, each with their own General Election manifestos. In turn, that would help the Labour family to organise more effectively for local ballots as well as elections to the Scottish Parliament and Welsh Assembly. A party that wants to embody the transfer of power to people must lead by example.

A truly federal Labour can begin to regain trust and command popular support. For instance, English Labour should learn from Labour council leaders in the Midlands, the north-east and the north-west on how to strengthen local democracy. The party could cautiously welcome the Tories' policy of city devolution but offer the country to go much further, introducing directly elected majors for every town and city with complete control over public services and economic development, including tax-setting and budgetary powers.

Central to a common good politics is Blue Labour's blend of political economy, statecraft and strategy. A Blue Labour political economy combines just reward for work with a greater distribution of assets. One way to achieve this is by linking wages to labour productivity growth and by promoting more profit-sharing models in the public and the private sector. This needs to be complemented by investment in through-life training and skills as part of an economy that values both academic and vocational formation, including hybrid education for professions such as law, medicine, finance and engineering. Combining skilled craft with high technology can foster innovation and generate value, not abstract wealth and low-paid jobs. By creating regional investment banks, all this can help bring about a rebalanced recovery and a diversified economy. Blue Labour also seeks to forge new social and economic coalitions at home around common interests such as shared prosperity. This needs to include more forms of social partnership between managers and workers, but also between funders, users and professionals as well as between consumers, suppliers and local communities. A new economic settlement has to be based on free association and accountability among all the stakeholders.

Linked to this is Blue Labour statecraft, which strengthens civic institutions that support internal practices and judgements and allow virtue and vocation to flourish without the domination of the market or the state. Blue Labour sees owners, managers, and workers as representing estranged interests that can be brought together in a negotiated settlement through new civic institutions, for example city corporations that are elected by both resident citizens and members of professions. This would involve a greater role for professional associations alongside legislators and regulators with the aim of improving self-regulation and to instil a culture of ethos and excellence that fosters the pursuit of virtuous ends – the goods that are internal to each activity. Associations offer professionals a framework in which they can negotiate rival ideas and interests and also agree on written codes of conduct as well as unwritten norms, which are reflected in good practice.

Statecraft also deploys government as an engine of radical decentralisation to self-governing towns, cities and regions where power lies with mayors, guild-corporations and citizen assemblies. This would include hybrids such as city-regions and county-corporations that reflect specific traditions such as naval colleges in Newcastle or ports in Norfolk that can trade with other European members of a recreated Hanseatic League. The trick is to 'politicise' existing cultural attachments and this could readily arise if regional assemblies became speedily associated with local pride, increased economic development and popular involvement in shaping regional character.

Concretely, local and regional self-government should have the power to vary business tax, reduce regulation and foster innovation hubs together with universities and enterprise. In relation to welfare and other areas, service provision would be more personal, local and holistic than the homogenised standards and uniform targets imposed either by central government or the European Commission (or both at once), which treats people as commodity consumers and mainly humiliates the poorest who cannot afford higher-quality alternatives. (Part of a more human approach would be a radical simplification of the tax system and significant tax cuts for low-income groups, especially the working poor who will be hit hardest by the Tories' hasty abolition of tax credits.) Thus statecraft is key to a radical public sector transformation based around productive value, virtuous leadership and support for families – for example through community institutions that can provide early intervention and childcare rather than tax and transfer.

In this manner, statecraft binds together domestic politics with foreign policy by devising a federal settlement for the UK and reaffirming Britain's destiny as a European and global power.[22] A Blue Labour strategy can bring about a more imaginative and courageous approach to international relations. First of all, Britain needs to connect its European and Atlantic links to its historic ties with the countries of the Commonwealth, otherwise it will lose its status as a global power based on a unique tradition of tolerance, freedom under the law, and public cooperation connected with Britain's 'mixed constitution' model of parliamentary monarchy.[23]

Second, the UK has to lead in Europe by ensuring that the EU's global outlook is not confined to the export of human rights but extends to more meaningful interventions. For example, in the Near East Britain should reach out to the great civilisations of Syria, Iran and Russia (even if their current regimes are profoundly problematic) and devise a long-term strategy that takes the fight to Islamic State by being pro-Kurdish and pro-Christian.[24] At home this requires not just a commitment to higher defence spending but also a renewed military covenant on the mutual obligations between the country and its armed forces.

Finally, UK leadership in Europe can complement the creation of a federal settlement at home by forging alliances with like-minded EU members such as Germany, the Netherlands, Scandinavia, and Poland to reverse the centralisation of power and make the Union an engine of devolution and accountability to its citizens. Over time Britain could even help rebuild the EU's political project around a European commonwealth of peoples and nations that can embed states and markets in civic institutions and relationships, which constitute Europe's unique polity.

Over-ambitious? Perhaps, but worth trying, because Britain's only other option is to tinker at the margins to preserve a system that has lost popular support and civic consent. To restore the United Kingdom and rebuild a Europe that is prosperous and peaceful, British politics needs a renewed idealism that is more realistic than mere pragmatism. For idealism is about the sustaining of noble traditions, shared purpose and character. It is about what kind of country Britain is and where Europe is going.

CONCLUSION

As the Labour leadership contest highlights, the danger is that the party will be stuck between the self-righteousness of the Blairite tribute band and of the hard left. Both offer false hope and will lead the party into oblivion. That is why Labour needs to go blue. Labour must recover its own best traditions and embody the values that resonate with the British public – north *and* south, urban *and* rural, native *and* immigrant, Saxon *and* Celt, religious *and* secular, working class *and* middle class, young *and* old, people *and* elites. The best response to Labour's current crisis is not some reinvention of Old or New Labour. Rather, the future for Labour is to be as radical as it is conservative and to take Blue Labour to the next level.

NOTES

1   Maurice Glasman, 'The good society, Catholic Social Thought and the politics of the common good', this volume.

2   On the Labour Party's origins in the 'radically conservative' tradition of the cooperative movement rather than the progressive tradition of the Liberal Party, see Martin Pugh, *Speak for Britain! A New History of the Labour Party* (London: Vintage, 2010); Maurice Glasman, Jonathan Rutherford, Marc Stears and Stuart White (eds), *The Labour Tradition and the Politics of Paradox: The Oxford London Seminars 2010–11* (London: Lawrence & Wishart, 2011), available at http://www.lwbooks. co.uk/journals/soundings/Labour_tradition_and_the_politics_of_ paradox.pdf; Jon Cruddas, 'George Lansbury memorial lecture', Queen Mary, University of London, 7 November 2013, available at http://www. newstatesman.com/politics/2013/11/jon-cruddass-george-lansbury- memorial-lecture-full-text (both accessed on 26 July 2015).

3   See Philip Collins' review of *Blue Labour*: 'Something Blue, something New', *Prospect Magazine* 229 (April 2015), pp. 70–1, available at http:// www.prospectmagazine.co.uk/arts-and-books/something-blue- something-new. By contrast, Duncan O'Leary argues more for a Blue Labour transformation of New Labour's legacy in his essay 'Something new and something blue: the key to Labour's future?', *The New Statesman*, 21 May 2015, available at http://www.newstatesman.com/ politics/2015/05/something-new-and-something-blue-key-labours- future (both accessed on 26 July 2015).

4   Alan Barnard and John Braggins, 'Listening to Labour's lost Labour voters', bbm research, July 2015. Available at http://www.scribd.com/ doc/271940748/Listening-to-Labour-s-Lost-Labour-Voters-bbm- Research-July-2015 (accessed on 26 July 2015).

5   James Morris, 'Why Labour lost and how it can win again', presentation delivered at a conference organised by the School of Politics and IR, University of Kent, on 27 June 2015 in the House of Lords.

6   Jon Cruddas and Jonathan Rutherford, 'There are no easy answers to Labour's defeat', *The New Statesman* (20 May 2015). Available at http:// www.newstatesman.com/politics/2015/05/there-are-no-easy-answers- labours-defeat (accessed on 26 July 2015).

7   Paul Hunter, 'Red alert: why Labour lost and what needs to change?', Smith Institute. Available at https://smithinstitutethinktank.files.wordpress.com/2015/07/red-alert-why-labour-lost-and-what-needs-to-change.pdf (accessed on 26 July 2015).

8   Jeremy Cliffe, 'Britain's cosmopolitan future. How the country is changing and why its politicians must respond', Policy Network, May 2015. Available at www.policy-network.net/publications_download.aspx?ID=9172 (accessed on 26 July 2015).

9   Rod Liddle, 'What Labour must do is estrange its awful voters', *The Spectator*, Coffee House, 13 May 2015. Available at http://blogs.spectator.co.uk/coffeehouse/2015/05/what-labour-must-do-is-estrange-its-awful-voters/ (accessed on 26 July 2015). Cf. Laurent Bouvet, *L'insécurité culturelle* (Paris: Fayard, 2015).

10 Frank Field, 'A Blue Labour vision of the common good', this volume, p. 57.

11 John Curtice, 'A defeat to reckon with: On Scotland, economic competence, and the complexities of Labour's losses', *Juncture*, Vol. 22, no. 1 (June 2015). Available at http://www.ippr.org/juncture/a-defeat-to-reckon-with-on-scotland-economic-competence-and-the-complexities-of-labours-losses#back3 (accessed on 26 July 2015).

12 Tristram Hunt, 'The forward march of Labour', speech to Demos on 20 May 2015. Available at http://www.demos.co.uk/press_releases/the-forward-march-of-labour (accessed on 26 July 2015).

13 John Harris, 'Who should Labour speak for now?', *The Guardian*, 13 July 2015. Available at http://www.theguardian.com/commentisfree/2015/jul/13/labour-party-2020-movement (accessed on 26 July 2015).

14 Jason Cowley, 'England is changing and the Labour desperately needs to change with it', *The Daily Telegraph*, 15 July 2015. Available at http://www.telegraph.co.uk/news/politics/labour/11739827/England-is-changing-and-the-Labour-Party-desperately-needs-to-change-with-it.html (accessed on 26 July 2015).

15 Michael Gove, 'What is good about the right?', The Legatum Institute, 12 March 2015. Available at http://www.newstatesman.com/politics/2015/03/whats-good-about-right (accessed on 26 July 2015).

16 Jon Cruddas, 'Love and work, these two things only', Speech to the Relationships Alliance, 29 January 2015. Available at http://www.joncruddas.org.uk/sites/joncruddas.org.uk/files/FINAL%20Love%20and%20Work%2028.1.15.pdf (accessed on 26 July 2015).

17 Adrian Pabst, 'Prosperity and justice for all: why solidarity and fraternity are key to an efficient, ethical economy', in Alberto Quadrio Curzio and Giovanni Marseguerra (eds), *Solidarity as a "Social Value": Paradigms for a Good Society* (Vatican City: Libreria Editrice Vaticana, 2015), pp. 125–59.

18   Jon Cruddas, Review of *Edmund Burke: Philosopher, Politician, Prophet*, by Jesse Norman, in *The Independent*, 17 May 2013. Available at http://www.independent.co.uk/arts-entertainment/books/reviews/edmund-burke-philosopher-politician-prophet-by-jesse-norman-8619001.html (accessed on 26 July 2015).

19   Cruddas and Rutherford, 'There are no easy answers to Labour's defeat', *op. cit.*

20   In Haldane's words, British company law 'puts the shareholder at front and centre. It puts the short-term interest of shareholders in a position of primacy when it comes to running the firm'. See Duncan Weldon, 'Shareholder power "holding back economic growth"'. Available at http://www.bbc.co.uk/news/business-33660426 (accessed on 26 July 2015).

21   Will Hutton, *How Good We Can Be: Ending the Mercenary Society and Building a Great Country* (London: Little, Brown, 2015), pp. 49–89 and 129–70.

22   Adrian Pabst, 'A new federal settlement for Britain and the EU', Policy Network, 23 April 2015. Available at http://www.policy-network.net/pno_detail.aspx?ID=4888&title=A-new-federal-settlement-for-Britain-and-the-EU (accessed on 26 July 2015).

23   Philip Murphy, *Monarchy and the End of Empire: The House of Windsor, the British Government and the Postwar Commonwealth* (Oxford: Oxford University Press, 2013); David Howell, *Old Links and New Ties: Power and Persuasion in an Age of Networks* (London: I.B. Tauris, 2013).

24   Maurice Glasman, 'This is a battle for civilisation… the UK cannot remain neutral', *Mail on Sunday*, 9 August 2014, available at http://www.dailymail.co.uk/debate/article-2720948/MAURICE-GLASMAN-This-battle-civilisation-UK-remain-neutral.html (accessed on 26 July 2015); 'The common good and foreign policy', lecture delivered at the University of Kent, 4 March 2015.

INTRODUCTION

Blue Labour and the Politics of the Common Good

Adrian Pabst

WHY BLUE LABOUR?

Since Labour's General Election defeat in May 2010 – their second-worst electoral result in over 70 years – there have been numerous attempts to rethink the Labour tradition. None has been more controversial and more significant than the movement known as 'Blue Labour'. Far beyond any other group, Blue Labour has questioned the current consensus at the heart of the Labour Party and British politics – the fusion of social with economic liberalisation under the joint aegis of the central bureaucratic state and the global 'free market'. The secular ideology that underlies this fusion promotes little more than freedom of choice, utility and short-term pleasure. Against this ideology, and its explicit or tacit support for both market commodification and state domination, Blue Labour argues for a new consensus – a politics of the common good that recognises the legitimacy of estranged interests and brings about a negotiated solution to conflict through civic institutions that promote virtue rather than vice. The aim is to shift the focus away from narrow self-interest and greed towards shared benefit and mutual flourishing. This essay collection provides a restatement of Blue Labour thinking from its key protagonists and from a number of new voices, including senior politicians, leading academics and activists, as well as influential commentators.

In the aftermath of the 2008 global economic crisis and the worst recession since the Great Depression of 1929–32, Britain has witnessed one of the most turbulent eras in politics since the Second World War. The Union is under threat from the forces of technocracy in both London and Brussels, as well as from a growing popular backlash that fuels support for populist parties such as UKIP or the SNP. In response, the three main parties in Westminster defend a politics that oscillates between the controlling centre and the controlled individuals so beloved of unadulterated liberalism. Faced with a twin crisis of identity and inequality, the failure of the 1945 and 1979 settlements is plain for everyone to see: neither nationalisation nor privatisation has delivered general prosperity and human flourishing. By contrast, Blue Labour seeks to craft a new vision that is centred on reciprocity and solidarity – a more mutualist model in which both risk and profit are shared, reward is rejoined with responsibility and individual virtue is linked to public acknow-ledgement. Central to this new vision is the promotion of vocation and good ethos across all sectors of the economy, the polity and society, combined inseparably with the honouring of interpersonal relationships, of place and of faith.

THE BLUE LABOUR NARRATIVE

Blue Labour is a narrative about fall and redemption. It is about the death of an old social-democratic politics in Britain and across continental Europe, and the loss of millions of voters who have deserted the party. And it is about reconnecting with people as they are – as human beings who belong to families, localities and communities and who are embedded in shared traditions, interests and faiths. Neither as lone egos nor as anonymous mass, but as relational beings who desire mutual recognition more than wealth and power, to paraphrase Jon Cruddas. If Labour wants to reconnect with people, then it needs to revisit its own history and the history of the United Kingdom, rejecting amoral cynicism and reclaiming an ethics of virtue.

Blue Labour seeks to reimagine both Britain and the Labour tradition. In this respect it continues the struggle between two rival traditions of politics – one rationalist, utilitarian and transactional and the other romantic, principled and transformative. The former may have triumphed at crucial junctures and dominated the twentieth century, but it never caught the imagination of the people. Whether in the late 1930s, the late 1960s or after 1994, it was the planners, managers and bureaucrats who won out over the visionaries and the creators. But now this cold rationalism is in crisis, and the tide is turning.

Blue Labour distinguishes itself from other forces within the wider Labour movement precisely on account of its commitment to a politics that is ethical, not materialistic. Its emphasis on the creativity of human labour, on the intrinsic importance of vocation and on the need to nurture virtuous action grows out of the British Romantic tradition embodied by William Morris. In his lecture on the legacy of the former Labour leader George Lansbury, Jon Cruddas tells this story as follows:

> The mass political party of the twentieth century that George Lansbury led is gone. The cultures and social formations of the industrial working class that gave it life and sustained it have gone. More recently, social democracy has suffered a cultural devastation – almost if you like, a social death – and while the structures of our party survive the meanings that gave them life have not.
>
> We are dwindling, and we have to change. We have to return to our exiled traditions and galvanise for the future. Indeed the One Nation tradition grows out of the moral outrage at the mechanisation of society. It begins with Carlyle's the Condition of England question in his essay on Chartism in 1839. His raging against the inhumanity of industrialisation gives first voice to the One Nation tradition: 'the condition of the great body of people in a country is the condition of the country itself'.
>
> Out of it grows the social novels of Gaskell, Dickens, Disraeli's Sybil or Two Nations, and Ruskin. It is the tradition of an English modernity of virtue and sensibility and Morris was its greatest exponent. It was given form within the ILP and Labour through Hardie, MacDonald and Lansbury. It lay deep within Attlee and the texture of his great transformative government. It is captured in the character of Lansbury more than any other and saved the Party at its moment of acute crisis.
>
> Politics is always first and foremost poetic because if it lacks the spirit to transform people and give them hope for a better life then it will fail to tackle the fundamental power relations that keep them in their place, however many policies it has lined

up. That's why to me Lansbury is so important, not just for
what he stood for but for his failures and the lessons we can
learn from his exemplary life.[1]

It is against the background of this continual opposition between the
transformative and the transactional that one has to understand Blue
Labour's appeal to the radical tradition of British Romanticism – of
William Cobbett, Walter Scott, Thomas Carlyle, John Ruskin and
William Morris, G. D. H. Cole and R. H. Tawney. There is in reality
no simple continuum of British radicalism stretching from Magna
Carta to the Peasants' Revolt and on to the Wars of the Roses and the
sixteenth-century Commotion Time uprising – or 'from the Lollards
to the Levellers and on to the Chartists and the suffragettes', as
Dominic Sandbrook has rightly remarked.[2] Rather, the more specific
Romantic tradition serves as a constant source of inspiration in the
battle against those forces that are determined to abolish the history
of both party and country in favour of abstract ideals such as progress
and freedom of choice (as John Milbank and Dave Landrum argue in
their contributions).

The invocation of Romanticism is vital because it highlights the
paradoxical nature of Blue Labour[3] – above all the idea that the old is
the new because renewal requires the recovery of exiled traditions, as
Maurice Glasman suggests in the opening chapter. Blue Labour's
restoration of a Romantic vision explains its rejection of the
utilitarian moralism and liberal economics that have characterised
both the left and the right for so long, and the recovery of a 'moral
economy' that promotes virtue and mutual flourishing even in an age
of austerity – an argument developed by Jon Cruddas in his chapter.

The Romantic legacy also helps explain why the Labour Party and
the wider Labour movement were not always on the side of progress
against tradition. On the contrary, Labour used to be a socially and
culturally conserving force that combined robust resistance to an
overly facile and uncritical progressivism (represented by the Whig
oligarchy) with a passionate defence of land, parish and work
(inspired by Morris' Romantic realism). In fact, Labour's roots are
much less to do with Victorian liberalism than with High Toryism
and the cooperative movement. David Marquand makes this point in
a review of Martin Pugh's *Speak for Britain! A New History of the
Labour Party*:

Labour was not just the heir of liberalism and the Liberal Party. It also drew on a long line of working-class Toryism: a rollicking, rambunctious, fiercely patriotic and earthy tradition, at odds both with the preachy nonconformist conscience that saturated the culture of provincial liberalism and with the patronising, 'we-know-best' preconceptions of metropolitan intellectuals. Working-class Tories were against the 'lily-livered Methodists' excoriated by the arch-Tory socialist Robert Blatchford, whose *Merrie England* (1893) was perhaps the single most effective work of socialist propaganda published in Britain before the First World War.[4]

Marquand is right that Labour has always been conservative in this sense of a genuine popular rootedness and belief in the best of the British legacy (a theme that is expanded in different ways by Rowenna Davis and Ed West). Blue Labour seeks to recover and renew the radical conservatism that defines England and resonates strongly with cognate traditions across the rest of the United Kingdom.

Thus Blue Labour is so controversial and significant precisely because its appeal to the British Romantic tradition challenges party orthodoxy and transactional politics alike – notably the individualist, pro-secular, pro-capitalist and pro-metropolitan outlook that is so closely connected with the party's embrace of social and economic liberalism and the current consensus. By contrast, Blue Labour reminds both the party and the country of the origins of the Labour movement and its contribution to national renewal. The practice of virtues such as courage, justice, honour and integrity shaped the workers' movement in resisting the worst excesses of the Industrial Revolution and laissez-faire capitalism, as Karl Polanyi first argued in his seminal book *The Great Transformation*.[5] His thought is at the heart of Blue Labour and runs through many of the essays in this collection.

Against the forces of the increasingly unfettered 'free market' and centralised state, workers set up burial societies to honour their dead and created cooperatives and mutuals to honour their communities and the places which they inhabited. They forged ties among Anglicans, Catholics, Methodists, other Nonconformists, evangelicals and Jews that gave rise to an internationalist movement of patriots who celebrate their country, its culture and history. It was a profound sense of mutual obligation and a desire for reciprocal recognition that gave rise to the tradition of solidarity and cooperation. In this way Labour grew out of popular movements of self-help and self-improvement, giving the voiceless a voice in the governance of the realm. It is this tradition that Frank Field invokes in his passionate plea for a new politics of the common good.

Such a legacy does not insinuate some form of reactionary nostalgia whose pessimism and fatalism is just as misguided as the idea of utopian progress, which underpins both state communism and market capitalism. That is why Blue Labour repudiates the old politics of both the secular left and the reactionary right, which are categories that were bequeathed to us by the French and the American revolutions. These two models are ultimately incompatible with Britain's unique legacy of a 'mixed constitution' which permits sovereign legitimacy to emerge at once from the popular will and from an objective sense of equity (underpinned by the Crown) and by reference to notions of eternal truth and goodness. Today the role of the established Church in guaranteeing this balance is consolidated by the contribution of other faith communities.

Thus Blue Labour marks a renewed resistance against the impersonal forces of liberalism that have disembedded the economy from society; re-embedded social relations in a transactional, economistic and utilitarian culture; and disturbed through incomprehension our ancient constitution in a manner that threatens both civil liberty and democratic involvement.

BRITAIN'S POST-LIBERAL POLITICS AND THE BLUE LABOUR VISION

Blue Labour emerged as part of a wider 'post-liberal' turn in British politics in the wake of the 2008 economic crash and the 2011 London riots.[6] A *New Statesman* editorial in March 2013 summarises this well:

> Ever since the Thatcher era, British politics has been defined by forms of economic and social liberalism. The right won the argument for the former and the left the argument for the latter, or so it is said. Yet in the post-crash era, this ideological settlement is beginning to fracture. The right is re-examining its crude economic liberalism and the left its social liberalism. This shift is characterised neither by a revival of socialist economics,

nor by one of reactionary conservatism. Rather, it is defined by a mutual recognition that liberalism, at least in some of its guises, does not provide all the answers to Britain's most entrenched problems: its imbalanced economy, its atomised society, its lack of common identity.[7]

Two thinkers, Phillip Blond and Maurice Glasman, and their respective factions – the Red Tories and Blue Labour – were quicker to recognise this than most. Mr Blond may no longer have the ear of the Prime Minister, if he ever did, but since the appointment of Jon Cruddas as the head of Labour's policy review, the Blue Labour faction has emerged as the dominant intellectual influence on the Labour Party.

[...] With its emphasis on abstract individualism, liberalism, the great driver of social emancipation and economic prosperity, now feels inadequate to this new age of insecurity. In his recent 'Earning and Belonging' speech, Mr Cruddas said: 'Simply opposing the cuts without an alternative is no good. It fails to offer reasonable hope. The stakes are high because when hope is not reasonable despair becomes real'. He is right: the stakes could not be higher but who is best positioned to lead Britain out of despair and create a new sense of purpose and belonging?

Blue Labour seeks to rebuild hope and a sense of direction by returning to long-neglected issues of ethical principle and character. Far from being nostalgic or reactionary, it appeals to perennial principles of the common good, participation, association, individual virtue and public honour. The task is to renew their meaning and craft institutions that can translate them into transformative practices of mutual assistance and cooperation across the country, as the chapter by David Lammy suggests.

Contrary to New Labour, Blue Labour hopes to demonstrate how Labour's strong civic traditions can point to a renewal of the movement as it seeks to forge a politics that meets the demands of our time. Beyond false binary choices, Blue Labour encourages a more robust and fundamental debate about a whole range of controversial and emotive themes, including welfare (Frank Field), globalisation and migration (David Goodhart), meaningful work (Ruth Yeoman), nature, science and conservation movements (Ruth Davis) as well as the central importance of the family (Michael Merrick). The goal of

the essay collection is to develop Blue Labour thinking and help forge
a new consensus around a vision of the common good. That vision is
informed not only by Catholic Social Thought, certain Anglican
strands and elements of the dissenting religious traditions and
cognate strands in Judaism and Islam, but also by the deepest legacy
of the cooperative and the trade union movement as well as the
practice of community organising, as Arnie Graf's chapter so vividly
illustrates.

What binds together all these traditions is the commitment to
resist the dominance of utopian ideology and sectional interests in
public life. Crucially, they share in common a concern with
honouring 'conservative' dispositions to defend the best in local
and cultural practices, resistance to the power of both market and
state transactionism, affirmation of the love of place as well as the
honouring of faith and institutional life. All these are elements of the
Blue Labour instinct, and we aim to show that they are irrevocably
part of Labour's political DNA.

As the quote from the *New Statesman* indicates, the ideology that
shaped UK politics for much of the post-war period is now fractured.
Together with other actors and movements, Blue Labour endeavours
to develop a new vision that will enable people to flourish and build a
common life by forming unexpected coalitions involving businesses,
the churches and the trade unions – as Tom Watson suggests in his
contribution. In this respect Blue Labour stands firmly in the
tradition of the wider Labour movement whose very existence –
forged from the turbulence of the Industrial Revolution – is a success
story in itself. Amid the current crisis and social dislocation, Labour
has once again a unique role to play in the civic, social and economic
transformation of the UK.

This essay collection is not an alternative party manifesto. Instead,
it aims to challenge Labour to rediscover its own best, exiled
traditions as a source of renewal for the party and the country. It is
part of an intellectual evolution rather than a fixed position. Blue
Labour is trying to sketch a new direction for the whole Labour
movement but it has much further to go.

For this reason, Blue Labour is neither a repackaged offering of
'Old Labour' nor the latest manifestation of 'New Labour'. These are
false dichotomies that privilege the status quo and bracket key ideas
from the wider debate within the Labour Party, the Labour movement
and British society. Nor is it but a gloomy diagnosis of the Blair and

Brown years, despite the vital reckoning that is required in relation to their legacy. It rather seeks to question some of the structural features of the Labour Party that have been barely queried over the past 70 years – rationalist planning, centralism and a progressive embrace of secular ideology.

But it asks questions of some of the key elements of Labour's history not in order to discredit the past but to shape the present and future. In an intervention in August 2013, Maurice Glasman put it as follows:

Only Labour has the traditions and values that can serve the country at this time of need. Yet the current Labour leadership seems to need reminding of these traditions and values. We forget at our peril that it was the Labour movement that built the burial societies so that the poor would not be abandoned to a pauper's grave. People clubbed together and founded building societies and mutual societies so that misfortune did not turn into catastrophe. Our values were respectability, loyalty, courage and, above all, work. Labour. We cared about it so much we named our party after it. These are the values we need now to rebuild trust and renew a sense of virtue and vocation in the economy and in politics. The Labour Party's future lies in reclaiming its inheritance. Our tradition is our future.[8]

Labour's 2010 General Election defeat demands a wholesale transformation of the party, not just some tinkering at the margins. Both in terms of ideas and organisation, Labour needs to change in line with its own best traditions – the workers' and cooperative movements and the manifold mutual arrangements with which they built a fairer Britain following the ravages of the agricultural enclosures, of the Industrial Revolution and of laissez-faire capitalism. Blue Labour seeks to renew and extend these traditions in order to envisage a more associationist possibility for this country's future, in both domestic and international terms.

It is in this spirit of renewal and transformation, peculiar to the Labour tradition, that we offer these essays as a contribution to the debate.

NOTES

1. Jon Cruddas, 'George Lansbury memorial lecture', Queen Mary, University of London, 7 November 2013. Available at http://www.newstatesman.com/politics/2013/11/jon-cruddass-george-lansbury-memorial-lecture-full-text (accessed on 25 August 2014).
2. Dominic Sandbrook, 'Family, faith and flag', *New Statesman*, 7 April 2011. Available at http://www.newstatesman.com/society/2011/04/labour-party-english-england (accessed on 25 August 2014).
3. Maurice Glasman, Jonathan Rutherford, Marc Stears and Stuart White (eds), *The Labour Tradition and the Politics of Paradox: The Oxford London Seminars 2010–11*, intro. Ed Miliband (London: Lawrence & Wishart, 2011). Available at http://www.lwbooks.co.uk/journals/soundings/Labour_tradition_and_the_politics_of_paradox.pdf (accessed on 25 August 2014).
4. David Marquand, Review of *Speak for Britain! A New History of the Labour Party*, by Martin Pugh, *New Statesman*, 2 April 2010. Available at http://www.newstatesman.com/books/2010/04/working-class-labour-party (accessed on 25 August 2014).
5. Karl Polanyi, *The Great Transformation: The Political and Economic Origins of Our Time* (Boston: Beacon Press, 2001 [orig. pub. 1944]).
6. For a lively telling of the story of Blue Labour, see Rowenna Davis, *Tangled up in Blue: Blue Labour and the Struggle for Labour's Soul* (London: Ruskin Press, 2011).
7. Leader, 'Liberalism now feels inadequate in this new age of insecurity', *New Statesman*, 27 March 2013. Available at http://www.newstatesman.com/politics/politics/2013/03/leader-liberalism-now-feels-inadequate-new-age-insecurity (accessed on 25 August 2014).
8. Maurice Glasman, *Mail on Sunday*, 18 August 2013. Available at http://www.dailymail.co.uk/debate/article-2396382/Lord-Glasman-Ed-Miliband-REAL-Labour-leader.html (accessed on 25 August 2014).

PART ONE

NARRATIVE AND PROGRAMME

CHAPTER ONE

The Good Society, Catholic Social Thought and the Politics of the Common Good

Maurice Glasman

THE POLITICS OF THE COMMON GOOD

Blue Labour was born of the desire for transformation and redemption, the very foundation of a good society and the politics of the common good. It was born of a recognition that the existing political economy, the existing system of the welfare state and a dominant financial sector was giving incentives to vice and not virtue, that it was leaving lives untransformed and unredeemed. The task of changing that involves finding another way of talking about the transformation and redemption of our politics, of a new political consensus based upon virtue and vocation, of a strengthening of relationships and society so that we are not dominated by money and public sector managers, so that the City of London and Westminster are not the sole geographical sites of power, and that political and economic liberalism are not the only definers of progress against which all other traditions are viewed as reactionary.

The generation of a new political consensus around the common good is a task of many hands, many different traditions, and we will be required to show an uncharacteristic civility to each other. The Labour, Conservative, Catholic, evangelical and civic republican traditions have not found a decent way of talking to each other, or even among themselves, for quite a time but they are the sources of nutrition out of which a new political consensus will be formed. The reconciliation of estranged interests is fundamental to a good society and to the common good and it is the work of no one institution alone.

The Labour Party has recently spoken a lot about public sector reform, the centrality of relationships, the decentralisation of power, the importance of accountability and participation of people in public life, so that they have some power and responsibility. In this context it is important to recognise that the contours of a new political consensus shared between the Labour and Conservative traditions are almost visible but also that this change will compel us out of our comfort zone. There will have to be coalitions between religious and secular, unions and employers, public and private sector, even Protestant and Catholic so that we can invite our exiled traditions home and have them engage with each other in creating the new institutions, relationships and practices necessary to treasure quality and equality, power and responsibility, virtue and vocation and above all the strange combination of democracy and liberty that distinguishes the English political tradition. Most particularly this concerns resistance to tyranny, understood as an unaccountable single interest that seeks to impose its will on others. The common good is also a retrieval of a political tradition that has served our country well for almost a millennium (the eight-hundredth anniversary of Magna Carta is in 2015), but has fallen into disrepute since 1945. It is time, perhaps, to domesticate the idea of a commonwealth that inspired the Tudor theorists before the Reformation.

It is a quirk of Blue Labour that we are fond of paradox, something that sounds wrong but is right, and in a rationalist, tin-eared and ungenerous Westminster village that has sometimes led us into trouble. Making statements such as tradition shapes modernity, faith will redeem citizenship, trust is the basis of competition, contribution strengthens solidarity, labour power improves competitiveness, decentralisation underpins patriotism can make us sound like highly educated idiots thus giving a new meaning to oxymoron.

Paradox is, however, necessary for understanding the politics of the common good because it will appear that strange people are in alliance, that incompatible ideas are working better together, and that – when these ideas cease to appear paradoxical but obviously right – political consensus change has been achieved. Perhaps the most important paradox is that the old is the new, that in interrogating exiled political traditions we will find the sources of our renewal. We don't need new policy but a renewed polity which recognises the legitimacy of interests and facilitates their negotiation through renewed institutions that give incentives to virtue rather than incentives to vice. This is the politics of the common good in a nutshell.

WHAT'S GOING ON? THE CRISIS AND THE CHALLENGE TO CONSERVATIVES AND LABOUR

In order to give some definition to what a good society might look like as a means of locating the common good it is perhaps best to ask Marvin Gaye's question of what's going on before we move to Lenin's subordinate question of what is to be done. I continue to be shocked by how Leninist our political class has become, how eager to engage in repetitive activity and how unwilling to reflect on where we find ourselves and why.

What's going on is that society is disintegrating in the face of the state and the market which are characterised by centralisation, concentration and commodification. Ugly words and ugly realities, but I can't find adequate alternatives. Both the market and the state centralise power in the name of efficiency and justice.

It is the tragedy of the conservative tradition since Burke that they have been unable to comprehend that the market centralises power, concentrates wealth and commodifies human beings and their environment. It has led to unaccountable power and the crash of 2008, that long-forgotten moment of clarity when the banks received the biggest subsidy in our national history, which was indicative of how dependent we had become on an avaricious and volatile banking sector with no alternative source of value in our economy. There has been a decimation of our regional banking system: not one of the demutualised building societies still exists as an autonomous institution. Northern Rock, Bradford and Bingley, Halifax, the Midland Bank, all dissolved into the City of London and the big six. Without constraints capital turns to oligopoly.

Equally important for the conservative tradition is that capital, through its pursuit of maximum return on investment, exerts tremendous pressure to turn human beings and their natural environment into commodities that are available at a price in fluctuating markets. Unless there are countervailing institutions with genuine power that can resist this there will be the systematic demoralisation and deceit that led to the financial crash. Without institutions such as families, churches, the army, universities, vocational colleges, professional associations and schools, that are founded upon a non-pecuniary definition of the good, that promote character, honesty, loyalty, skill and faithfulness, that create virtue and incentives to virtue there will be no space between the individual maximiser and the external aggregator, the market and the state. There will be no society at all.

The Big Society foundered on its inability to understand tradition and institutions as embodiments of the good, as countervailing forces to vice. It put all its eggs into the volunteering basket and the message got scrambled. That is the challenge of the common good. It is time for the conservative tradition to recognise the weaknesses as well as the strengths of the market that manifest themselves in poverty wages, usurious interest rates, the disintegration of skills and the subordination of character to the temptations of cheating and greed. There is a need to rediscover the virtue of institutions, local tradition and relationships rather than an exclusive concern with maximisation of returns and quarterly balance sheets. Our economy has been voided of value and fuelled by debt. A good society and a common good requires a change towards value and vocation.

This leads to the challenge to Labour and its uncritical turn to state administration and public spending as a default orthodoxy. In an almost exact parallel to the degradation of what is noble in the conservative tradition, Labour has, at times, been unable to understand how the state can undermine responsibility, agency and participation; that redistribution without reciprocity is just another form of domination and leaves its recipients untransformed. The Labour movement was born in opposition to the free market economy and the Poor Law State and under New Labour, it seems that we forgot both. I have received an astonishing degree of abuse for suggesting that the biggest mistake was the 1945 government – centralising, dominated by public sector managers and impervious to the traditions of labour and their organisations.

Germany went a different way after the war, building its approach around Catholic Social Thought and a form of social democracy that was social and democratic. It embraced subsidiarity and federalism in its politics, a radical form of decentralisation that enabled responsibility and power to be exerted at a local level. It endowed and established regional and sectoral banks that were constrained not to lend outside their region. They developed a partnership model between capital and labour in its corporate governance system that allowed for cooperation and conflict in the negotiation of interests and they retrieved a conception of vocation in their labour market entry that allowed for the preservation of status and skill and the reproduction of knowledge. Family, place and work were all recognised and honoured in a way that they have not been in England since 1945. We won the war, but have lost the peace.

The Good Society and the politics of the common good need to look soberly at vice and virtue and how to give incentives to the latter and not the former, as has been the case until now. Labour needs to repent of its exclusive reliance on an administrative state and the redistribution of money often through transfers to the private sector. Relationships, responsibility and reciprocity should be the guiding principles of welfare reform where contribution plays a central role in the renewal of solidarity.

1945, 1979 and 1997 were all false dawns that led to centralisation and demoralisation in our polity. We have an economy built around debt, a stagnation in wages, a deficit that refuses to shrink, a disaffection with politics, a degradation of previously trusted institutions amidst a backdrop of a generally subdued howl of powerless outrage. That is the background that frames the discussion of what needs to be done.

CATHOLIC SOCIAL THOUGHT

There is no more reasonable tradition from which to begin an analysis of the strengths and weaknesses of the Big Society and no more fertile terrain out of which to begin to fashion a politics of the common good than Catholic Social Thought. It provides durable materials, appropriate practices and profound insights in a synthesis that can challenge and defeat the combination of economic and political liberalism that has subordinated diversity to homogeneity, institutional mediation to individualised care packages, vocational training to transferrable skills and neglected entirely the conditions necessary for flourishing markets and democracy. Above all, it offers a system that challenges the debt and demoralisation that are the twin characteristics of the prevailing economy. It preserves and renews an approach which places institutions and tradition as necessary aspects of modern life and combines this with a robust and subtle conception of vocation, virtue and value, which are the missing practices in our economy and state.

In articulating the necessity of a balance of power between interests within institutions which pursue internal goods, Catholic Social Thought offers the possibility of a common good which is not an aggregate of prevailing interests, or a median point between conflicting views, but a negotiated ethical position that is built upon institutions, interests and practices in which the balance between tension and cooperation is always alive. It is redemptive but anti-utopian in that it views relationship, tradition and vocation as constitutive of a meaningful life but does not posit a world in which negotiation and tensions between interests have been overcome.

The fundamental insight is that while both a market economy based upon private property and price-setting markets, and a state based upon the rule of law and its enforcement are seen as necessary and a condition of justice and prosperity, they are also seen as a profound threat to a fulfilled human life and as sources of power that can dominate people. The tragic paradox of Catholic Social Thought is that while there is no alternative to capitalism, capitalism is no alternative. Also, while there is no alternative to the state, statism is no alternative for it is also, potentially, a collectivist instrument of oppression that can overrule and subordinate traditional institutions, which uphold a non-pecuniary good. The double paradox was resolved by a commitment to the strengthening of that which all forms of progressive social science insisted was doomed, namely society. Society, through the development of institutions built around the preservation and nurturing of status, solidarity and subsidiarity, of reciprocity and responsibility, could mediate the logic of both state and market which was to subordinate all self-organised societal institutions to their mutual sovereignty. Democratic decentralisation played a constitutive role in the formation of Christian Democracy as a political movement. This is a radically different idea to that of the Big Society and is, in fact, far more constitutive of the Labour tradition.

It was the threat to the possibility of a moral personality, of the dignity of the individual that led to the politics of the common good that would distinguish Catholic Social Thought, and the threat came from both capitalism and statism. The threat can be summarised as commodification in terms of capitalism, and collectivisation in terms of the state. Commodification refers to the process through which something that is not produced for sale in the market, human beings and nature for example, a body or a forest, are turned into tradable commodities with a price. The logic of capitalism is to achieve the highest possible rate of return on investment, which asserts a relentless pressure to create commodity markets in labour and land. In the 1830s in Britain vocational status and customary practice were subordinated to freehold title and clearing markets in the economy. Vocational traditions upheld by institutions and land holdings held by custom were viewed as an impediment to justice and efficiency. They were abolished in an alliance between the state and the market that imposed the dispossession of enclosures and the exploitation of industrialisation. The understanding of the way in which capital has a tendency to centralise ownership is well understood within the tradition and was institutionally mediated by the generation of local banks bound by trust to region or sector.

The state, through the demand of impartial administration, also generates an imperative to homogenise procedure and undermine relationships through its collectivist logic. The state can destroy those institutions of the body politic that allow reciprocity and responsibility to be strengthened if it is the exclusive instrument of delivery.

Catholic Social Thought, in other words, argued that those things held to be impossible under conditions of modernity – a sense of place and of human-scale institutions that was pursued through subsidiarity, a continued emphasis on vocation and vocational education and the pursuit of a balance of interests on the boards of companies and welfare institutions – preserved a sense of status that interfered with the prerogatives of capital and its managers from the point of view of classical economic theory and class consciousness for Marxists. A common good underpinned by a diverse range of decentralised democratic institutions embedded in the economy was the distinctive Catholic response to the twin perils of the state and the market, commodification and collectivisation. This was summarised under the heading of solidarity in which a common good was forged through common institutions that were diverse and decentralised in form.

It was Lamennais, a Catholic intellectual and activist who founded the journal *L'Avenir* in Paris in the 1830s, and not Marx who first coined the phrase 'proletariat' to refer to a class without status, assets or power and asserted the importance of mediating institutions that could preserve a sense of honour, skill and belonging in a dehumanised world, which was also a disenchanted, secular and rationalised world. Further, and most importantly of all, Catholic Social Thought remained faithful to a theory of labour value, labour understood in terms of experience, skill and expertise, rather than simply physical energy and time, that was held to be anachronistic and antithetical to the division of labour and managerial rationalism. Catholic Social Theory wagered everything on the relevance and strengthening of that which was held to be rationally impossible and it won. Further, its victory belongs to reason.

Both state and market were held to be necessary and wicked, capable of exploitation and oppression as well as justice and prosperity, and in that tension Catholic Social Thought has generated a unique gift to the modern world: a balanced view. There is not only a distinction to be made between society and the state, but also between society and the market economy, and most importantly, finance capital. It is impossible as well as wrong to have two contradictory systems, one based upon unmediated collectivism and the other upon unfettered individualism. Catholic Social Thought, through the idea of mediation and subsidiarity, represents interests through democratic institutions in the economy and the welfare system thus giving substance to the notion of society, making it not only bigger but more robust and less open to being preyed upon by the state and the market and their mutual desire for unfettered efficiency through the exclusion of institutions.

The reintroduction of institutional mediation is the task of a contemporary statecraft that seeks to generate a common good. The combination of finance capital and public administration, the market and the state, the public–private partnership, which has been the dominant driver of employment and growth over the past 30 years, has not generated very much energy or goodness. Of the £1.3 trillion lent by banks in the British economy between 1997 and 2007, 84 per cent was in mortgages and financial services. The practical predicament we confront is that in the combination of household debt and debt held by our financial institutions we are indeed a world leader and this 'competitive advantage' has been building for a long time. Private indebtedness was the most recent method by which we borrowed against our future to serve the present and it has reached its limit.

The theoretical predicament is that on their own, neither a Keynesian nor a neoclassical approach has the conceptual means of understanding the importance of institutions; of vocation, virtue and value in generating competitive advantage, reciprocity as the foundation of good practice and the importance of long-term relationships between capital, labour and place in generating growth and innovation. Catholic Social Thought gives us both a plausible explanation of crisis and a genuine alternative that can guide action.

The assumption that globalisation required transferrable skills and not vocational speciality, that tradition and local practice were to be superseded by rationalised administration and production was mistaken. The denuding of the country and its people of their institutional and productive inheritance by the higher rates of returns found in the City of London, and then the vulnerability of those gains to speculative loss, is the story we confronted in 2008. Further, the practice of relationships, reciprocity and responsibility were not present. The money managers of the financial sector functioned, within the corporate governance of firms, without oversight or accountability. Organised interests within the speciality and expertise of the firm are a far stronger basis for accountability than accountants and absentee and disorganised shareholders.

For the Catholic anthropology that underpins the theory that we are fallen and capable of both sin and grace and the balance between them is given by human relationships and human-scale institutions within which a balance of power prevails, where the individual proclivity to cheat and lie is tempered by an interest in long-term stable relationships based upon trust, mutual interest and oversight. Redemption is not a unilateral exercise but is, of necessity, relational. The corporation, corporatism, the body politic that animates the discussion of association within the tradition is not dominated by the mind alone but made up of various parts, dependent but undominated.

In Pope Leo XIII's encyclical *Rerum Novarum* of 1891 this is captured by the idea of one hand washing the other, of the conflict and cooperation required for the common good, between organised interests within common institutions. There can be no account of the crisis of capitalism that does not refer to the failure of corporate governance within the financial sector, the lack of virtue and value present within it, the excessive self-regard and the perversity of its incentive structure that allowed the money managers to function outside of all constraint so that risk-taking became a synonym for recklessness and innovation a toxic cocktail of greed and deceit.

The answer is not new and better forms of regulation, but a reconstitution of corporate governance based upon a balance of interest in which there are incentives to virtue. Such incentives can engage with the organisation of interests and the priority of long-term stable faithful relationships in the economy rather than the faithless promiscuity that is the inevitable outcome of undomesticated capitalism. Perhaps the most startling conclusion that Catholic Social Thought leads us to is that having pursued bad for 300 years as a means of achieving good, it might not be such a bad idea to pursue the good more directly.

LABOUR AND THE GOOD SOCIETY

It will come as no surprise that it comes down to Labour in the end. The important and original work by Bishop von Ketteler in Mainz in the 1860s and then developed by Pope Leo XIII in *Rerum Novarum* and developed so profoundly since then was the link established between the Catholic theory of the person, of personality and the institutional arrangements required for the reciprocal development of personality and association organised around the idea that work is transformative of both nature and self. 'By your sweat shall ye live' is our fallen fate. The priority of the value of labour over capital is central to this thesis. In *Laborem Exercens* Pope John Paul II wrote that

> Man is a person, that is to say a subjective being capable of acting in a planned and rational way, capable of deciding about himself and with a tendency to self-realisation. As a person man is the subject of work [...] these act to realise his humanity, to fulfil a calling to be a person that is his by reason of his humanity [...]. Labour is a primary efficient cause, while capital, the whole collection of means of production, remains a mere instrument or instrumental cause.

It will also come as no surprise that I argue that the distinction between predatory and productive capital is central to the position. This has two fundamental components. The first is to assert the ethical rejection of usury, the use of money to prey upon the vulnerability of the poor. This can only be understood if money is conceived as a power. In London Citizens we used to talk about 'living wage' and an interest rate cap of 20 per cent as the floor and the ceiling of the common house. Earning enough to feed your family and limiting the damage of debt is central to preserving a human order. Faith and citizenship are mutual traditions and not, ultimately, antagonistic. The living wage and an interest rate are examples of the state laying down a simple limit, not of regulation but of balance. The second component is to recognise, following the crash, that unconstrained financial capital does not lead to efficiency or growth but severed from practices that tie it to relationships and place generates a volatile nihilism that leads us to where we are: isolated, powerless and disappointed, abandoned without vocation and value before the demands of an unrepayable debt.

The lack of appreciation of the impact of deregulated markets on stable patterns of association, family life and traditions is one that goes back to Burke and has not been resolved through the Big Society. It is hard to engage in public life if you have to work two jobs because you are not paid enough to live. There seems to be no conceptual means for understanding the inequality of power within the market itself. In terms of its political economy, the Big Society is nowhere.

The same critique applies to welfare reform. A move needs to be made from a dualistic structure of public and private towards a Trinitarian structure. Any public institution is made up of three components: funders, users and workers. The state has interests, in justice and avoiding corruption, in the pursuit of wider and integrated forms of social policy but it should not be dominant and should have a third of the seats of the board on any public institution. Similarly, the workforce is a necessary aspect of the good of an institution and necessary for effective delivery. The workforce should, therefore, have a third of the seats on the board that decides strategy and delivery. Similarly, users need responsibility and power in the delivery of service and should not be passive recipients but actively structure the content of delivery. The domination of any single interest is to be avoided if we are to be faithful to the tradition.

So, for example, I argue that Labour's response to free schools should not be to dismiss the power of parents in school governance but to bring that into relationship with teachers and funders in an institution that is committed to the common good. The same is true of hospitals and care homes. Relationships, reciprocity and responsibility are the key terms and are central to the Catholic Social Thought tradition as concerns the balance of power and interests in institutions. It is historically proven self-governing institutions, such as Cambridge University, with its endowments, trusts, college system and chaplains and the Catholic Church with its myriad decentralised orders, churches and institutions that can resist the domination of the state and the market and which, potentially, are allies in doing so.

A good society is based upon a balance of interests rather than the domination of any single interest. It is underpinned by a sense that your own interests are served if there is a sense that it is tied up with the well-being of others. A sense of shared fate that can generate sacrifice and solidarity. This is not a natural condition but is generated and sustained by a range of institutions that support the good. A good society is also a human-scale and humane society, where people can participate in having some power over their lives through working with others. We used to call it democratic politics, but I am sure we can work on the language.

The first condition of a good society is that power is decentralised so that a sense of place is restored, in which people can earn and belong to specific institutions and localities. Subsidiarity, the exercise of power at the lowest level possible commensurate with the performance of its function, which has its counterpart in federalism within the republican tradition, is a necessary condition of redistributing power and responsibility.

We need to return citizenship to the city and cease talking about its national meaning. We are subjects of the Crown, but emphasise that citizenship is civic status, it is natural to cities. Self-governing cities with embedded universities, vocational colleges, banks, parliaments and budgets that are governed by their citizens are part of that. We can imagine, for example, the City of London, with its mayor, guildhall, livery companies and aldermen representing all of London, in which all Londoners are citizens and where the democratically elected mayor lives in Mansion House and the Guildhall is London's Parliament. The old is the new.

Renewed country hundreds with power and control over the countryside is its complement. People require institutional expression of their interests and the power to act in the world to pursue those interests. The flooding in the West Country in 2014 speaks of a lack of local power over their shared needs and a centralised power that had other concerns. Dredging rivers should be part of the local calendar and fulfilled by local people upholding their responsibility and duty to the good. In specific institutional terms the common good can be pursued through the corporate governance of all schools and hospitals consisting of one-third funder, one-third user and one-third workforce: the three constituent parts of any institutions who negotiate a common good and hold each other to account. So in any school a third of the seats on the governing body would be held by the funder, whether that be the state or the local authority, a third by parents and a third by the teachers.

This is linked to a recognition of work, and most particularly of vocation as a central aspect of the preservation of value, whether that is understood in the determination of price or by the ethics of the person who embodies the vocation. The importance of work and the work ethic is something that should be at the heart of the Labour Party: labour is constitutive of our humanity in terms of childbirth and family life, the transformation of things through skilful action, the meaning of going to work.

It is vital that the vocation of teaching is restored, but where is the institution that upholds the tradition, the practice and the craft of teaching and enforces it within the sector? There is none. That is why we need to establish a college of teaching run by teachers, for teachers, to restore the vocation from the conditions of proletarianisation that have been imposed by a coalition between government and the teaching unions since the war. The consequences of pursuing decentralisation, vocation and a common good in education are surprising. It requires different pathways at 14 and a new respect for a vocation that leads to an apprenticeship in a specific skill. It requires labour market reform that gives to plumbers the same market status as dentists and accountants. It requires a substantive reform of higher education which could involve turning half our universities into vocational colleges run and funded by a partnership between local business, unions, and civic institutions that employ local people such as hospitals and universities and city governments. The generation of mutual interests where there is now estrangement is one way of conceptualising this. Renewing vocation is another.

The common good will also be carried by the need for new financial institutions and the problem of debt. Pope Francis called usury the way that the rich prey upon the problems of the poor, and that is the case when Barclays lend to the Money Shop at 7 per cent and they begin their lending at 5,500 per cent. The Pope has spoken out, and Archbishop Justin has also led courageously on this issue and wishes to build an alternative banking system through the credit unions.

Guy Opperman is helping set up a community bank in Hexham. Unite is supporting the establishment of the Bank of Salford, bound to lend within Salford, and has consolidated the credit union funds; the local authority is putting its payroll through it and it is taking deposits from local people. A politics of the common good would reconcile the churches and trade unions in upholding a status of the person through building institutions that serve the interests of the poor. The unions would redefine themselves as having a civic function within society rather than an exclusive concern with the party and the state. The Church would fulfil its calling as an embodiment of the good. The bank would lend to local businesses who have suffered from the disintegration of local banking systems and the lack of affordable credit. Businesses, unions, churches, mosques, local authorities, all seeking a common good through the sharing of resources and local leadership and initiative. Participation, enterprise and a renewed sense of solidarity are the results of building local institutions together, which is another way of talking about the politics of the common good.

When I see Justin Welby speaking alongside Len McCluskey in the shared pursuit of the good of the city I will know that the agenda is really taking form. The future should be shocking and full of surprises.

CONCLUSION

The new consensus, built around the common good, will be pro-business and pro-worker, it will be patriotic and localist, it will be based on lower tax but higher participation, a balance of interests that facilitate negotiation. One of the paradoxes I mentioned at the beginning of this essay was that tension is necessary to reach a common good, we have to learn to stay in the room and represent our interests and explore how they can be reconciled with others. The fundamental insight is that we cannot do it alone. We need relationships, institutions and other people to fulfil ourselves.

CHAPTER TWO

The Blue Labour Dream

John Milbank

PARADOXICAL POLITICS

Within the British Labour Party, 'Blue Labour' is the crucial factor in the emergence of 'One Nation Labour'. Such paradoxical combinations are characteristic of the new 'post-liberal' politics in the United Kingdom, which seeks to combine greater economic justice with individual virtue and public honour. Blue Labour rejects the double liberal impersonalism of economic contract between strangers, and individual entitlement in relation to the bureaucratic machine. Instead of the combination of contract without gift, plus the unilateral gift from apparently nowhere that is state welfare, it proposes gift-exchange or reciprocity as the ultimate principle to govern *both* the economic and the political realms.[1] This would restore in a new version the ancient and medieval idea of the political as ultimately an extension of friendship within a shared *ethos*.

But an ethos can only develop over time, and so post-liberal advocates like David Goodhart have called for a new recognition of the role of tradition and the contract between the generations.[2] The Labour Party is grounded in the notion of solidarity amongst labour and it sees all human beings as workers, because, as Maurice Glasman has said, in line with Catholic Social Teaching, it is with respect to work that we see the *personal* origin of all of human society and culture.[3] Yet work also takes time: it requires learning from the past, induction into inherited lineages of good craft and relating to fellow workers; an initial submitting to leadership if one is eventually to lead in one's turn. It is for this reason that Labour affirmation of civil society in terms of solidarity and mutuality requires a linkage with certain Burkean thematics if it is not simply to fade back into the current hegemony of liberal notions of isolated freedom of choice.

The same consideration applies to notions of equality. How can we decide to own some things in common and to divide up other goods equitably if we do not know what constitutes a good and what broad ends of flourishing human beings should agree to pursue? Of course we have no fixed or final knowledge of such things – but tradition gives us some intimation of their nature and education allows us to refine and debate this intimation. Without a concern for formation and virtue which is not in itself democratic – because the genuine good remains the good even if all vote against it – we lack the precondition for democracy and for democratic discussion which will further refine our sense of what it is that renders us human.

And without the possession of virtue whose key mark is Aristotelian *phronesis* or a kind of moral art or tact, we will remove social judgement from the hands of humans as workers or craftsman and assume that everything must be precisely legislated. Soon we will suppose that right and wrong can be exactly defined and that all that is wrong must be legally outlawed, while all that is not outlawed is not only permissible but valuable. Soon after that we will imagine that we should only be allowed to do that for which we have a legal licence. These drifts can readily be seen to be at work in the recent debates over gay marriage and also in those over surveillance, whistleblowing and the indictment of military decisions before courts of human rights. All of this witnesses to the bankruptcy of the liberal rights perspective and the lack of attention to non-formalisable, non-legal judgement. To give an example: governments have no absolute right in the name of security to know everything, but neither are rights of privacy absolute in relation to the public good. Soldiers who reveal injustice in battle should not be treated as mere breakers of a contract, but neither can army commanders treat protection of their troops' lives as an absolute (since a soldier, by definition, has signed up to possible sacrificial death) in the face of other considerations, like not alienating a civilian population.

THE LIMITS OF MODERN LIBERALISM

These are some summary indications of what post-liberalism might mean and why, in my view, the Labour tradition is naturally aligned with it. But to understand more deeply what this new politics involves, it is necessary to attend closely to the intended sense of both 'post' and 'liberal'. 'Post-' is different from 'pre-' and implies not that liberalism is all bad, but that it has inherent limits and problems. 'Liberal' may immediately suggest to many an easy-going and optimistic outlook. Yet to the contrary, at the core of a searching critique of liberalism lies the accusation that it is a far too gloomy political philosophy. For liberalism assumes that we are basically self-interested, fearful, greedy and egotistic creatures, unable to see beyond our own selfish needs and instincts. This is the founding assumption of the individualistic liberal creed, derived from Grotius, Hobbes and Locke in the seventeenth century.[4]

Such a position sounds, as it is, secular and materialistic. However, another important root of modern liberalism, traceable for example in Adam Smith, derives from Calvinistic and Jansenistic theologies. For this theological outlook original sin is so extreme that human beings must be considered to be nearly or totally 'depraved' and incapable by nature of acting out of virtue to produce economic, social or political order. Instead, in a kind of proxy operation, divine providence must manipulate our egotistic wills and even our vices behind our backs, in such a way as to make will balance will and vice balance vice to produce a simulacrum of economic and political harmony, even though this had never been originally intended by self-obsessed individuals.[5] Here is the ideological root of Smith's 'hidden hand'.

In this way we can see how liberalism has been doubly promoted by both hedonists and puritans. Today the British Conservative Party, which has long since abandoned Toryism for liberalism, remains something of an uneasy alliance between these two different character traits, even if the puritans are fast losing ground.

However, neither label would exactly seem to apply to the *Guardian*-reader-type granola-eating liberal, whom we more usually take today to define liberalism as such. Why does the fit appear so poor? The answer is that there is another, 'romantic' variant of liberalism that was invented in the late eighteenth century by Jean-Jacques Rousseau. He inverted Thomas Hobbes by arguing that the isolated, natural individual is 'good', lost in contemplative delight at the world around him, satisfied with simple pleasures and provisions. He is not yet egotistic, because that vice arises from rivalry and comparison. However, Rousseau took the latter to be endemic once the individual is placed in a social context. Accordingly he transferred pessimism about the individual into a new pessimism about human association. This encouraged scepticism about the role of corporate bodies beneath the level of the state: for it is only the state that can lead us to sacrifice all our petty rivalries for the sake of the common purpose or general will which will return to us, at a higher level, our natural isolated innocence.[6]

The problem with this vision is that the state will not really stand above the interests of faction and sectional intrigue. And meanwhile the concentration of all power in the centre will just as effectively undermine the immediate bonds of trust between people as does the operation of impersonal market forces. Recent British governments have apparently exulted in this erosion of trust because it tends to increase their power to control individuals both directly and en masse. Accordingly they have increased the power of the market, decreased the power of local government and voluntary associations and, as Goodhart has related, permitted immigration without integration in such a way as tends to make the inhabitants of these islands more and more strangers to each other.[7]

The invocation of Rousseau allows us more easily to locate the *Guardian* reader. While the *Financial Times* sort of 'right-wing' liberal takes a basically gloomy view of the individual, the *Guardian* reader takes a basically gloomy view of society. But this verdict seems to have things back to front. Isn't the political right suspicious of anything public and the political left unwilling to trust individual liberty very far?

Yet at the deepest level the contrast is the other way round: right-wing liberalism is so cynical about individual motivation that it entrusts social order to the public mechanism of the market and to an inflexible legal protection of property by the state. The liberal left, on the other hand, so distrusts shared tradition and consensus that it endlessly seeks to release chaotically various individual desire from any sort of generally shared requirements, which it always tends to view as arbitrary.

This is most of all shown by the New Left, which ever since the 1960s has pursued a politics not of solidarity but of emancipation. Such a politics endlessly seeks to show that an overlooked 'exception' – of gender, sexuality, race, disability, religion or culture – does not and cannot conform to a shared norm and therefore that its specificity (regarded at once and incoherently as arising both from given nature and pure preference) must be released. Equally, this politics misreads the necessity of hierarchically organised care, that is intrinsic to our temporality and variety of formation and talents, as unacceptable patriarchal domination.[8] But by doing so it cannot promote an extreme libertarianism (crossed with and confused by multiculturalism) without at the same time reinforcing and assisting the cause of right-wing liberalism which it claims to oppose.[9]

In this instance, as in others, right and left liberals converge far more than they imagine. For in either case what is basically celebrated is random individual desire. And in either case human association or relationship is distrusted, since it is held that it is bound to be perversely motivated. The right holds that the remedy for warped relationships is the hidden hand of the marketplace; the left the manifest hand of the state. But in either case 'society' is bypassed and human beings are mediated indirectly, by a third pole standing over against them – the neo-liberal 'market-state'.

We can contrast this liberalism with George Orwell's genuinely socialist trust in 'common decency'.[10] People have always lived through practices of reciprocity, through giving, gratitude and giving again in turn. By way of this process people achieve, in a simple way, mutual *recognition* and relationality. Most people pursue association, and the honour and dignity of being recognised in significant ways, however lowly, as their main goals, and are relatively unconcerned with becoming much richer than their fellows or achieving great power over them. Indeed, most people wisely realise that such things will only increase their anxiety and insecurity – they prefer a less spectacular but quieter life. They are basically hobbits. Nevertheless, the temptation to pursue the goals of pride at the expense of danger is there in all of us; in some more than others and in some to an overwhelming degree that can threaten the social fabric. Deep down people are 'decent' and rejoice in relationality, yet in all of us a destructive imp of the perverse always lurks.

Orwell suggested that a good society is one which erects safeguards against such perversity and especially against the overweening, reckless individual, and he pointed out that most tribal structures are built on just this 'warding-off of danger'. Inversely, the positive structures of a social order should seek to build upon our natural and given practices of reciprocity – not destroying, but augmenting our natural capacity for association. For Orwell this more prevailing human instinct was the root of genuine, popular socialism. But liberalism does just the opposite to what Orwell recommended: it tries to remove intermediate social practices of mutual assistance, while augmenting our tendencies to pursue wealth and prestige instead of human and divine love. It ignores the fact that human life as such depends upon a bedrock of gift-exchange and that it develops in time through the astonishing and gratuitous irruption of new charisms.[11]

In the nineteenth century, working people and some intellectuals started to grasp this. They were inspired by a spontaneous sense that something was missing from liberal modernity. What was lacking was relationality, creative fulfilment in work, festivity and joy. They did not, like some conservatives of 'the right', wish to return to the bastard feudalism of the *ancien régime,* but they also rejected the individualism of the modern liberal 'left'. Now to pursue above all relationality is to risk being *wounded* by the other: thus the mood is often going to be indeed 'blue'. The market and the state encourage us to think that we can be insulated from such hurt by the impersonality of economic and bureaucratic or legal transactions.[12] But without embracing the likelihood of some or even much sorrow, there can be no openness to real joy either. Through a bland buffering, participatory power is removed from ordinary people.

A further problem with specifically statist buffering is that it is resigned to treating the market as an evil monster that can be partially tamed but never rendered benign and docile. This is one crucial manifestation of the liberal idea of the priority of evil to which I have already alluded. Within the terms of this assumption it is thought that the main instrument of social justice must be government redistribution. But that can only realistically be carried out in a period of guaranteed economic growth – for otherwise, within the norms of capitalist operation, it will tend to damage profits and so national productivity. Partly because sustained strong growth is not in prospect in the UK for the foreseeable future, Ed Miliband is rightly abandoning this view for notions of 'pre-distribution' – or in other words attempts to produce a just economy in the first place as the major vehicle of material equity.

LIBERAL ECONOMICS AND THE LOGIC OF DIMINISHING MARGINAL UTILITY

But this is only true in part, because pre-distribution makes more radical sense in any case. An inherently just economy would provide more stable financial security for most people, providing stronger incentives to work effectively, and at the same time it would escape the logic whereby the social goals of the state and the supposedly amoral, wealth-increasing goals of the market are seen to be in inherent tension with each other. A further good consequence would be the removal of many people from welfare dependence – something that neo-liberal policies only *create*.

What is more, ever since the 1890s, statist solutions have often been just as committed to the marginalist ideology of neoclassical economics as have those of the 'free market'.[13] According to this ideology human beings exercise 'rational choice' in terms of their calculation of utilities. Beyond Jeremy Bentham it is allowed that humans' ideas of what makes them happy can be incredibly various, but it is still thought that in order to fulfil our desires we make a cold calculation of gains and losses. Inevitably this means that the typical object of desire is still thought of as a commodity consumable by the individual in isolation. Such objects were deemed by the marginalists to be subject to the 'law of diminishing returns': over time we get less satisfaction from consumer durables and their rarity value diminishes as other consumers catch up with us.

To propose this notion was to ignore those goods which are 'relational' in character – family, friendship, erotic unions, warm communities. Equally it was to fail to distinguish the enjoyment that we get from high-quality goods like works of art or literature or the exercise of artistic talents from other objects of consumption. High-quality goods and the realisation of skill through long practice tend to deliver a more solid kind of happiness and also the kind of happiness in others which we most tend to admire and want to emulate. This 'higher' happiness was dubbed *eudaimonia* or 'flourishing' by Greeks such as Plato and Aristotle. So, as Jon Cruddas has argued, perhaps the crucial question in contemporary British politics is whether the main aim of government should be to increase people's freedom of market choice, largely in the sphere of measurable material happiness, or whether its main aim should be to seek to encourage human *eudaimonia*.[14]

A couple of footnotes to this diagnosis are in order here. First, if it is correct, then the main issue of contention in modern politics *is no longer* 'state versus market'. For in many ways we can now see that this was a sham debate. The proponents of marginalist economics were just as often of the left as of the right, and the crucial reason for this is that neoclassicism can favour statism just as easily as it can markets freed from all state interference. For the central theory of neoclassicism is that when the individual calculators of utility are acting rationally, then markets will achieve perfect equilibrium, balance or clearance. To the degree that they fail to act rationally, then the state can make adjustments. This much is common to marginalists of both the right and the left – the difference arises in terms of how far it is supposed that the conditions for perfect market operation arise automatically through market processes themselves and how far they have to be politically engineered.

Thus both the invisible hand of 'providence' and the visible hand of the state is deemed by this outlook to be seeking the same goal of perfect rational equilibrium that coordinates egoistic wishes, without any mutual agreement as to the common good. It is for this reason that even neo-liberal theorists who dogmatically rejected the role of the state still often *modelled* the ideally free market in terms of how a socialist state would distribute material goods *if* it enjoyed perfect information. Conversely, the socialist states of the old Eastern bloc generally conceived their citizens as utilitarian rational actors, rather than in the humanistic terms of the young Marx.[15]

Even when 'market socialisms' were advocated and practised, especially in Yugoslavia and Hungary, the model remained highly rationalistic. So much so that part of the argument put forward was that if property remains in some way publicly owned and if individual firms are democratically organised, then the market in goods and labour can operate with a much more genuine 'freedom', after the model of Adam Smith.[16] So although there is still something to be learned from these examples, they lacked any sense that excessively 'prideful' economic action, leading to monopolistic conglomerations of monetary power, can only be prevented through a reciprocal determination of economic prices, wages and shares linked to a sense of inherent moral value.[17] This element was only really inserted into 'market socialism' by the Catholic-inspired Solidarnosc in Poland.[18]

The second footnote concerns the relationship between the social and the political. Aristotle declared that 'man is a political animal'. Augustine, on the other hand, discovered that human community is more fundamentally 'social' than it is 'political' because it is always united by a 'certain object of desire' that is prior to specific laws and coercion.[19] Thomas Aquinas, who was decisively influenced by both thinkers, seemed to synthesise them by translating Aristotle's 'political animal' in Greek (*zoon politikon*) into 'social animal' in Latin (*animal sociale*). However, Aquinas still thought that any constituted society would have to possess a ruling and legal authority in some sense or other. So in agreement with Aquinas it can be suggested that, while 'society' is the primary human reality, we cannot realistically imagine human associations existing entirely 'before' the state (in whatever sense) any more than we can imagine cultural individuals existing prior to the state, as in the misleading 'social contract' thought-experiments of Hobbes, Locke and Rousseau.

This reflection has implications for Labour's perspective upon the 'big' or 'the good' society. Primarily, as I have already suggested, it is committed to 'the public realm', which is both social and political. For while this realm does indeed first of all exist in civil society and belongs to the people themselves (which Labour has largely forgotten since 1945, as Glasman has argued), it remains crucial to a specifically Labour or socialist case that the social *is of political relevance* if the prime purpose of politics is to promote human flourishing.

By this I mean that the real economic, cultural and ethical conditions of human beings are the proper concern of government, as they most certainly were for Aristotle. But liberals have always tended to deny this – including such highly sophisticated and nuanced liberals as Alexis de Tocqueville. For them, economic, ethical and cultural circumstances have to be left to the private sphere.[20]

It is here, perhaps, that one can glimpse a further element of the 'blue' in Blue Labour and the Disraelian component in One Nation Labour. For while a new ethos has to spring up mainly from below, as Glasman has insisted, it is also the case, as he would agree, that governments cannot just remain neutral with respect to ethos, but must both encourage the good and discourage the bad in various ways – through education, institutional formation and legal frameworks. In this way a 'Tory paternalist' political element as recommended by Robert and Edward Skidelsky is a paradoxically natural partner of greater democratic co-determination of human society.[21] For the alternative here is really a liberal, supposedly 'neutral' state that is in reality on the side of the barren and barbarous elitism of income and technical expertise. There simply is no third possibility. But in modification of this 'paternalism' it needs to be said that between a genuinely good government and a virtuous people a constant feedback should operate all the time.

Yet can a new emphasis on the common good and the promotion of human flourishing be truly relevant to hard economic questions? It can, because liberalism itself, as Adair Turner has hinted, is subject to that very law of diminishing returns which it has itself articulated.[22] We can see this especially with respect to finance. *At first*, as the history of the modern world attests, liberalisation of financial markets leads to growth, but in the long run, as we now see, *too much* financial liberty tends to anarchy. The components of this condition are over-abstraction from the real economy, self-interest that can in reality (contra marginalism) be aligned to market failure rather than market success, the non-constraint of capital by labour and a multitude of transactions that are only about shifting around the existing monetary symbols of wealth, not about creating new wealth.

Generalising this point about finance to the whole history of liberalism, one can say that while to begin with in history the release of individual negative freedom removes many oppressions and allows for new manifestations of creative talent, in the long run it too much tends to stifle the exercise of trust that is crucial to all human association, while eroding belief in the objective values that creativity might seek to instantiate. A lack of trust and belief in objective metaphysical truth and goodness then engenders high-level criminality, greater inequality and fear-driven rivalry. Such an atmosphere actually starts to inhibit people's inventiveness and entrepreneurship and therefore their capacity for freedom – even for freedom of choice. In the same way the spirit of greed tends to replace small businesses with large and monopolising ones which are reluctant to pursue innovations for fear of damaging existing products.

Here one can note something that usually goes entirely overlooked. Anglo-Saxon capitalism is essentially *passive* and *not* dynamic because it is built upon an Enlightenment philosophy which only acknowledges the reality of impersonal *givens* like material reality and human reasoning power. It can only acknowledge the *gift* of human creativity as an abstract and valueless power of will. The primacy of capital over labour follows from this: it exalts an economy perversely driven by the willed stockpiling of the mere means of production in land, technology and finance. Eventually this leads to stasis, lack of products to invest in, excessive speculation and a cycle of debt – reinforced by the lack of grounding of money in any objective standard or disinterested legal system ever since 1944.[23]

By contrast, two of the most successful economies in the last half-century – those of Germany and Italy (despite the recent and to an extent German-imposed problems of the latter) which tend to define our lifestyles in terms of automobiles, domestic technology, food, cafés and clothing – are not really the products of the Enlightenment but of a Renaissance that remained in continuity with the Middle Ages. What I mean by this is that they combine a Renaissance exaltation of the creativity of human labour with a medieval sense of constitutional corporatism that is neither statist nor merely free-market in character. Worker participation in management, control of entry conditions to labour by voluntary associations, and high-status technical education are all predicated on the relative primacy of labour with respect to capital.[24] And labour, not capital is the dynamic factor, because it is to do with release of personal, creative human power. This is quite different from the negative freedom of the Anglo-Saxon will – for creativity goes along with the power to judge and discern the aesthetic and social value of one's product. This is exactly the difference between German cars and Italian food and design compared to the American equivalents. Of course many American products are excellent – but then the Middle Ages and the Renaissance survive even in the United States...

So without trust and the primacy of labour it turns out that the economy as a whole cannot function. This is true also because an economy comprises not only markets, but also *firms* which are inherently cooperative exercises. Recent attempts to run them on internally agonistic lines, setting employees at each other's throats, have not proved a great economic success – least of all in universities.

POPULAR SOCIALISM AND THE 'CIVIL ECONOMY' ALTERNATIVE

So could it be that a more ethical economy, like a more creative and aesthetic economy, is also a more stable economy, more viable in the long term? A crucial argument here is that this has in some degree always been the case. Anglo-Saxon and French economic theory has largely followed liberal presuppositions. But Italian economists, standing in a more classically humanist and Christian tradition, unbroken since the Middle Ages and the Renaissance, have often, ever since the eighteenth century, thought in much more associationist terms. For them, an economic contract itself can be a sympathetic negotiation about shared value and community benefit as well as self-interest – which is itself more socially and so realistically construed.[25] In terms of this more reciprocal model of contract it is arguable that much of the *actual* market economy of the modern world has operated more like the Italian theorised 'civil economy' than like the Anglo-Saxon fantasised 'political economy'. This means that perhaps we have never been as 'capitalist' as we imagine, and in fact the more the market economy becomes dominated by capital the less functional it is shown to be.

Crucially, a capitalist economy, as Stefano Zamagni explains, does not pursue the common good but 'the total good'.[26] That means the sum total of individual utilitarian happiness in the aggregate. People counted one by one, not in their real relationships. But an abstract sum means a sum of numbers, the total wealth of a community, which may accrue to some more than to others, to a small minority rather than to the vast majority. The British GDP is evidently *not* the common good of the British people.

Yet a true market economy can be described, after Zamagni and his co-writer Luigino Bruni as a 'civil economy'.[27] That kind of economy really does, in principle, pursue the common good: the good of each and every one of us as we concretely are in our families, workplaces, communities. But how can we do that by labouring and trading in the market? The answer is that one can be both pursuing a reasonable profit for oneself, and at the same time trying to offer to other people a social benefit – in return for a social benefit that they are offering you. One can trade in real human goals as well as in hard cash. Likewise a contract can be a reciprocal agreement about a shared goal and value, not just the joint meeting of two entirely separate individual goals. The latter applies when I take a cab: I want to get to the station, the taxi-driver needs to feed his children. But it does not apply if I and my neighbour agree to put up a hedge between our gardens that we both want. More pertinently, it does not apply if villagers collectively agree to use some vacant land to build a new village hall or if a town-council and a business consortium agree to encourage the growth of a certain industry as appropriate to the town's needs and capacities. It does not even apply if you know the taxi-driver or if you offer him an unnecessarily generous tip.

It follows from this contrast between the capitalist economy and the market economy that the challenge now is to move away from neoclassicist utility in either its neo-liberal or statist versions, towards a specifically recognised and deliberately augmented 'civil economy' based upon reciprocal exchange and the virtuous pursuit of a true economic wealth that contributes to human flourishing. Such an economy would also be a more stable one, relatively freed from cyclical fluctuations that are ultimately to do with a clash of interests between capital and worker, producer and consumer, supply and demand. These clashes can be avoided or mitigated where economic contracts are the subject of ethical and sometimes legal negotiation and all parties feel that they have been fairly dealt with and share a common stake and pride in the success of an enterprise and the quality of its products. Human beings want recognition for excellence and social contribution much more than they wish to pursue primal hoarding. This is a much more fundamental Anglo-Saxon truth, first articulated in the great Anglo-Saxon epic *Beowulf*.

Moves towards such a civil economy need to include, amongst other things, the following elements:[28] 1. The sharing of risk in all financial transactions – including house mortgages – between lenders and borrowers, investors and owners, shareholders and managers, employers and employees; 2. The rewriting of company law to demand statement of social purpose and profit-sharing as conditions of trading; 3. A new public institutional 'trust' for the pooling of technological knowledge to replace the current patenting system;[29] 4. Ethical as well as economic negotiation of wages, prices and share-values amongst owners, workers, shareholders and consumers who would all be given real political and economic stakes in every enterprise. Such practices would be encouraged by legal and taxation arrangements, while disputes over such matters would come more within the purview of the courts of justice; 5. Passing through vocational training and membership of various recognised professional vocational associations, encouraging an honourable ethos, being made conditions of entry to business practice.[30] 6. A contributory welfare system whose mutualism would preclude any need for means-testing to ensure a safety net. Such a system would again enshrine reciprocity and have the further merit of encouraging people to take greater risks in business, in the knowledge that, if they failed, not all their gains would be lost.[31]

To propose such things is in effect to suggest a rather novel mode of 'civil economy socialism'. What do I mean by such a claim? It can be contended that there have been two major phases of socialist thinking. The first, running up to 1848 and then somewhat beyond, was in quite severe reaction against a basically 'Smithian' economism, exacerbated by Malthus and Ricardo. So much was this the case, that 'socialism' was often seen as an *alternative* to economics. 'Social' solutions were sought, whether of a semi-anarchistic or state-led kind, which sought in various measures to bypass such economic categories as price, income, shares, interest, property and even money itself. Marx's 'communism', to be arrived at beyond the envisaged first state-led 'socialist' phase, remained within this paradigm.

However, the second phase of socialism, in part because it was far less Christian and religious in various modes, tended, as already discussed, fully to ascribe to the rationalist utilitarianism of neoclassical economics. This was just as true of Soviet economics as of Fabianism. The thinking of this phase rightly regarded Marxian economics as not an economic advocacy, but rather as what Marx had said it was, namely 'a critique of political economy', and so as the theoretical aspect of the critique of capitalism, taken to be an 'economism'. In consequence, Marxism was seen as not very relevant for building a socialist economy, and even (with more revisionism) as not sufficient for knowing how to arrive at the Communist future.

This was instead to be done in rationalist and utilitarian terms that involved the joint operation of state and market in various combinations. As a concomitant of this approach, certain 'economic' realities were after all accepted in differing modes and to different degrees. Gorbachev's mode of market socialism (which was *not* initially covertly capitalist) proposed to restore the entire gamut – private property, wage, shares, interest, etc. of such operational categories.[32]

Compared to these two socialisms, 'civil economy socialism' could inaugurate a third model which would *for the first time* offer a socialism that was both practicable and humane. For it would combine the realistic acceptance of economic categories of socialism 2, with the focus on immediate human reciprocity and solidarity of socialism 1. But unlike socialism 1 (to an admittedly varying extent), it would realise that the economic can also be the site of the reciprocal. It must be said here that many practices of the Italian cooperative movement in the past and the present would conform to this third model, even though they have often not identified themselves as 'socialist', in their refusal of the anti-economism of socialism 1.[33]

In this way, the Labour Party could start to reinvent the socialist and cooperative tradition itself. But if we need a mutualist market, we also need a mutualist state. To some degree Labour local councils especially are starting to deliver this both by using the Coalition Government's localism measures, and subverting its transferred cuts to work in partnership with social enterprises and voluntary associations. At the state level we need the kind of strategic instead of tactical intervention that I have already mentioned, including a renaissance of vocational education and an integrated transport policy linked to mutual associations of operators, workers and transport users.

And again in keeping with the 'High Tory' aspect of One Nation Labour, we need to restore the notion of an honourable elite. For as the implausibly High Tory Tony Benn always insisted, besides the elected delegates of a people, the other valid contributors to government are a professional body who have inherited a dedicated commitment to serve the national well-being. Our civil service is in something of a mess, as the repeated train operators' debacle has proved. To improve it, greater democratic answerability is only half the solution, because in a representative democracy those who take the decisions can never be entirely called to popular account. In addition one requires a renewed sense of honourable public service and pride in position at the top of our bureaucracy. Even a meritocracy requires a sense of *tradition* if it is to function well and virtuously.

At the centre of this new mode of action lies a linking of the renewal of our culture and of pride in our regions with economic recovery. For if we are still sick in the UK then it is a psychological and not just an economic sickness. We need to recall who we are as a nation: the people who invented constitutional government and gave it to the world and should continue to help to do so, freed from the shackles of excessive US influence. We also need to recall who we are in our localities. In Nottingham where I work, this means a place of free manufacturing all the way from medieval alabaster statues supplying the whole of Europe through lace-making to modern bicycles and drugs to the world market. A place of craft, skill and greenwood fraternity and sorority. Without that kind of pride and self-belief we will not want to work in the future to any purpose.

And instead of relying mainly on state redistribution we need to forge an economy that operates justly and fairly in the first place:

both through the internal ethos of firms and professional associations, and through a new legal framework that demands that every
business deliver social benefit as well as reasonable profit. But this
does not imply that the state has no role. Alongside ideas of the Big
or the Good Society we need a new notion of the 'public' that slides
between society and state-direction or answerability. It is here that,
following Glasman's ideas, at the centre of the emerging Blue Labour
programme, could stand the idea not of tactical government
intervention but of the strategic shaping of new economic
institutions: of systems of apprenticeships; of entry conditions to
work through the operation of professional bodies, of new
polytechnics, more visionary business schools, regional banks and
partnerships between such banks, local business and new city-based
parliaments.

Of course such true economic equilibrium cannot be achieved by
one country alone, because international capitalist forces would tend
to undercut it. For this reason, the adoption by Labour of a civil
economy approach would imply an unprecedented and more
creative foreign policy. Such a policy would regard London's
geopolitical and geo-economic situation as a vortex of meeting and
competing forces as an advantage rather than a drawback. With the
EU and with the Commonwealth and the former French (and
perhaps also Spanish) dominions *together* we could try to craft an
alternative international network of expanded 'fair trade' and legal
guarantee whose ability and success could eventually bring even the
United States and other countries into its orbit. If the EU could
abandon its current commitments to neo-liberalism and to formal
regulation and absolute rights, and support at an interstate level the
communitarian and constitutionally corporatist elements in
Germany and Italy, then it could find the courage to cancel its
own internal and external debts, fund more adequately its own
scientific leadership and assume genuine power in the world for the
good. Instead of an absolute free trade in capital and labour it could
substitute reciprocal agreements for mutually beneficial protection-
isms for certain things in certain nations and regions. Such a politics
of shared sovereignty would be the international equivalent of
subsidiarity within nations and could form the nucleus of a
governing network that is potentially global.

A BLUE LABOUR VISION OF RENEWING THE BRITISH COMMONWEALTH

In my view, 'One Nation Labour' will fail unless it has this truly bold scope. As Goodhart argues, it needs a vision for Britain if everything is not to fall apart in the face of now extreme divisions between the British nations, between north and south, between secular and religious, between young and old, between men and women, between town and countryside, between culture and culture and between the EU and its constituent nations. I have already tried to indicate aspects of what this vision might be.

More controversially, I do *not* think that this vision can be simply a version of the American dream or an essentially post-imperial 'Little Britain' one. For this would be to misunderstand who we are and how we have come to be – which is not out of a big revolutionary explosion, as Goodhart has rightly noted. Rather, our slow-burning genius, as both English and Celtic, since before the Norman conquest (but always of a part-Christian inspiration) is political, it is to know how to govern, based on a flexible rule of law and on constitutional free association at many different levels. It is this long legacy of interweaving consent with leadership, and freedom with community that has most of all given to the world modern democracy – and by comparison the revolutionary legacies are rather inadequate parodies, on which what is best in France and the United States does not really depend.

Therefore we have to tell a long-term story about ourselves – not simply a Whiggish and capitalist recent story that is superficial and misleading. Part of this story is the strange truth that we have never been a pure nation state – have never been based on a narrow ethnicity – but also lacked for a long time and never completely acquired, as Carl Schmitt noted, the crucial marks of modern statehood – 'police' control by the state, juridical formalism, state-administered finance and civil politeness: this is why we are still so rude and robust in debate.[34] Instead, the British Atlantic empire, like the Spanish one, arose in continuity with its *medieval* empire, where a group of diverse local territories, ethnicities and cultures was already held together by a common set of symbolic loyalties, values and acceptance of a certain jurisprudential horizon which was rather different from that, for example, of France.

There is therefore a historic sense in which 'empire' can be more benign, plural and inclusive a reality than that of 'nation

state'. Of course the international British Empire was overwhelmingly to do with capitalist expropriation and it eventually
tried to impose precisely 'statist' features on a global scale.
However, it also from the outset mitigated through politics,
diplomacy and cultural negotiation a more naked exploitation on
the part of freebooting entrepreneurs. Equally, given the limits of
its military and personnel resources, it perforce had to encourage
the emergence of more plural and indigenous modes of political
control, while also fostering a certain cross-cultural and international modulation of an originally merely British ethos. This
should be inversely contrasted with the fact that every nation state
is as much the upshot of originally violent seizure as is every
empire. Meanwhile the obsession since the mid-nineteenth century
with matching state boundaries to linguistic and cultural ones has
led to all too familiar and bloody mischief both in Europe and in
the Near East – in part thanks to the decadence of romanticism,
which had originally, with Herder and Novalis, favoured
regionalism rather than nationalism.[35]

For this reason it is shallow to think that the legacy of empire has
no positive and equitable potential, or cannot naturally be turned
towards mutual and cooperative notions of international commonwealth – and in fact there are historical links between the emergence
of the British Commonwealth, of Francophonia and of the European
Community (originally envisaged in some ways as a substitute for
recently lost Habsburg control in the East and a attempt to restore
an ancient Carolingian unity of France and Germany in the West.)[36]
It is assumed that our international influence must necessarily wain,
but those who assumed this in the 1960s would be staggered by the
degree to which it still persists today. Empire is always about to
finally end and yet interestingly never does so and in certain modes
– like the underwriting of foreign business by British law – reinvents
itself in some positive new ways, in contrast to the post-imperial
corporate and oligarchic ravages which we have disgracefully
supported.

Indeed the most penetrating historians have argued that much of
our loss of influence was down to miscalculation, loss of nerve and
absence of vision on the part of a decadent establishment and not to
historical inevitability.[37] Today we are likely to be the most populous
country in Western Europe by mid-century and the increasingly
culture-dominated character of international politics considerably

favours our global legacy and current global strengths. Equally, it is shallow to suppose that the break-up of the UK follows automatically upon the end of empire. For a British and even a British Isles dimension in both culture and politics stretches right back to the early Middle Ages – as historians rather than Hollywood-made movies so clearly attest.

If British identity has tended to lapse in favour of Celtic and now English ones with the rise of UKIP and the establishment of the SNP, then this is not, I submit, inevitable. But rather, it is the result of a southern English failure to offer a vision of British identity which has to include a new version of our looking outwards in order to seek pan-federal, international equity true to our destiny – because without this maritime destiny we are just not being ourselves, in contrast, perhaps, to the Americans. That this destiny has often been pursued with brutality and was abandoned so recklessly and irresponsibly – with dire consequences in the Near East – only precludes us trying to pursue it in future more charitably and cooperatively if we act out of guilt, which is always to act in bad faith. Outside Western Europe (which is itself not immune) the world now exhibits a general slide into corruption, criminality, state and corporate tyranny, the collapse of equity and the rule of law. To retreat to an insular powerlessness in the face of these things would be to betray our own identity and incidentally threaten our own long-term security.

It is here notable that recent Scottish-based articulations of the common good, such as those found in J. K. Rowling's *Harry Potter* sequence or Bill Forsyth's film *Local Hero,* tend to update an essentially conservative vision of virtue. They cling to older British values which the metropolis and the ruling elites in London have abandoned. Traditionally the Celtic countries have if anything looked yet more outwards than England, and while they all require home rule, to cut themselves off from England and London would be to risk losing this vital part of their own legacy. For they could only then pursue a futile liberal internationalism like Sweden or Éire, not a culturally dense, virtue-orientated and therefore more effective one.

The reasons then for sustaining the UK are the same reasons for remaining in the EU, and yet for not abandoning our links to international Anglophonia (including the United States). Here, as elsewhere, Blue Labour should call us to abandon false and dysfunctional either–ors in favour of strangely possible paradoxes.

Not state or market, religion or the secular, Anglophonia or Europe, or nation versus the global. Instead, intimate reciprocities in ever-widening circles from the local street to the planet, fusing economic, political and ecological purpose in the name of the flourishing of each and every person and their combination as workers to erect a shared and beautiful cosmopolis.

BONDS OF RECIPROCITY

Behind all of these ideas lies the view that a true practice of the ethical – as the training of character towards the realisation of the common good which includes bonds of reciprocity – is not an inhibitor of economic and political success. Instead, it is a necessary condition for such success. So if Labour, following the Blue Labour inspiration, can recover its ethical and religious roots, then this will also help it in future to govern well and to remain in power to good purpose. We can renew our country if we renew our love for each other and for our common quest. And by rejoining gift to contract we can recover at once our ancient British festivity and our spirit of genuine economic enterprise.

NOTES

1.   For this neo-Maussian perspective, see (amongst many others) Jacques T. Godbout with Alain Caillé, *The World of the Gift*, tr. Donald Winkler (Montreal/Kingston: McGill-Queen's University Press, 1998).

2.   David Goodhart, *The British Dream: Successes and Failures of Post-War Immigration* (London: Atlantic, 2013).

3.   Maurice Glasman, 'Politics, employment policies and the young generation', in A. Quadrio Curzio and G. Marseguerra (eds), *Rethinking Solidarity for Employment: The Challenges of the Twenty-first Century* (Vatican City: Libreria Editrice Vaticana, 2014), pp. 255–70.

4.   See Jean-Claude Michéa, *The Realm of Lesser Evil: An Essay on Liberal Civilisation*, tr. D. Fernbach (Cambridge: Polity Press, 2009). Michéa is important for much that follows. For a similar thesis see also John Milbank, *Theology and Social Theory*, 2nd ed. (Oxford: Blackwell, 2006 [orig. pub. 1990]), pp. 9–47, 278–442.

5.   See Serge Latouche, *L'Invention de l'économie* (Paris: Albin Michel, 2005); Milbank, *Theology and Social Theory*, pp. 26–47; Adrian Pabst, 'From civil to political economy: Adam Smith's theological debt', in P.

Oslington (ed.), *Adam Smith as Theologian* (London: Routledge, 2011), pp. 106–24.

6. See Jeremiah Alberg, *A Reinterpretation of Rousseau: A Religious System* (London: Palgrave-Macmillan, 2007).
7. Goodhart, *The British Dream*, pp. 261–341.
8. Arguably, collective self-organisation and resistance needs to ally itself with a recovery of a sense of architectonic and educative responsibility amongst leaderships and elites. The left must remember that no advanced political system is conceivable without these phenomena, as Marx himself recognised in his *Critique of the Gotha Programme*. On this point about Marx, see Raymond Geuss, *Philosophy and Real Politics* (Princeton, NJ: Princeton University Press, 2008).
9. This is a critical commentary upon Nancy Fraser's essay 'A triple movement? Parsing the politics of crisis after Polanyi', *New Left Review* 81 (May/June 2013), pp. 119–32. The most defining product of the New Left was 1960s student revolution: the ultimate Rousseauian gesture, which rejected even the temporal hierarchy of education (and in time reversible, as the taught can later teach). Since this hierarchy is ontologically unavoidable, all this has led to in the long run is students being treated as consumers whose right to complain obscures from them the reduction of their education to standardised process which supposedly guarantees their fitness to enter the labour market.
10. George Orwell, *The Road to Wigan Pier* (London: Penguin, 1989).
11. See Luigino Bruni, *The Wound and the Blessing: Economics, Relationships and Happiness*, tr. N. Michael Brennan (New York: New City Press, 2007).
12. Bruni, *The Wound and the Blessing*, passim.
13. See Johanna Bockman, *Markets in the Name of Socialism: The Left-Wing Origins of Neoliberalism* (Stanford, CA: Stanford University Press, 2011).
14. As Jon Cruddas MP put it, 'Labour is a political tradition that allows us to realise our potentials, to flourish as human beings – to live more rewarding lives'. See his lecture, 'Earning and belonging: two challenges to progressive politics', The Resolution Foundation, London, 6 February 2013. Available at http://www.resolutionfoundation.org/media/media/downloads/Jon_Cruddas_speech_to_the_Resolution_Foundation.pdf (accessed on 25 August 2014).
15. See again Bockman, *Markets in the Name of Socialism*.
16. Bockman, *Markets in the Name of Socialism*, pp. 76–132, 157–214.
17. Bockman herself does not embrace this point but seems to advocate a neoclassical market socialism.
18. See Maurice Glasman, *Unnecessary Suffering: Managing Market Utopia* (London: Verso, 1996).

19. See Milbank, *Theology and Social Theory*, pp. 382–442.
20. See Domenico Losurdo, *Liberalism: A Counter-History*, tr. Gregory Elliott (London: Verso, 2011), pp. 195–205.
21. Robert and Edward Skidelsky, *How Much is Enough? The Love of Money and the Case for the Good Life* (London: Allen Lane, 2012).
22. Adair Turner, *Economics After the Crisis: Objectives and Means* (Cambridge, MA: MIT Press, 2012).
23. On the latter point see Jomo Kwame Sundaram and Felice Noelle Rodriguez, 'Structural causes and consequences of the 2008–2009 financial crisis', in C. Calhoun and G. Derluguian (eds), *Aftermath: A New Global Economic Order?* (London/New York: SSRC/NYUP, 2011), pp. 97–117; Régis Debray, 'Decline of the West?', *New Left Review* 80 (March/April 2013), pp. 29–44.
24. Glasman, 'Politics, employment policies and the young generation', pp. 255–70.
25. See Luigino Bruni, *The Genesis and Ethos of the Market* (London: Palgrave-Macmillan, 2012).
26. Stefano Zamagni, 'Catholic Social Teaching, civil economy, and the spirit of capitalism', in D. K. Finn (ed.), *The True Wealth of Nations: Catholic Social Thought and Economic Life* (Oxford: Oxford University Press, 2010), pp. 63–93.
27. Luigini Bruni and Stefano Zamagni, *Civil Economy* (Bern: Peter Lang, 2007).
28. For a longer exposition of these arguments, see John Milbank and Adrian Pabst, *The Politics of Virtue: Post-liberalism and the Human Future*, chap. 4, forthcoming.
29. I am indebted to the fine journalism of Will Hutton in *The Observer* for this and other ideas in this section.
30. One might though distinguish here between 'compulsory' professional associations safeguarding a minimum of good practice and 'free guilds' which would be voluntary and exist in order to shelter and encourage more stringent standards which could in the long term give a market advantage, encouraging membership.
31. Nevertheless, a way needs to be found of quantifying the equally crucial 'contributions' made by those who stay at home to care for children, old people and the disabled and who also often make a strong input into local civil society. See John Milbank and Adrian Pabst, 'Post-liberal politics and the alternative of mutualising social security', in Nick Spencer (ed.), *The Future of Welfare: A Theos Collection* (London: Theos, 2014), pp. 90–100. Available at http://www.theosthinktank.co.uk/files/files/Reports/The%20future%20of%20welfare%20a%20theos%20collection%20combined.pdf (accessed on 25 August 2014).
32. See Bockman, *Markets in the Name of Socialism*, pp. 189–214.

33. See Bruni, *The Wound and the Blessing*.

34. Carl Schmitt, *Hamlet or Hecuba: the Intrusion of Time into the Play*, tr. D. Pan and J. Rust (New York: Telos Publishing Press, 2009), pp. 63–5.

35. See Elie Kedourie, *The Chatham House Version and Other Middle Eastern Essays* (London: Ivan R. Dee, 2004).

36. Of relevance here is Jan Zielonka, *Europe as Empire: The Nature of the Enlarged European Union* (Oxford: Oxford University Press, 2006).

37. Corelli Barnett, *The Collapse of British Power* (London: Faber, 2011); Kedourie, *The Chatham House Version*.

CHAPTER THREE

A Blue Labour Vision of the Common Good

Frank Field
(August 2014)

THE BLUE LABOUR CHALLENGE

Labour's leadership may not have thought through the challenge Blue
Labour poses. But it can be easily stated. Blue Labour confronts the
cultural war successive Labour leaderships have waged against the
moral economy of Labour's core working-class voters. Blue Labour
therefore poses the most fundamental of challenges to the Blairite
electoral strategy that, despite changes in personnel, remains in place.
Had the leadership given serious thought to Blue Labour, its worry, if
not annoyance, would have quickly turned to alarm. For if Blue
Labour prevails it will herald a new centre-left electoral strategy based
on a different meaning of the term progressive and how this
progressiveness will be enshrined in policies promoting the common
good. Alternatively, if the Blairite electoral strategy is maintained, and
past trends are in any way a guide to the future, Labour's core vote
will continue to disengage. But from now on there is likely to be a
second sting in the tail of departing Labour voters. Instead of joining
the great army of non-voters, the march of Blue Labour voters may
turn directly to UKIP who offer an alternative vision of the common
good that is more akin to their own.

THE WRITING ON THE WALL

British post-war politics are often discussed in terms of the
electorate's disengagement from the two major parties. This is true,
but it is only part of what I would contend is a much more serious

Table 1: Number of votes cast in General Elections since 1950

	Votes (millions)[1]					Total Votes	Electorate	Non-voters
	Con[2]	Lab	Lib[3]	PC/SNP	Other			
1950	12.47	13.27	2.62	0.03	0.39	28.77	34.41	5.64
1951	13.72	13.95	0.73	0.02	0.18	28.60	34.05	5.45
1955	13.29	12.41	0.72	0.06	0.29	26.76	34.85	8.09
1959	13.75	12.22	1.64	0.10	0.16	27.86	35.40	7.53
1964	11.98	12.21	3.10	0.13	0.24	27.66	35.89	8.24
1966	11.42	13.07	2.33	0.19	0.26	27.26	35.96	8.69
1970	13.15	12.18	2.12	0.48	0.42	28.34	39.34	11.00
Feb. 1974	11.83	11.65	6.06	0.80	1.00	31.34	38.73	7.39
Oct. 1974	10.43	11.46	5.35	1.01	0.95	29.19	40.07	10.88
1979	13.70	11.51	4.31	0.64	1.07	31.22	40.07	8.85
1983	13.01	8.46	7.78	0.46	0.96	30.67	42.19	11.52
1987	13.74	10.03	7.34	0.54	0.88	32.53	43.18	10.65
1992	14.09	11.56	6.00	0.78	1.18	33.61	43.28	9.66
1997	9.60	13.52	5.24	0.78	2.14	31.29	43.85	12.56
2001	8.34	10.72	4.81	0.46	2.03	26.37	44.40	18.04
2005	8.78	9.55	5.99	0.59	2.24	27.15	44.25	17.10
2010	10.70	8.61	6.84	0.66	2.88	29.69	45.60	15.91

1. For elections up to 1992, the Speaker of the House of Commons is listed under the party he represented before his appointment. From 1997 the Speaker is listed under 'Other'.
2. Includes Coalition Conservative for 1918; National, National Liberal and National Labour candidates for 1931–5; National and National Liberal candidates for 1945; National Liberal & Conservative candidates 1945–70.
3. Includes Coalition Liberal Party for 1918; National Liberal for 1922; and Independent Liberal for 1931. Figures show Liberal/SDP Alliance vote for 1983–7 and Liberal Democrat vote from 1992 onwards.

long-term threat to the stability of our democracy. A number of voting patterns are detailed in Table 1. I have taken 1950 as a starting point for this analysis as the 1945 election was fought in wartime conditions with millions of voters displaced at home and millions more in the services overseas.

Four major trends can be discerned from these post-1950 voting figures. The first centres on the Conservative vote. Up until 1997 Conservative votes fluctuated between 12.5 and 14 million – with a total vote well above the 13 million in five post-war general elections. This level of support collapsed in 1997, reaching its lowest point of 8.3

million votes cast for Conservative candidates in the following 2001 election. In the past two elections the Conservative vote has risen by 2.4 million.

Second, in terms of numbers of votes cast, the Labour Party has never registered greater support in the votes cast for it than it gained in 1951. The 1997 election recorded 13.5 million Labour supporters, but this was still nearly half a million below the 1951 high point and during this period the number of voters increased by 9.8 million. Since 1997 Labour support has fallen by 5 million votes – and I promise you that it is not a misprint. There has been a fall of 5 million votes in the space of three general elections. And this was at a time of a further rise in the numbers of voters – by an additional 1.8 million. As voters disengage in significant numbers from the two major parties, the size of the electorate has been rising. Since 1950 the electorate has risen by over 11 million. The total vote going to the two main parties since that election has fallen from its peak by over 8.5 million at a time when the electorate has risen by nearly a third.

A beneficiary of this disengagement from the two major parties was the Liberal Democrats. Liberal Democrat support has grown from 2.6 million votes in 1950 to 6.8 million votes at the last election. Here is the third movement in party support which can be gleaned from the table. This trend is unlikely to hold in the next election, and is anyway not as spectacular as the fourth trend. The total of non-voters has nearly tripled from 5.6 million in 1950 to 15.9 million in 2010 – a greater number than the total votes cast for all Labour and Liberal Democrat candidates. It is true that this total is down from the peak of 18 million in 2001, but this fall looks as though it has overwhelmingly benefited the Conservative Party whose vote increased more than the decline in the number of non-voters.

THE NOT SO STRANGE DEATH OF LABOUR'S SKILLED WORKING-CLASS VOTE

Of course this trend may peter out. Looking at the table, the ebbs and flows in party support are clear. So this increase in the Tory vote may not be maintained. Indeed, it might be reversed. But my concern with Tory Party fortunes is limited to how they might impact upon Labour Party support. Again, this horrendous decline in Labour support over the last three elections may be reversed. But I want to suggest that it won't be unless one looks, first, at which groups have been

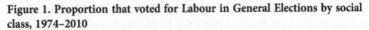

Figure 1. Proportion that voted for Labour in General Elections by social class, 1974–2010

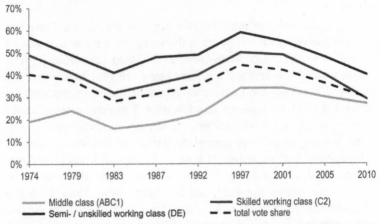

Source: These data from MORI/Ipsos MORI election aggregates 1979–2010. 1974 figures taken from a Louis Harris poll. The data underlying this chart are available on the IPSOS-Mori website: http://www.ipsos-mori.com/researchpublications/researcharchive/poll.aspx.

disengaging fastest and then, at Labour policies that might attract them back. Here we need to disaggregate the Labour vote by social class, and then, secondly, consider which policies around the theme of the common good might reverse those trends. The breakdown of the changing level of class support for Labour candidates since the election of 1974 is given in the graph in Figure 1.

What do the trends in the graph tell us about the collapse in Labour support? Three important trends are at work. The overall decline in the semi- and unskilled working-class Labour vote has been in line with the overall decline in the party's vote. The poorest in the electorate have been deserting candidates in line with Labour's overall decline. So much then for being 'the party of welfare', as the Tories like to dub us. Yet, this false link which is all too firmly made now by large numbers of voters has not resulted in an electoral reward from the very group that gains most from the welfare state.

The group of the electorate most likely to see Labour as the party of welfare is the skilled working class, and as we can see from the graph it is this group that is punishing Labour most trenchantly. The decline in Labour's support amongst the skilled working-class electorate is shown to be greater than the decline in Labour's overall vote, particularly from the 2001 election onwards. Between 2005 and 2010 Labour's proportional share of the skilled working-class vote is less than its overall share in the total vote.

Finally, the third trend apparent in Figure 1 is that while Labour's share of the middle-class vote has declined, it has done so much more slowly than the overall decline in the party's vote, and particularly its vote from the skilled working class. This is the group least disaffected by Labour's vision.

POLITICALLY HOMELESS LABOUR VOTERS

Where is this core vote going? Again the answer appears disarmingly simple and is given in Table 1. For most of the period an ever-greater proportion of Labour's core voters has become politically homeless with the vast majority of departing voters appearing not to vote at all. Hence the decline in turnout, which I have commented on as one of the most significant trends in recent British politics.

Once voters are on the move this process seems to gain its own momentum. Party bonds are rarely cast asunder by a single event. The breaking of loyal bonds often begins imperceptibly. When R. H. Tawney was shot and left for dead in one of the all too numerous shell holes that pockmarked the Western front, he realised, indiscernibly at first, his roots in life were being loosened and that, later, he would never feel quite the same about death. So too with the transference of political loyalty. Once friends who were keen supporters start expressing their doubts it becomes easier to express one's own doubts and doubts can all too often lead to disengagement.

A movement from party loyalty to the status of being politically homeless, where no vote is cast, is dangerous enough for a party's future well-being. But homelessness does not necessarily define a permanent state of being. It is from this homeless group that an even greater danger is now being posed to Labour. A number of these voters are calling a halt to their homelessness, or their non-voting status, and are deciding to move to another party. A significant proportion of the homeless amongst ex-Labour supporters is now voting UKIP. At the European election a fifth of the UKIP vote was from those who had previously stopped voting. And a significant part of those Labour voters alienated by New Labour is choosing UKIP.

Here they see a home in which their values are displayed on every wall, if not by the wallpaper itself.

The economic pull that Labour exerts remains. Working-class Labour voters believe that they would be better off financially under Labour. Yet while the views of this group on Labour's economic competence are important, the party now finds that the cultural push away from Labour is so strong that the economic pull is negated for a significant and what looks likely to be a growing proportion of this group of the electorate. A sizable part of ex-Labour voters have been repelled by the policies promoted by a largely non-working-class party elite with whom these ex-voters find it difficult to sympathise and vice versa.

VALUES TRUMP MONEY

These trends challenge the now conventional wisdom on which New Labour's electoral strategy was based. The decline in the overall Labour vote in the period from 1966 was to be countered, reasonably enough, by reaching those parts of the electorate that had turned their face against the party. In doing so, it was assumed, dangerous as it turned out, that this process of wooing middle-class voters could be pursued and the needs and responses of Labour's core voters ignored. The view that these voters had nowhere else to go was the comforting phrase chanted by Labour's chattering classes. But as we have seen, Labour voters have a mind and determination of their own, as increasing numbers of them move party. So why the move?

Let me reinforce the view I hinted at in the opening paragraph. This decline in Labour's vote has not been driven by economic alienation, although that clearly has played a part. A more fundamental force has been at work. This force is primarily cultural and ethical, not economic.

A significant proportion of deserting Labour voters, and a significant proportion of working-class voters who remain loyal to the extent that they continue to vote for Labour candidates, are hostile to the kind of society they perceive Labour is now in business to promote. They do not see Labour as being committed to the flag, i.e. being proud of the country; as having a clear stand in defending the country's borders, i.e. they are soft on immigration; or as promoting a welfare state where rewards have to be earned, i.e. they cater largely for the freewheelers, rather than hard-working families.

They witness a Labour Party that all too often stands for a distribution of public services that they find repulsive; a housing allocation system that favours the newcomer and the social misfit over good behaviour over decades. They see Labour as soft on vulgar and uncivilised behaviour that plagues their lives and from which the rich shield themselves. Moreover, they witness a leadership that never expresses the anger they feel as the world they stand for is mocked and denigrated by hoodlums for whom official Labour always seems to have an understanding word.

Hence the disengagement from a Labour vision that repels working-class voters who once saw, or who wish to see, decency as the cornerstone of Labour's Jerusalem. This movement from voting Labour to non-voting, and then to another party, stands on its head the Marxist assumption that has unquestioningly underpinned Labour's electoral strategy. It is values, not economic interests, which are now determining party loyalty for a significant proportion of Labour and ex-Labour voters. In the period up to the 1960s Labour's economically based social strategy reflected the moral economy that governed a very large part of working-class family life. That is no longer so and it is working-class social values, rather than economic interest, that now take an increasing hold of working-class voting loyalty. Four values predominated this vision of the common good.

- A pride and love of one's country and a near-blind loyalty in taking its side against whatever is thrown against it.
- A loyalty to old friends, particularly those who have always been prepared to fight on one's side, rather than occupy the opposing trenches.
- A central belief that duties beget rights and that privileges have to be earned.
- An emphasis on making contributions as a means to earning entitlements and that it is in joining in, so to speak, by making contributions that defines society's borders, both socially and geographically.

Late in the day the Labour leadership has begun to wake up to the threat its values-based programme poses. But the fundamental significance of this challenge remains misunderstood and under-valued. Not surprisingly therefore the party's response has been inadequate. So what policies are necessary to demonstrate to footloose and would-be footloose Labour voters that their values will regain their old primacy in whatever coalition of voters Labour attempts to put together? I would suggest four initiatives are fundamental to underpin and appeal to that new coalition of voters, built around Blue Labour's conceptions of the common good. Each of these approaches encapsulates an idea of the common good in everyday politics.

First, the threat the current scale of immigration poses to our national identity has yet to be met. There is no way the clock can or should be turned back. But without a fundamental control of the borders there is nothing to prevent another inflow of seven million people coming into Britain during the next decade and a half, to match the seven million who have entered the country since 1997.

Here the style of Labour's fight back is crucial. The party has recently tried to respond to the concerns of the whole country on the issue of immigration, and particularly those of its core voters, by listing a number of detailed and worthwhile reforms. But the reforms are out of time. Had they been proposed in 1997, they might have been seen by the electorate as a robust response. Not so now. The politics of regaining Labour's core vote entails the use of initiatives which speak sacramentally to voters. The party's outward policy announcements have to be seen to reflect an inward change in the attitudes and beliefs of the Labour leadership. How might this be achieved?

Labour needs to commit itself to the end of the free movement of labour within the EU. No one will underestimate the size of this task. Those who caution this objective as unachievable, and maintain that the leadership should not embark upon it, seem to ignore totally the impact such a stance would have on the attitude of Labour's lost voters. The party's core voters will give Labour the thumbs up for trying to defend their interest instead of standing idly by and witnessing yet further erosions of their living standards, and particularly so when the leadership wants to fight the election on the decline in living standards. Battles might be lost, but the core voters will mark Labour's card as trying to promote their idea of the Good Society. The aim, of course, should be to win such major battles.

Second, the primary role of the family has to be reasserted through policy commitments and not simply through words. Core voters accept the diversity of family life. But the traditional model remains for most working-class Labour voters the ideal to aim for, and itself to a full employment strategy, with higher-paying jobs being central to this objective. Some of those jobs will be created by a commitment to build by the end of the Parliament 300,000 social houses each year – the Tory commitment in 1951. A building programme of housing would also be one that strengthens families. It is difficult to survive, let alone thrive, in the semi-slum conditions into which all too many families are now condemned.

But, likewise, running an exchange rate policy will be significant to achieving this employment objective. Exchange rates do not only help to determine the level of exports. They are also crucial for building an effective import substitution strategy. An effective exchange rate policy must also be concerned with preventing imports, including food, basic materials, as well as manufacturing. Being obsessed by the level of exports is important, but is only part of the story. Employment levels are directly affected by both the level of exports and also imports.

THE FORWARD MARCH OF BLUE LABOUR

A Blue Labour strategy is not one simply about shoring up Labour's core voters. It is certainly that. But it is also a strategy on which elections can be won. The moral economy to which Blue Labour voters attach such importance is one which has a universal appeal. Why do I say this?

Public and private ethics in this country are the product of a Christian inheritance. While during the nineteenth century the country slowly took leave of Christian dogma, it ensured that much of Christian teaching was secularised. The agent of this successful secularisation was the growth, and then for a period, the dominance of English idealism to which most party leaders subscribed, as did their followers.

This left us with a common ethical code onto which party divisions were imposed. The decency therefore that has driven so much of Labour's vision of both private and public common good is one shared by the members of other classes. The appeal to country, loyalty to old friends, the belief that duties beget rights, are all sentiments that appeal across classes. It is on this universalism of Blue Labour's common good that Labour should begin rebuilding that wider coalition of voters that is so crucial to general election successes.

PART TWO

LABOUR – PARTY AND POLITICS

CHAPTER FOUR

Blue Labour: A Politics Centred on Relationships

David Lammy

INTRODUCTION

Blue Labour has been a source of controversy and renewal for the Labour Party in opposition. Maurice Glasman, who coined the term, describes it as 'a completely agitational idea to provoke a conversation about what went wrong with the Blair project'. For me this is the best way to understand it. You do not have to like the term, or take a particular stance on issues like immigration, to engage in the conversation that it has begun.

That conversation, at heart, is about how we build a politics centred on relationships. In a more individualistic society Blue Labour asks a simple question: how should we treat one another? Can we imagine a society built on mutual respect and mutual responsibility? Can we forge a politics where people trust and listen to one another? Can we rediscover the ethical instincts that make us good parents, good neighbours and good colleagues?

The context for this discussion is vital. Modern Britain has been shaped by two social revolutions. The first was cultural: the social liberalism of the 1960s. The second was economic: the free market revolution of the 1980s. Together these two revolutions made Britain a wealthier and more tolerant nation. But they have come at a cost, combining to create a hyper-individualistic culture, in which we do not always treat each other well.

The riots of 2011 were one expression of this culture. Many of those who took part in the looting lacked decent jobs, good prospects or a realistic chance of owning their own home – they had little stake in society. But they also demonstrated shockingly little regard for others as they attacked police officers, burned down people's homes and ransacked shops. The riots were the product of a 'me-first', take-what-you-can culture.

The financial crisis was another expression of the same culture. Just as the riots were caused by selfishness and social breakdown, not just poor policing, the financial crisis was the product of greed, not just bad regulation. Of course the riots and the financial crisis cannot be compared directly, but they were both driven by an ethic of personal gratification, not mutual respect and responsibility.

It is this culture – and Labour's recent responses to it – that Blue Labour seeks to address. It argues that while Labour has been strong on promoting individual rights and defending the welfare state, it has often overlooked the importance of our relationships with one another – in families, neighbourhoods, workplaces and so on. Because of this, Labour became too detached from people's everyday lives and experiences while we were in government.

Of course, no one need remind me of the value of individual rights or a generous and supportive welfare state. My mother arrived in Britain in 1970. Just two years on from Enoch Powell's 'Rivers of Blood' speech, Britain was far from a picture of racial harmony. Nor were the odds stacked in favour of a woman entering the workforce without much in the way either of money or formal qualifications. At a time when comics would routinely insult black people on television, she relied on the left to help her stand up to racists and bigots. When my father left, she became responsible for looking after five children alone. The same people who fought against racism were those who also spoke up for single mothers. They were the counterweight to Tory politicians and their friends in the media.

Meanwhile, there were bills to be paid. At times Mum did three jobs to get by and was, of course, a beneficiary of the Equal Pay Act, passed in the same year she arrived in Britain. Like countless others, she trusted socialists to stick up for her when the child benefit was frozen. She relied on public libraries to nourish the minds of her children. She watched proudly as the first generation in our family was given the opportunity to go to university. Later in life she was cared for wonderfully by the NHS, which treated her with dignity and compassion. No one in our family needs to be persuaded about the value of individual rights, or that the state can be an enormous force for good.

LIBERTY, EQUALITY...FRATERNITY

But Blue Labour is a reminder that our party stands not just for liberty and equality, but also fraternity. Something important exists in between the state and the individual – our relationships with one another.

When my mother arrived in Britain it was not just the state that stepped in to help her. A friendly trade union official from NUPE helped her into a course of learning that made it possible to find work that could provide for a family. The local church provided a sense of fellowship and community. Friends and neighbours looked after her children while she juggled life as a single mother. When she was ill doctors in the NHS treated her illness, but Macmillan nurses also provided invaluable care. As she grew older she relied more and more on her children, just as we had once relied upon her. All these relationships made the difference to her life. This is what Blue Labour is trying to get at.

The focus on relationships explains why, despite the overlap with strands of liberalism, Labour is not a liberal party. Unlike the Lib Dems we do not see people simply as free-floating individuals. Our politics is not orientated towards an unrealisable version of freedom where we can each do whatever we please. Instead Labour politics is built on the idea that people are social beings, dependent on one another. We are not born free, but dependent on our parents. As we grow older, a good life depends in large part on family, friends, neighbours, colleagues and strangers. We never stop being mutually dependent. How we treat each other matters.

Because relationships are so important to people's lives, they must be important to our politics. Labour, for example, needs a story about the family. Of course we care passionately about women's rights and children's rights but that's not the end of the story. We have to seriously raise the volume and the focus on the value of strong relationships between adults, good parenting and care for the elderly. We are at our best when we speak to that ethic of care, as well as a language of liberation. We can't be satisfied by talking about children in care and retirement homes – the workings of the state. There is just more to it than that.

In the workplace there should be the same emphasis. Of course we stand for workers' rights – on pay, on leave, on flexible working and the rest. But if the conversation between employers and employees never gets further than the right to strike versus the right to sack an employee then we have big problems. The reason worker representation on company boards is such a powerful idea is that it holds out the promise of constructive, respectful relationships based on give and take. Workers taking responsibility for the success of firms. Firms taking responsibility for the well-being of workers. Again, it's not just about the state telling employers and employees what to do. It's also about the quality of the relationships between employers and employees within firms.

In other areas of life, the same principle holds. We support free speech but that doesn't mean we have given up on the idea of a society with civility and mutual respect. We support personal and religious freedom but we also understand the importance of an integrated and harmonious society. Too easily a language of individual rights can regress into a shrill and anti-social individualism. Labour politics fails when these ties we have to one another fray. If families disintegrate, if workers do not have a voice, if neighbourhoods are divided and strangers fear and mistrust one another then our politics is stone dead. We end up willing the ends for social justice, but the means are impossible. People retreat into their own lives and any sense of the common good disappears.

Blue Labour's insight is that solidarity is both important and fragile. It must be constantly worked at. We can't just wag our finger and demand that people be good to one another, we have to take seriously the things that make mutual respect more difficult than it should be. This means listening to people and what they tell us. So when someone says that immigration is a problem in their area then the instant response cannot be to simply brand them a racist. Our job is to question why neighbour is set against neighbour in the scramble for scarce homes, jobs and services. Rather than judging people for airing their concerns we should be interested in how to ameliorate the things that cause these tensions.

Likewise when someone says that the family has come under pressure since women have entered the workforce, we shouldn't simply shout them down. Rather, we should ask how we can help families adapt to a world in which women rightfully have the chance to pursue their ambitions and earn a living. In particular, we might through which their happiness is maximised. The point is not only that it is within this framework that most children are best nurtured. Working-class women, in particular, stress the importance to their happiness of having a partner in full-time work so that their work can be fitted around the needs of their family. For it is within this social and communal world that working-class women, and now an increasing number of middle-class women, say their greatest happiness is found. This fundamental realignment of Labour's policy is not a disguised plea to begin discriminating against other types of families and households. It is, rather, to cease discriminating against the traditional family, and particularly so through the welfare state.

There are also powerful fiscal and social reasons for a recommitment to the traditional family. Child poverty is a major problem in modern-day Britain, yet there are almost no – repeat, no – poor children in households where one partner works full time and one part time. 'If you do not want your children to be poor, you need a partner who works' should be part of our social highway code.

Third, the working-class belief that it is the performance of duties which gives rise to rights has to be enshrined in our welfare state. The leadership's welcome phrase of 'something for something' has to be enshrined in more robust policies.

The galloping spread since 1979 under both Tory and Labour government of means-tested assistance in the form of social security, tax credits and housing and council tax benefits, have to be seen for what they are. They amount to a full-frontal attack on a working-class moral economy that believes in work, effort, savings and honesty, and that these great drivers of human endeavour should be rewarded rather than penalised. The welfare state has to be reconstructed away from means testing onto a National Insurance basis. Such a revolution cannot be achieved overnight. But the first steps in a clearly marked 20-year route map have to be taken, and a commitment to that route map given.

Any contributory benefits system does more than begin to rebuild support for a welfare state. It also defines acceptable behaviour, membership of a community and also, not least importantly, begins again to draw the lines around national identity. National borders can be enforced not only by geographical boundaries and border agencies but by welfare as well.

Fourth, work is crucial to human dignity, the good functioning of the family and the prosperity of the nation. Labour must commit consider how we help fathers take on more of the caring at a time when mothers do more of the earning. Feminism and 'the family' don't have to be at odds. We often slip into the same trap where faith is concerned. When a person or an organisation draws their values from a particular faith then the reaction cannot simply be to dismiss them. People can disagree with faith groups on social and ethical matters but still join together to campaign for a cap on lending rates, or against the commercialisation of childhood.

There is, of course, still racism, sexism and religious bigotry to be found in Britain. The battles our party has fought against discrimination of all kinds have been historic and hard won and they are not over yet. But when we decline the opportunity to enter into conversations about issues like the family, immigration or faith we undermine our own political project. If Blue Labour reminds us of this then it has already achieved a great deal.

BIG SOCIETY ... BIG BUSINESS

If one half of the coalition doesn't understand the importance of fraternity, the other half forgets that it should apply in markets too. Part of the problem with the Big Society is that it does not understand that the voluntary and public sectors often work in partnership.

The other fundamental weakness of the Big Society is that it has nothing to say about the marketplace. 'Big Society not Big Government,' says David Cameron, leaving Big Business out of the picture altogether. It leaves his government with little to say about ethical consumerism, good work or responsible business practices. Blue Labour seeks to address this through making corporations more accountable to the society around them.

Blue Labour stands opposed to anyone being used simply as a means to an end. That explains why employers should not treat staff as commodities to be exploited, but rather human beings to be respected. People should have a voice at work and be paid a wage they can live on. It explains the opposition to loan sharks who exploit people's poverty, enticing people into debt that they will never be able to escape from. It explains the offence at companies who target advertising at other people's children, manipulating young girls and boys. It explains why the public are so angry that the banks were able to hold the country to ransom.

This is what the Tories do not understand when they talk about people making 'free choices' in markets. A choice between eviction and a loan shark is no real choice. A choice between two bad jobs is no real choice. A choice about whether to let banks go down with millions of people's savings, or to bail out the richest people in the country is no real choice. None of these reflect relationships built on give and take: they are about the powerful bullying and exploiting the powerless. Collective action is how we stand up to those who profit at the expense of the rest of society. We do it together, through trade unions, cooperatives, consumer movements, civil society campaigns and of course, government at national and international level.

But collective action is not easy. Again we have to be careful how we build the trust and the solidarity and the momentum to take on those who abuse their power in the marketplace. Finger-wagging will not work here either. We have to find connections with people's lives as they live them. There is a national campaign for a living wage because, first of all, there was a specific, tangible campaign against certain firms in the City of London. Momentum grew from there as people joined the dots between excess in the City and poverty for those who cleaned the offices of the 'masters of the universe'.

Stella Creasy is running a brilliant campaign not just against loan sharking in general, but also some credit companies in particular. It gives the campaign a sense of vibrancy and a practical orientation, while the Tories have continued to vote measures down in the House. The Billingsgate campaign that Jon Cruddas has been involved in is another good example. One response to the market porters would be to nod sagely and promise to do what we can at the next G20 summit. Another is to campaign for their cause at a local level, as well as pressing for international action.

In my own constituency I have worked hard to prevent Tottenham Hotspur from leaving the area. The more people get involved in that campaign, the more the momentum builds for proper representation of fans on the boards of all football clubs. In the local party we are campaigning against betting shops swamping local high streets and, despite the Tories and Lib Dems voting down my amendments to the Localism Act, building support for a change in the law. We are also looking at the dangers of fixed-odds betting terminals in bookies – the real driver for the clustering of betting shops in high streets. These are national issues, but they play out in different ways in our neighbourhoods.

The point is that we shouldn't be afraid of the particular and the local. This is where people live their lives. It is when discussions about justice and equality become abstracted from everyday life that they lose their persuasive power and political purchase. Labour was founded as a movement to civilise capitalism – what Blue Labour reminds us is that this must take place in workplaces, in neighbourhoods and in civil society as well as rooms in Whitehall.

LABOUR TRADITIONS

Blue Labour is not a panacea. But the debate it has started is an opportunity to reconnect with some of the ideas our party was founded upon, after 13 years in government and a political project that challenged many of the party's traditions and shibboleths. The danger is that this introspection has almost exclusively focused on its controversy rather than its continuity. It has found itself portrayed as an appeaser of the English Defence League, willing dismantler of Attlee's welfare state and staunch believer in hierarchy and social order (particularly with regard to gender roles). Even its name suggests a project advocating the last great New Labour triangulation to the right. In the minds of much of the wider Labour movement, Blue Labour has become a project bent more on rolling back the victories of liberalism than building upon them.

Many will say this doesn't matter. They will point to the Blue Labour themes that are being weaved through Ed Miliband's 'One Nation' Labour project and brand it a success. It is of course cheering, but if Blue Labour's ideas are to be the Labour Party's keystone that bridges the gap between itself and the aspirations and values of the British people, it will need more than just the ear of a sympathetic leader. It needs grassroots support and organisation if it is to outlast the immediate political moment. Yet until it can convincingly explain the difference between being 'post-liberal' and 'anti-liberal' this is unfathomable.

This is no pitch to recast Blue Labour in the philosophy of individualism. There can be no straying from the fact that the challenges of the future have emphatically collective solutions – the consequences of globalisation, climate change and an ageing population will not be blunted by conferring more 'rights'. But just because the great questions of the twenty-first century will almost certainly have post-liberal solutions does not mean we stop looking for the answers to questions left over from the twentieth century. Blue Labour not only needs to acknowledge liberal triumphs against sexism, racism and homophobia, but must be clear where it will stand when those advances come under assault. It has to be clear that there are still 'liberal' battles to be won and it has to be unequivocal that it stands with the forces of progress.

Beyond accusations of xenophobia and sexism, less withering critiques include the suggestion that Blue Labour is overly nostalgic about the past, rather than projecting something modern and forward looking. They believe it hankers for a world that has gone and isn't coming back. Others question whether it has enough to say about self-improvement – that it gives the impression that people should be satisfied with their lot, rather than encouraged to strive for something better.

These have to be taken seriously and worked through. But even here we should be careful not to repeat some mistakes from our recent past. The Labour Party always needs a forward-looking agenda, but we lose touch with people when we promote change for its own sake. When people see their job become more insecure, when they see their family less and when they feel they no longer know their neighbours, this doesn't always feel like progress – and Labour needs to show it understands that.

We should take Blue Labour's arguments on their merits, rather than mistake it for something it is not, or dismiss it on the basis of an ill-conceived name. The Labour Party has always been a coalition – of trade unionists, Fabians, Christian socialists, NGOs and local community activists, human rights campaigners, environmentalists, feminists and anti-racists. These traditions compete and coalesce with one another, enriching our party in the process. Blue Labour has something important to offer, alongside our traditional defence of individual rights and a robust defence of the modern state. It should be engaged with in that spirit.

CHAPTER FIVE

Community Organising and Blue Labour

Arnie Graf

INTRODUCTION

For over 40 years my public home has been the Industrial Areas Foundation (IAF). The IAF was founded by the late Saul Alinsky in 1940. For most, Alinksy is considered to be the father of community organising. The IAF is the oldest national and international network of community organising in existence today. I came to the IAF in 1971. Although I came to the IAF with some previous organising experience, almost all of what I have learned about organising has come from the IAF. Since the IAF builds local self-determining political but non-partisan organisations, all of my experience before 2011 has been in the civic sector.

In 2011 Lord Maurice Glasman asked me to come to the UK to meet Labour leaders and Ed Miliband, the leader of the Labour Party. In my meeting with Ed, he asked me to undertake a root and branch analysis of local parties throughout the country. I agreed to do this and proceeded in the summer of 2011 to travel the country meeting with over 1,000 civic and Labour staff, members, and supporters either individually or in small groups. After completing my travels I came back to the US and wrote to Ed my assessment and recommendations. It was from that point on that I began my odyssey with the Labour Party and my relationship with Ed Miliband.

This essay will describe my understanding of some of the basic universals of good organising and why these universals resonate so vibrantly with Blue Labour. I have one caveat. In writing about the universals of organising, I am going to contrast different ideas for the sake of clarity; however, in doing so, I trust that everyone knows that most universals are not entirely one way or the other.

WHAT IS COMMUNITY ORGANISING?

To begin with, I am going to contrast mobilising with organising, even though there are aspects of mobilising in organising and vice versa. In a paper by Richard Rothstein, what is seemingly obvious is stated: 'organizers organize organizations'. I wish that this was so. Unfortunately, the 'organizer' in many organisations has very little to do with organising or expanding the organisation. With some wonderful exceptions, this is true for many community groups, trade unions and political parties.

More often than not, the organiser's role is either to service the members or to be the person who is in charge of mobilising members and supporters to do something, e.g. leaflet, door knock, find the venue for a meeting or rally, organise refreshments, make sure the agendas are prepared and printed, do 'turnout' (more and more by email), keep data, etc. All of these tasks have very little to do with organising an organisation through the development of local leadership.

For the most part, decisions are made by a relatively small core of people. It is the organiser's role to implement their plan. This scenario requires the organiser to be a mobiliser. It is his/her role to bring people to an event, to train and educate people on how to build an organisation, how to develop a following, how to conduct effective actions aimed at a target, how to develop allies, how to think strategically, how to research an issue, or how to develop their own voice and gifts. This is why so many members of community groups, trade unions and political parties talk in the third person when referring to an organisation that they belong to.

Mobilisers work with members and volunteers to accomplish a particular task; organisers educate and train members to become leaders. The leaders become the co-creators of powerful, broadly based, culturally, economically and racially diverse democratically run organisations in the community and in the workplace. These organisations are multi-issued, action-oriented and are run by a broad collective leadership team.

While successful organisers must have the ability to mobilise large numbers of people at times, he/she is doing it well if 60–75 per cent of the turnout is produced by the leaders. If the organiser is responsible solely for 60–75 per cent of the turnout, then it is clear that the leaders have not been the co-creators of what is going on.

The role of the organiser is to recruit, educate and develop leaders. Nicholas von Hoffman, an organiser with the IAF in the early 1960s said, 'Leaders are found by organizing and leaders are developed through organizations'. He stressed that leaders are not born, they are developed. Successful organisations that stand the test of time are developed and continue to grow through the work of a good organiser and a collective of strong leaders. These leaders, and by leader I mean a person who has a following that they can deliver, are always in search of new leaders to develop.

How does an organiser build and continually develop leaders? Many organisers organise around a task as opposed to a relationship. While this is necessary at times, it is for the most part a mistake. Building public relationships precedes power. Power is built on organising people in a way that can be delivered with a focus, constantly and persistently. Major issues are not won quickly. They are not won by mobilising for a few demonstrations.

To build and to sustain power over the long haul takes not only a pressing issue, but also a network of relationships that can sustain and grow the organisation until victory is realised. Organising around relationships first is a hard concept to digest; however, it is crucial to building power because people respond to relationships more than they do to tasks. Every human being responds to his or her self-interest and it is more in people's self-interest to relate than it is to respond to a task. Most of us are not overly excited about going to another meeting or taking one more request outside of our work and family obligations.

People were born to relate. To paraphrase the well-known biblical scholar Martin Buber, all real meaning in life is in meeting (note he did not say 'meetings'). It is through relationships that we find love, meaning, and the power to organise around common concerns that bring quality to our lives. Too often organising consists in telling people what needs to be done instead of listening to what people identify as their concerns. The successful organiser organises more with his/her ears than with his/her mouth.

This is why the most radical tool in building an organisation is the individual 30–45 minutes face-to-face meeting. This meeting is not a chinwag, it is not prying into a person's life, it is not learning a person's résumé and it is not an interview. It is a focused conversation aimed at the other person's self-interest. The important question is not 'what' or 'how', but 'why' does he/she think the way they do, why do they act or not act, and what is the story behind their action, passion or apathy.

While every person's self-interest is driven by those things that they do for survival, e.g. provide for food, shelter, safety, etc., we are also driven by our need to relate, to be recognised, and to experience meaning in our lives. Every place that I have ever worked or lived in – whether it was in a rural village in Sierra Leone or in urban Baltimore, Maryland – I have found this to be universally true.

THE STORY OF MS MARIAN DIXON

Who are you looking for in an individual meeting? You are looking for Ms Marian Dixon. Ms Dixon was most certainly not an activist. She was not involved in community organisations or any other form of politics; however, she was a leader in her Roman Catholic parish. She was a public-school teacher and a teacher of religious education at her parish. I met Ms Dixon in 1980 when I was hired as the lead organiser of BUILD, the IAF affiliate in Baltimore, Maryland. Ms Dixon's sister, who was active in BUILD through a different parish, suggested that I conduct an individual meeting with her sister. Ms Dixon met with me only because her sister asked her to do so. When I met with Ms Dixon, she told me that she had no interest in politics of any kind. She just wanted to work at her school and her parish. I knew that she was a leader in her parish, so I persisted in setting up follow-up meetings with her. Around our fourth individual meeting, as we began to build some trust, she told me a story.

Ms Dixon was a black Roman Catholic devoted to her faith. She grew up on the eastern shore of Maryland when racial segregation was in full bloom. As a child, when she went to her church for Mass, she was required to sit in the back of the church. One day, without telling her parents, she walked into the church and sat on the front pew. The congregation was abuzz with disapproval. Some of the leaders went to the pastor who was preparing to enter the church to begin the service. They told him that a black girl was sitting in the first pew and that he had to remove her. The pastor came out and asked this 14-year-old girl to please go to the back of the church where she belonged. When she quietly refused, the pastor had some of the male leaders of the parish pick her up and place her on the last pew. By the time Ms Dixon arrived at her home, the pastor had called her parents. Her parents asked her what had happened. To her surprise, her parents listened to her and said nothing.

From then on Ms Dixon repeated her behaviour of walking down the aisle to sit on the first pew only to be lifted by some leaders and carried back to the last pew. This went on for three months. Finally the pastor and the leaders gave up. They did not bother her any more. Ms Dixon at 14 years old had integrated the seating in her parish. If BUILD was a mobilising effort, I would never have met with Ms Dixon. If I was looking for an activist, I would never have found her. She had never participated in a demonstration. She had never been involved in anything outside of her family, her parish, and the school where she taught, but her story told me all that I needed to know about her. As I met other members of her parish I learned of the high esteem she was held in. She had taught religious education to many of the members' children. She had a huge network of people who admired her commitment to their children and to the parish.

After a number of meetings with Ms Dixon she began to come to some actions that BUILD was engaged in. Two years later Ms Dixon became the second president of BUILD. She led the organisation with the same dignity and grit that she had shown as a 14-year-old girl. After she died, the organisation got the city to name a street in her honour in a distressed community where BUILD had constructed 600 new affordable homes. If you go there today, you will see a street named Marian Dixon Way. Ms Dixon was a leader. Through her network of relationships she developed a core team of ten leaders who could turn out 300 people to an action. If you recruit, train and develop 15 Ms Dixons, you can have a powerful organisation that can move mountains.

COMMUNITY ORGANISING AND THE 'LIVING WAGE'

I want to tell one more story that shows the power of the individual meeting. It is the story of how the living wage came about. When I met Ed Miliband for the first time, he told me that he ran his leaders' campaign on the support of the concept of the living wage. It was the BUILD organisation that had developed the idea and was the first organisation to get the city of Baltimore to pass a living wage law in 1994. This came after a year-long fight with the mayor and the city council. The law required all private companies who contracted to do city work to pay the living wage. This wage was far above the national minimum wage. The law was set to remain a certain percentage above the poverty level for a family of four, a figure that was set by the national government. Unfortunately, a person working full time at the minimum wage in Baltimore fell far below the poverty level.

BUILD's premise was simple. No one should have to work for their poverty. Ed was curious as to how the idea of a living wage came about. He wondered if the idea came from a think tank or from a university professor. I told Ed that the idea came from organising low-wage workers. By doing this we had accumulated a great deal of social knowledge that can only be learned through the lived experience of relating and acting in the public arena.

In this case, it came via a brilliant organiser, Jonathan Lange. I had met Jonathan in the 1980s when he was the associate director for the clothing workers in the south. In 1991, I recruited Jonathan to come to Baltimore to help us understand why so many families were coming to the many church feeding programmes that were being established. Jonathan and a group of leaders from BUILD began where we always begin. We started conducting individual meetings with the people and families who were dining in the church basements of the congregations that belonged to BUILD.

After hundreds of individual meetings, Jonathan and the team had heard numerous stories and began to get a picture of what was going on. While there were multiple dimensions to the causes of the problem, one thing stood out. In the city's drive to save money, they decided to contract out much of the work done by city employees to private companies. While the city was proud of the savings this brought them, they did so by impoverishing thousands of workers and their families.

These workers, once released by the city, lost their union membership in AFSCME, the US union akin to UNISON. This meant that in 1992 a former city employee and union member went from earning US $9.00 an hour with health benefits and a pension to US $4.25, the minimum wage at the time, with no benefits. No wonder many of their families were now forced to seek free meals at the church. In conducting hundreds of individual meetings with the former city employees, our team not only got lists of names of other workers, but we were also able to spot leaders and potential leaders.

This process led Jonathan and his team to ask those who showed the most drive to call together fellow workers to meet in small groups. We did this for three reasons. First, we wanted to see who had a following that he/she could deliver; second, we wanted the workers to get to know each other and to share their stories; and third, we wanted to hear their ideas about what they thought should be done.

One suggestion that came from some of the workers was to push for the state of Maryland to raise the state's minimum wage. After a good deal of discussion, the realisation came that a small increase to the minimum wage would have a negligible effect. Out of these discussions and a lot of organising came the idea of the living wage. This made absolute sense and after a long fight, the first Living Wage Law in the US was passed and signed by the mayor into law.

It is important to note that through this entire organising effort, BUILD's partnership with AFSCME was crucial to our success. This was a partnership based on the self-interest of both organisations. For BUILD, it was to restore the wages and benefits to many of its members and to the neighbours where their congregations were located. For AFSCME, it was a drive to stop the privatisation of the work done by AFSCME members. In fact, as the living wage rose each year as well as the power of BUILD, hundreds of privatised workers returned to city employment and therefore to AFSCME.

COMMUNITY ORGANISING AND BLUE LABOUR

These two stories have summarised the importance of organising as opposed to mobilising, the power of the individual meeting, the power in understanding all facets of a person's self-interest, the development of leaders and a bias toward action.

What does the above have to do with Blue Labour? At the heart of Blue Labour are two very important ideas. The first is the belief that the centralised power that resides in the market and state sectors is fundamentally destructive to creating a healthy democratic society. Picture a three-legged stool. If all three legs are sturdy, you can sit on the stool with no worries; however, if one of the legs is weak, the stool will collapse. If one leg of the stool represents the market sector and one leg of the stool represents the state, unless the third leg of the stool, which represents the civic sector and its voluntary institutions and organisations, is strong, the stool will collapse. Unfortunately, time and time again, the stool collapses on a majority of the people.

Blue Labour

People on the right generally believe that to fix the stool you must break up the power of the state. You must leave the market alone so that it can work its magic and you must stop encouraging people to shirk their responsibilities by relying on the state for assistance. People on the left generally believe to balance the stool, you must break up the power of the market sector. They believe that only through a powerful state will you be able to tame the power of market forces. They also believe that it is the state's role to provide assistance to people who have multiple needs. The market views people as customers, the state views people as clients, Blue Labour views people as citizens. Blue Labour knows that people have a powerful drive to relate, to love and to be co-creators of their own destiny.

Secondly, Blue Labour believes in the concept of subsidiarity, a concept that it borrows from Catholic Social Teaching. Subsidiarity is the belief that the best and most effective decisions are made at the most local level. When asked what his ideology was, Alinsky said it was his belief that given the right circumstances and information, most people will make the right decision. He believed that to realise democratic ideals you had to build mass organisations that are broadly based and leader led. To create a balanced society, Blue Labour stands for a sturdy balanced stool. As fewer and fewer people belong to political parties, as fewer and fewer people trust the state or the market, a large space opens for the dangerous populist movements on the Right or the Left that tap into people's anger and mistrust. Blue Labour believes in the universals of organising because it seeks the politics of the balanced stool.

Through mass participation of people on regional bank boards and workers on corporate boards, and by the state devolving power to local authorities, and finally by calling on people to take responsibility for citizenship, Blue Labour is leading the way to building a healthy democratic society.

CHAPTER SIX

Blue Labour and the Trade Unions: Pro-Business and Pro-Worker

Tom Watson

I can still remember my first party card, proudly handed to me by Mum for my fifteenth birthday – a coming of age that showed I knew my class and tribe. But we have to accept that these totemic expressions of belonging are not as potent for the next, digital generation, whose members expect parties to work harder for their loyalty.

The Labour Party has wrestled with the need to reform in order to be relevant to that generation. This debate does not end with an internal constitutional reform, it has barely started. We need to build a party that sets out a sense of long-term national purpose and mobilises broad political support. To govern effectively in the digital age will require a Labour Party working with lots of other organisations in order to build coalitions for real change and lasting transformation.

This is not solely a challenge for the party I love, but for politics as a whole. And with 24-hour political news coverage, it is impossible to have an internal debate about this challenge without the inevitable headlines about party splits, as we saw in the latest iteration of the debate on how the trade unions and the party relate to each other.

My concern is to dig deeper into a debate broader than the important nitty-gritty about affiliation and member participation. For if we are going to make politics relevant and real again, I believe there are only two options that stand a chance. Parties must either broaden their bases – becoming more pluralist and actively engaging members in innovative ways – or change the electoral system to allow smaller parties into Parliament. The results of the AV referendum do not bode well for the latter, so we are back to the party.

There is an unwise third option, preferred by David Cameron: to do nothing. It is tempting for a prime minister to make this choice because the effects will not be felt on their watch. But the result of inaction – membership decline, electoral disengagement, civic institutions withdrawing from political debate – would be to decrease parliamentary legitimacy.

Reform of the Labour Party must not be reduced to a debate about opting in or opting out of trade union affiliation, as sometimes appeared to be the case in the debate of 2013. That would be to miss the point and to scupper the opportunity – it is the tactics of mid-level media managers. What we need is an overarching strategy.

I think it is important the Labour Party retains a clear and serious link to organised labour. Unions have always provided a pool of people who learn how to represent and debate – outside the party machine – and who could then challenge the dominance of intellectuals in the party, which leads to a party bound to a progressive and liberal worldview. This worldview is largely alien to the constituents I represent in the Black Country. In addition to the countervailing influence of the workplace-empowered shop steward, unions brought organisation and campaign support too. You simply cannot run an authentic electoral machine without workers.

It goes deeper than that though. Labour was built by workers to represent the interests of people without many assets, who work for a living. Labour must represent a vision of a prosperous country that does not only work in the interests of capitalists, whether they be media owners, venture fund owners or the owners of football clubs, but resists this domination through democracy. Labour is the instrument of that resistance and we have lost that vision. The idea was never to dominate. Unions stood as a bulwark against communism. In the 1930s it was Labour that stood firm against both fascism and communism at home and then abroad, and the people elected a Labour government because it was in line with their values and experience. Ernest Bevin was a great Labour politician and a great patriot. We are in danger of losing the natural support of working people and that does not imply breaking the link with trade unions but engaging on the renewal of both party and unions.

When you join Labour, you are still joining a movement that stretches beyond the narrow definition of political party. And that means building a place where everyone can feel at home, where decisions are dealt with transparently and people are given a fair hearing. Our sense of mutual responsibility should be at the heart of our culture.

Still, we must find more ways to work in partnership with civic institutions. Look at the incredible work of Maurice Glasman, pulling together faith and community groups to use their power to improve the lives of those around them. He wants to give power back to people in their communities by building new institutions. This is the challenge of our age and it is one that Labour should be equipped to meet, with our history emerging from working communities to confront the powers of the day. Yet talk to the average Labour political adviser these days and Glasman is dismissed. This task has only just begun. Unions need to think about their potential role in a wider movement, involving civic and faith groups and other non-state institutions. The nascent Bank of Salford is just such a venture. Here is an example of a union collaborating with other organisations to create a new institution for the future. When the Christians of Nineveh were being slaughtered it was vital that the unions and the churches came together to show solidarity.

When I was Campaigns Coordinator I worked closely with the Chicago community organiser Arnie Graf to implant a new culture at the heart of the party. It is bottom-up, it values relationships, collaboration and mutual self-help, develops new activists who never stop listening, and creates lasting partnerships with civic actors outside the party. It is more exciting than a stale debate about the Labour rulebook. Such an approach could build Labour's base and give the party and the country a new sense of purpose. But as we broaden our reach to new institutions and movements, as I asserted in the debate about internal party reform, what is needed is more affiliation – more cooperation – to challenge the party's internal machine, not less.

The unions need this too. Where the leadership is elected by less than 10 per cent of the membership there is a lack of connection between union members and activists. The same approach as that pioneered by Arnie Graf is required. A strong stress on leadership development of workers, a far more relational approach to the culture of the union can lead to a far more amenable culture to partnership and training so that unions can be a constructive and vital force for the renewal of society. We used to call it socialism and maybe we will do so again.

In addition to developing a distinctive form of community organising Labour needs a new political economy. The German economy, with its co-determination in corporate governance and pension fund management and its vocational labour market entry, provides an instructive roadmap. Of course we cannot transplant every institutional and cultural arrangement from Germany into the UK ecosystem. However, given the broken neo-liberal model whose ruins we live amidst there are real principles that emanate from Germany which we can embrace, agitate for and integrate into the Labour offer. This also builds upon Christian traditions that have long been dormant and ignored within Labour: ideas of vocation, subsidiarity and the balance of power.

What is required, therefore, in the United Kingdom is a new pro-business and pro-worker political economy. This approach is less focused on external regulation and more concerned with relational accountability within the governance of the firm and sector, and less focused on tax and fiscal transfer and more on giving incentives to vocation and value through building decentralised institutions such as vocational colleges and regional banks.

What would such an agenda look like? First, Labour should champion a partnership model that gives a constructive role to trade unions and to workers in vocational training and corporate governance. This would build on the work of Dr John Lloyd when the AEEU pioneered the partnership approach to industrial relations. Yet, the challenge is serious: we need to be bolder and go much deeper.

To make this a reality, it is necessary to give a primary role to work and labour value in the corporate governance of firms so that there can be an active negotiation of strategy that does not exclusively benefit the managers of firms. One of the principal causes of the crash was a lack of accountability, which led to cheating and excessive risk. The workforce are the only people with internal expertise and an interest in the flourishing of the firm. A third of the seats on boards should be elected by the workforce. That would also give them 'skin in the game' when it comes to the sacrifices required for profitability.

Furthermore, there should be a decisive change in our attitude to vocation and skills. As Maurice Glasman has asserted, half of our universities could be closed and turned into vocational colleges jointly governed by business, unions and local authorities. This could renew the skills lacking in our workforce. UnionLearn could yet become the most significant and vibrant wing of the Labour movement.

Finally, we should establish regional and sectoral banks so that there is stable access to capital in regions that can support local business with an awareness of their specific needs, which was a key recommendation of Labour's small-business taskforce and it is a radical one. The work that Unite is supporting with the Bank of Salford is commendable and needs to be built on.

This then is the common good approach to renewing Labour that reconnects unions and the party with their civic roots. As a party we must get ready for the next generation. To be relevant in the digital age, the Labour Party must be more pluralist and retain and build upon its trade union links. A pro-business and pro-worker agenda restores economic vitality and ensures Labour is a vital and indispensable partner in national renewal. Labour needs to value labour and business and seek a common good between them. That is the new Labour political economy. Blue Labour? Post-liberal? I don't really care what these ideas are called. However, they have the potential to fire Labour with a transformative mission once again.

The stakes are high. UKIP is growing in strength in Labour areas. We also need to bring the white working class together with Sikhs who are running soup kitchens, black Christian churches that believe in and promote the common good and environmental groups that are campaigning around preserving forests and clean rivers that people love. In the end, that is what we need to stand for. Relationships of mutual responsibility based on love, and we should not be ashamed to say that. For a century Labour has risen to the challenge of serving the country in the interests of locals and immigrants, faith and secular, cities and provincial. It is time to do so again.

PART THREE

POLITICAL ECONOMY

CHAPTER SEVEN

The Common Good in an Age of Austerity

Jon Cruddas

INTRODUCTION

I will start with a basic proposition: that here today in the United Kingdom we face a twin crisis of inequality and identity. This is not simply a question of the distribution of material goods. Rising inequality is not just an economic problem. It also violates our deep sense of democratic inclusion, justice and fairness. Likewise, Britain's fragmented identity threatens not only social cohesion. It now threatens our very political unity – reflected in recent elections and future referenda. For it appears that we no longer know how to define who we are or what we stand for; we are losing our ability to live together, work together or help one another – and indeed to talk about this.

In this context it is vital that we restore and reshape a vision of Britain that everyone can sign up to – Michael Gove for example has repeatedly talked about the need to re-establish core British values. To this end I suggest we need to look to an idea deeply rooted in Christian life and thought. The idea of the common good. The common good is concerned with personal and mutual flourishing in terms of our talents and vocations. It is about treating people as they really are: as human beings who belong to families, localities and communities, and to shared traditions, interests and faiths. We must challenge the concept of abstracted, rootless, atomised individuals that governs neoclassical or neo-liberal thinking – the thinking that dominates our life.

To begin this essay I would like to make two basic points. First, the more that I am involved in politics the more I realise that it is this later viewpoint regarding isolated human activity that has won out; it conditions our public philosophy. I remember some 30 odd years ago, just before his death, Michel Foucault argued that neoclassical economics, or neo-liberalism, was becoming 'bio-political' – in that it was being naturalised. Seen as eternal and beyond political contest; not situated in time or place. How right he was. This needs to be contested. That is why the notion of the common good is so vital today. It questions the very foundations of this liberal economic worldview – of what it is to be human – of 'rational economic man'.

Second, politics has become increasingly instrumental and economistic. Therefore, a discussion of the notion of the common good helps us retrieve a language around what it is to live a good life. It provides a very different texture to our public conversation. Let me give you an example. No one identified this better than Bobby Kennedy at the University of Kansas on 18 March 1968 when he dared to suggest the following: 'Even if we act to erase material poverty, there is another great task, it is to confront the poverty of satisfaction – purpose and dignity – that afflicts us all'. He went further:

> the gross national product does not allow for the health of our children, the quality of their education or the joy of their play. It does not include the beauty of our poetry or the strength of our marriages, the intelligence of our public debate or the integrity of our public officials. It measures neither our wit nor our courage, neither our wisdom nor our learning, neither our compassion nor our devotion to our country, it measures everything in short, except that which makes life worthwhile.

So we are becoming more economistic in politics; it is a specific type of economics that dominates.

GLOBALISATION VS ISOLATIONISM

The need for a transformation in our thinking has, I believe, become ever more urgent in the context of a rapidly globalising world. The main problem with current neo-liberal globalisation is that it detaches economic and political power from locality, tradition and inter-personal relationships. That's because it makes a fundamental assumption about human nature: that we are essentially selfish, greedy, isolated individuals who seek to maximise our own individual happiness or short-term pleasure. Ayn Rand has won if you will. Purely individual interests ultimately clash. This conflict is then supposedly resolved by the 'invisible hand' of the market and the visible hand of the state. In consequence we are left with an increasing centralisation of power, a growing concentration of wealth and an ever-more atomised society.

Faced with this crisis of inequality and identity, we are seeing two dominant responses. Some demand ever more market globalisation, in the forlorn hope that it will promote the 'greatest happiness of the greatest number'. The 'if-it's-not-working-let's-intensify-it' approach. Others suggest a retreat into a nation state that promises greater self-determination and protection from foreign meddling in domestic affairs – a modern national isolationism. Both are equally dangerous. They back the impersonal forces of state and market against the interpersonal ties of society. They do nothing to reduce inequality or to project a positive vision of our identity.

It is rather by embracing a specifically rooted vision of the common good that Britain can reclaim a positive vision of itself. This is Ed Miliband and Labour's vision of a country committed to the promotion of the flourishing of all peoples within its borders – his agenda described as 'One Nation' – and by extension of all peoples across the whole globe.

COMMON GOOD IN AN AGE OF AUSTERITY

People will claim that this is not possible. They will say that the debt burden means we must ruthlessly retrench social provision, whilst withdrawing all restraints on the very market systems that created the recession. This is the coherent response of the liberal political economist – it just misreads human nature. On one thing we can agree however: austerity is a reality. The state of our public finances is not acceptable. But this problem is precisely the opportunity to change things, to shape a new, fairer Britain. It provides a space in which to transform both the operation of the global market and the central state. A vision of Britain built on pure economic liberalism can never recognise, let alone serve the common good. In its purest form it does not recognise the concept and its economics can never provide for it. For most wealth accrues only to the top 1 per cent.

So it's the whole logic of economic liberalism that is in question. British GDP is evidently not the same as the common good of the British people – to return to the Bobby Kennedy of 1968. And there is an alternative to this type of economy that increases inequality and erodes our shared identity. That alternative is a true market economy which genuinely pursues the common good. The good of each and every one of us, individually and combined. We owe much of our thinking about the common good to philosophers in antiquity. So what can Christianity and other faiths add to our understanding of its nature?

Three crucial contributions I would suggest. And I would like to reference here the work of John Milbank. First, religions generally insist that human beings are partial, rooted creatures who live in concrete, inherited conditions. Yet they equally insist that we are in search of universal, transcendent principles such as justice, kindness and forbearance which apply to all human beings. These ideas do not for religious outlooks exist as pure abstractions. How else could we distinguish between good and bad craftsmen, good and bad Brazilian football players, good and bad statesmen or even politicians, good and bad neighbours?

So one could say that religions offer exemplary stories springing from particular soils and particular pasts that can nevertheless inspire everyone from whatever background. Such stories are more effective than abstract notions that move no one in particular. So without these stories we tend to be left at the mercy of biased, chauvinistic narratives that celebrate only national heroisms and caricature the other as an enemy. To seek to follow religious stories – to dare to be yourself an Abraham, a Samson or a Good Samaritan – is not about subjective will or personal preference. It's about an inward desire and drive that can be nurtured through educative guidance, often over several generations. Hence the importance of rooted institutions and practices that take the stories forward – not left to market vagaries pulled from the textbook.

Second, Christianity and other faith traditions also teach us that the common good concerns the relational. Not lone egos, nor an anonymous mass. But instead shared bonds that are both convivial and sacrificial. That is because human beings flourish as persons who freely associate with others in groups, communities and nations. So to the centrality of story as example, we can add the importance of relational covenants. Indeed many of the stories in the biblical legacy and other monotheistic traditions are stories of covenant – from Abraham through Moses to Jesus and Mohammed. The word covenant is vital here – as it expressly moves beyond the transactional so beloved by the economic liberal.

Third, religions remind us that we are not necessarily selfish, greedy and prone to violence. Nor, however, are we purely selfless and unconditionally cooperative. Rather, most people naturally and rightly seek mutual recognition – a fulfilling of themselves alongside others. They want to be at home in the world, but they don't usually want to destroy the other home-dwellers. Thus to the story of covenant we can add the inner content of covenant, which is mutual sharing. Religion has told a positive story about how human beings have made an agreement with God to agree amongst ourselves to celebrate each other and to share in justice the good things of life.

Exemplary story. Relational covenant. The principle of reciprocity. These aspects of our religious legacy are crucial to the rediscovery of a sense of identity and economic justice in the UK today.

ETHICAL ECONOMY AND MORAL, MUTUAL MARKETS

This threefold vision can be the starting point for a transformed market economy. The politics of the common good rejects the idea that markets are necessarily either immoral or amoral. Instead, the common good promotes the idea of an ethical economy as also the most plausibly successful economy. That means a model which combines private profit with public benefit by sharing reward, risk and responsibility amongst all stakeholders: owners, managers, workers, consumers, suppliers and members of the local community. Our – Labour's – commitment to put workers on remuneration committees is just one example of this.

Such a model requires a rise in productivity to guarantee also a rise in salaries or wages, encouraging a greater sense of pride, duty and genuine calling in every workforce. In turn, this creates efficiencies, including higher retention and lower hiring/firing costs. This guarantee will be achieved through a combination of legislation to redefine corporate organisation, fiscal encouragement of good practice and educative creation of a new business ethos.

By similar means we will encourage more vocational training and higher-quality vocational qualifications. An ethical economy will also link small firms in wider associations working both for mutual benefit and mutual upholding of high standards. Such an aim necessarily seeks to resist the routinisation of mental as well as physical labour through the misuse of technology. Rather, technology is more efficiently employed when it is used to enhance the scope of individual creativity and personal engagement. The notion of the dignity of labour itself is vital here.

We will also reform the banking sector by recognising and rewarding the social benefit of making capital more widely and responsibly available. In these ways and others we will create a new economic covenant based on the mutual sharing of risks, rewards and responsibilities. This approach is pro-business, pro-worker and pro-aspiration. This covenant will strengthen solidarity within firms and banks and between them. Greater cooperation between economic institutions will allow small businesses to offer to employees the long-term securities now only possible for large organisations. In such a fashion we will challenge the false story told by neo-liberalism that greed engenders more wealth and more wealth for all.

Instead the truth can be told that solid and lasting prosperity is built upon foundations of virtue. Many exemplary narratives – such as that of the Rhineland model in the German economy – illustrate this today.

PLURALISING THE STATE AND RENEWING SOCIETY

And what does the common good mean for the governmental sphere? Much of modern politics has been about notions of the 'popular will' or the 'general will'. These notions treat us all as isolated individuals whose interests can somehow be defined by mass convergence. In reality this tends to mean that executive power subverts the supposedly sovereign power of the people in whose name they pretend automatically and instrumentally to act. Britain has never fully embraced this new tradition.

In this country the executive power of prime ministers and ruling parties remains accountable to the inherited sovereignty of the Crown in Parliament. Parliamentary sovereignty personally represents the complex democratic will and interests of the people in terms of an evolving sense of the common good that stretches from the past into the future. This sense has included a notion of the ultimate answerability of all of us – singly and together – to a God of Justice. So, governance in the name of the 'common' is about interpreting and interrelating the multiple, plural goods that grow out of interpersonal relationships – whether between free persons or in groups and associations.

The trouble is that over the last 100 years, the British state has become ever more centralised, even as democratic participation has withered away and the power of the executive has increased. All this in spite of our unwritten constitution. The European Union has suffered from the same disease. As a consequence voters have turned to parties like UKIP to express their anger with Brussels and Westminster alike. People feel powerless and ignored. There are many estranged interests that neither participate in our polity nor are represented by anyone. We are facing a crisis of legitimacy.

In this circumstance Labour's politics of the common good requires three big changes. First, no more top-down reorganisation. Instead, locally run and organised schools, hospitals, house-building programmes and habitats. Second, no more outsourcing of relational services to those parts of the private sector that are driven purely by corporate profit rather than a social purpose. It is quite staggering that some £10 billion of public contracts – of taxpayers' money – is allocated to some 20 private companies. Rather, we need to forge cooperative ties with ethical enterprise – such as cooperatives, mutuals, and social businesses.

Third, combined local authorities will be given greater control over tax revenues to invest, grow their revenues and fund their own priorities. By decentralising both taxes and services, we can simultaneously get rid of public debt and increase popular power. Cutting out middle and higher tiers of bureaucracy and managerialism reduces waste. And giving people more responsibility for what is spent ensures greater responsibility and exercise of thrift: a Public Accounts Committee in every community if you will.

This is the proposed social covenant to match the economic one. Like the latter, it belongs in a different and truer story. Not the old one of zero-sum alternatives in which you have to choose between state debt or loss of services. Or between public security and personal freedom. Instead, a truer story in which mutual care and financial prudence belong naturally together; in which your freedom of opportunity and expression is inseparable from the same freedom for your neighbour. A story exemplified in our everyday experience – a story of decency and neighbourliness.

THE INTERNATIONAL DIMENSION

I have spoken of a new covenant situated in a different, less abstract and more common-sensical narrative of our past, present and future. A narrative based upon the truth of the common good, which is that sharing and success belong together. We already know that the opposite assumption has destroyed sharing; now we are seeing that it also destroys success. The new story of the covenant of reciprocal sharing applies both to the economic and the public realms, as we have seen. But in the longer term we could move towards a third, international covenant, whose principles could already begin to guide and shape British foreign policy.

This could be a voluntary agreement amongst participatory nations to meet minimum standards of the sharing of rewards, risks and resources in both the economic and the social realms. Also to meet certain shared standards of 'subsidiarity', or of decentralised control and responsibility. Part of that covenant could be a pooled promise of financial assistance under inspected control, if any nation found it hard to meet such standards. Such an extended covenant for social and economic justice could indeed be a way to revive and rethink the UK as a united association of different self-governing nations. A version of the same idea could make the EU work for and not against nations, regions and individual people. And might it not even be a new way to reinvigorate the British Commonwealth?

CONCLUSION

If we continue to think in the old, pessimistic ways that assume the reign of selfishness and mere quantitative aggregates, then an age of austerity can only be a period of reduced ambition. But if we think in both more optimistic and more realistic terms of the common good, then austerity is converted into opportunity and innovation. An opportunity to rediscover the story of our best British selves. As a people, partly under religious inspiration, covenanted with each other in the interests of mutual benefit. A people who aspire to wealth in the sense of an improved and shared material and spiritual well-being for all. A people who aspire to good public services – to increased interpersonal care and greater democratic participation. A people who aspire to be a beacon to the rest of the world and to collaborate with other nations towards the same, shared ends. In this way austerity can allow us to recover and redefine a covenantal destiny – it is about Big Reforms without Big Money. It begins to answer what is the purpose of Labour without growth but with austerity. In this way a more generous Britain can also be a more successful Britain. In a genuine sense, it can be great again.

I will conclude where I started. Not with Kennedy but with his great adversary Lyndon Johnson. Four years before the Kansas Speech I mentioned at the start of this essay, Johnson spoke in Michigan of an 'opportunity to move not only toward the rich society and the powerful society, but upward to the Great Society'. Here material justice is simply the beginning. It tells a deeper story of human enrichment – of 'the desire for beauty and the hunger for community'. And where 'the meaning of our lives matches the marvellous products of our labor'. He recites Aristotle – he considers the city, the country and the classroom where this Great Society was to be forged to overcome a 'soulless wealth'. It required a new statecraft – 'new concepts of cooperation, a creative federalism, between the national capital and the leaders of local communities'. The task being to 'help build a society where the demands of morality, and the needs of the spirit, can be realised in the life of the Nation'.

That Great Society has at various times in this country been called the Good Society. It is what might have been with the idea of Big Society – remember that. Or we could just settle here today with the notion of the common good. Where we push back against a desiccated materialism – our 'soulless wealth' – and contest the very foundations of economic liberalism and reintroduce the notion of obligation and duty to each other as citizens and humans. It should not be a choice but an obligation.

CHAPTER EIGHT

'Civil Economy': Blue Labour's Alternative to Capitalism

Adrian Pabst

MORAL ECONOMY

If the Labour Party does not look like an opposition ready to govern again, it is because it has so far failed to craft a proper political economy that recognises the nature of the current crisis and offers a realistic alternative. More than any other force within the wider Labour movement and British politics, Blue Labour has led the way in showing that the economic crash reflects a wider social and ethical crisis which has to do with a culture of incentives and rewards for vice – especially vanity and greed. (Dante had it right when he described the former as 'love of self perverted to hatred and contempt for one's neighbour' and the latter as 'excessive love of power and money'.) Accordingly the only genuine alternative is a renewed 'moral economy' that offers incentives and rewards for virtue, above all sympathy, forbearance and courage.[1]

Linking these and other virtues is the principle of reciprocity. For Blue Labour reciprocity is key because it outflanks in advance all the binary terms such as left vs right, state vs market or individual vs collective that are but diverse expressions of the same underlying logic: the disembedding of the economy from society and the re-embedding of social relations in a culture that is rationalist, utilitarian and transactional – as Karl Polanyi first diagnosed.[2] This primacy of politics and the economy over society is the mark of contemporary liberalism, notably the fusion of social with economic liberalism that has defined Britain's political consensus since 1997. While increasing individual freedoms and opportunities, liberal modernisation has also led to an economy that is dominated by debt and despair and a society that is characterised by ever-greater interdependence and atomisation.

By contrast, the principle of reciprocity underpins the social nexus that is more primary than the cash nexus or the power nexus. The focus on mutual recognition more than wealth and power chimes with popular English and British cultural traditions that never embraced the self-serving creed so characteristic of the new elites who consider themselves beyond the rules applying to everyone else. Contra false opposites such as selfishness and selflessness, recognising reciprocal needs and promoting practices of mutual assistance can help reintegrate ethics at the heart of the public realm while also avoiding a pious moralism and a misplaced cynicism as to people's most consistent motives.

Reciprocity is at the heart of the 'civil economy' tradition that has recently shaped Catholic Social Thought on which Blue Labour draws.[3] In this essay, my argument is that the 'civil economy' model provides the best alternative to its neo-liberal and Keynesian rivals. Beyond the rather sterile opposition between more market austerity and more state stimulus, neither neo-liberalism nor Keynesianism has much to offer in terms of breaking Britain's addiction to debt (both public and private) or enabling the country to compete in a global race to the top – in relation to excellence and to ethos. For the same reason, the 'civil economy' also goes further in building a post-crisis vision than the ordo-liberal approach that underpins the German 'social market economy' which was enshrined in the 2009 Lisbon Treaty. A 'civil economy' ties economic profit to ethical and social purpose, and it seeks to ethicise exchange by instituting just prices, fair wages and non-usurious rates of interest. In the same spirit, it replaces the separation of risk from reward with risk- and profit-sharing models which, for example, require the indexing of salary levels to growth in labour productivity.

In both respects it publicly requires an economic pursuit of honourable practice and genuine benefit rather than just abstract wealth and power. It argues that the seemingly utopian pursuit of the truly good is in natural alignment with the various goods of concrete flourishing (work, housing, food, health) and higher fulfilment (work satisfaction, subtle cuisine, beautiful environment, educational development) that human beings everywhere naturally seek. For this reason the 'civil economy tradition' believes that the real economic task is the shared coordination of all these pursuits in terms of a 'common good' which bends and integrates the vivid colours of social life – rather than washing them away in favour of the grey paste of utility.

Thus honourable behaviour – precisely because it inspires and runs with the natural grain of human endeavour – tends to foster higher innovation, higher productivity, higher growth and higher remuneration. All this is *only* utopian in terms of the current capitalist logic and liberal ideology, but it can be achieved under the carapace of a different set of ideas and institutions that combine novel incentives and rewards for virtue with punitive action for vice (e.g. revoking licences to produce and trade in the event of criminal behaviour) that would command wide assent. In this manner, Blue Labour rejects immoral capitalism and the liberal version of a supposedly 'fair' economy that benefits the few in favour of genuinely moral markets in which mutual obligations beget individual entitlement, trust – not compliance – enhances efficiency, cooperation is the basis of competition and workers' representation improves competitiveness. Thus Blue Labour's paradoxical politics can provide 'One Nation Labour' with an overarching narrative and a series of transformative policy ideas.

THE NATURE OF THE CURRENT CRISIS

Clearly the continual economic crisis does not foreshadow the end of capitalism. However, it both reminds us of something well known and reveals something new. It reminds us that capitalism is subject to a peculiar sort of periodic crisis: a crisis of speculation that is linked to the inner contradictions of expansion and contraction, notably the episodic over-accumulation of capital linked with declining rates of return, as Adam Smith recognised long before Karl Marx.[4] But the crisis also reveals that globalisation since the 1970s has so expanded and speeded up the processes of capitalist change as to engender something qualitatively different. More than ever before, global capitalism erodes the 'moral economy' of mutual obligations on which economic exchange ultimately depends. By further reducing everything and everyone to a tradable commodity, capital constantly expands the reach of the market into new areas and creates more opportunities both nationally and globally. But by the same token, it undermines relationships, reciprocity and responsibility, without which markets cannot generate lasting prosperity or combine private profit with social benefit.

Moreover, unrestricted movements of international finance now severely curtail government freedom of action in a way that puts popular democracy itself into crisis. The manner in which excess capital can be transferred from one part of the world to another and back again in a matter of milliseconds using high-speed computer trading has in large part generated the recent severe economic destabilisation and also expanded the possibilities for outrightly criminal behaviour.[5] In response to the collapse of the subprime mortgage market and the 2008 global 'credit crunch', national states bailed out transnational banks by taking over their debts in a manner that locks politics itself yet more tightly into this sheerly financial logic. In consequence, government has less and less regard for the specifically political ends of human well-being and interpersonal communication, while the long-term needs of the national polity and society are subordinate to the short-term interests of global wealth accumulation. The economic turmoil of 2008–9 had its roots in a much deeper political and cultural crisis that is fundamentally about values, not primarily money.

Indeed, popular protest such as the Occupy movement has been triggered not only by deprivation linked to the recession but also by moral outrage against all those in the public and the private sector who have betrayed traditional social norms and obligations of substantive justice and the common good – bankers, politicians, regulators, journalists, policemen and managers at institutions that used to enjoy high levels of public trust. More than six years after the financial crash, much of the country remains caught in a spiral of debt, demoralisation and despair. In the UK and elsewhere there is a growing, albeit inchoate, sense that 'Big Business' and 'Big Government' have colluded at the expense of the people. For example, the Corporation of London represents the interests of finance to the detriment of all vocational trades, strengthening the City's capture of the Treasury and the Treasury's domination of government policy, as Maurice Glasman has argued.[6] In this manner, the Corporation has turned London from a self-governing *civitas* at the centre of the British Commonwealth into the capital city of global finance.

Just as global finance is disconnected from ethical goals, so too the state has extended the rule of the political and the economic over the social. For half a century, governments of the left and the right have either replaced mutualist arrangements among workers with centralised, bureaucratic welfare or outsourced the delivery of public goods to private service providers – or indeed a fusion of both. In this manner, the elections in 1945, 1979 and 1997 led to settlements that ended up exacerbating the centralisation of power and the concentration of wealth which characterise the UK – with both income and asset inequality rising at exponential rates.[7] Moreover, during the boom in easy credit in the late 1990s and 2000s governments shifted debt from the public sector to private households.[8] After the crash, taxpayer-funded bailouts saved the banks but governments and families were left saddled with a debt burden that depresses the kind of sustained strong growth which alone can reverse Britain's long-term economic decline. That is why protesters have rounded not just on bankers but also regulators and politicians who have all been complicit in the bubble cycle of boom and bust that has imploded with such devastating consequences. From the outset, the economic turmoil of 2008–9 was part of a much deeper moral crisis that has to do with perverse incentives for vice such as vanity and naked greed.

BRITAIN'S BROKEN ECONOMY

The recovery that started in late 2013 changed the mood music but represents little more than a continuation of the pre-crisis model. After the longest downturn since the Great Depression of 1929–32, renewed growth marked a snap-back rather than a level change, as national output went up thanks to deferred consumer spending, cheap credit and house-price inflation in London and the south-east. With few notable exceptions, Britain still has a low-wage, low-productivity, low-innovation and low-growth model that is now undergoing a 'zero hours' intensification. It is true that certain manufacturing businesses are booming and that there are new industrial and manufacturing hubs and corridors in southern England. But if anything this adds to the deepening North–South divide. In any case, it is not yet sustained by sufficient long-term investment or by sufficient demand through wage growth in line with productivity, which remains very weak compared with other countries. We are seeing a slight revival of spirits after a long recession, not a genuine and lasting return to health.

On the contrary, the deep dysfunctions that have beset the British economy since the 1970s persist:

(1) A continual process of de-industrialisation has reinforced a two-tier economy and labour market that are increasingly divided between high- and low-skill groups; meanwhile middle-skilled groups such as former machinists and tradesmen lost their jobs and joined the army of cashiers and call-centre workers; the low-skilled (both indigenous and immigrant) form a new 'precariat' for whom opportunity and flexibility is synonymous with insecure employment and low pay.

(2) The rising costs of living that outstrip wage growth are closely connected with a monopoly or cartel capitalism that pushes up prices and cuts salaries; in this way, 'Big Business' and the super-rich extract rents, while the rest of society are confined to new forms of indentured labour.

(3) The growing precariousness and the increasing cost of living are further fuelling the vicious cycle of debt and demoralisation, with the poorest 10 per cent owing four times as much as they own in financial assets; millions are forced to choose between the exploitation of usurious payday loans and the humiliation of food banks.

(4) The excessive reliance on finance and other services reinforced a 'great risk shift'[9] – transferring insecurity from government and large businesses to small- and medium-sized enterprise and households; this, coupled with the separation of risk from reward, has concentrated the benefits in the hands of the super-rich, while farming out to the mass of people an ever-augmented share of the dangers attendant upon it such as hunger and homelessness.

(5) The process of privatisation, liberalisation and deregulation to which every government since Margaret Thatcher has subjected the country constitutes a massive transfer of previously public assets into private ownership; this transfer has resulted in 'the great divestiture', with levels of inequality and social regression not seen since the 1920s.[10]

Britain is facing the paradox of a richer economy with poorer people. By any historical comparison since the Great Depression of 1929–32, economic growth is low and long-term unemployment high. Those aged 18–25 or older than 50 especially struggle to find jobs, not to mention all those who are under-employed (in involuntary part-time jobs or on zero-hour contracts) and those who have given up on finding employment altogether (including those on disability benefits or in early retirement). Thus there is a very real prospect that this generation of 18–25-year-olds and their children's generation will be worse off than their parents' and grandparents' generation. Even some of the baby-boomers who are now retiring will be worse off than previously thought. Furthermore, the financial precariousness that was exposed by the crash combines with long-standing feelings of social dislocation and cultural disorientation to produce a dread of abandonment. All this adds to the support for populist forces on the radical left and the radical right such as UKIP.[11]

Crucially, Britain has joined a global 'race to the bottom' in terms of wages, employment conditions and low taxes on the top 1 per cent that reinforces the ever-widening income and asset inequality which characterises capitalism, as the French economist Thomas Piketty has shown.[12] Since wealth begets wealth, inequality trends are like a self-perpetuating upward spiral. While the wealthy now split between the super-rich and the super-super-rich (as corporate executives compete with billionaires to drive up the wealth spiral), the middle classes struggle to make ends meet and the poor are seen as surplus to requirements.

Beyond mere exploitation, we now live in an 'economy of exclusion' that treats unproductive people as 'outcasts' and 'leftovers', as Pope Francis rightly warned in his Apostolic Exhortation *Evangelii Gaudium*:

> [h]uman beings are themselves considered consumer goods to be used and then discarded. We have created a 'throw away' culture which is now spreading. It is no longer simply about exploitation and oppression, but something new. Exclusion ultimately has to do with what it means to be a part of the society in which we live; those excluded are no longer society's underside or its fringes or its disenfranchised – they are no longer even a part of it. The excluded are not the 'exploited' but the outcast, the 'leftovers'.[13]

Since Pope Leo XIII's encyclical *Rerum Novarum* in 1891, the tradition of Catholic Social Thought has consistently made the point that the dominant economic system is economically unsustainable and ethically indefensible – most recently in Pope Emeritus

Benedict's social encyclical *Caritas in veritate*. At present, the prevailing model does not even pretend to aim for higher purposes. It combines the nakedly honest pursuit of power and wealth for the few with a legal licence for objectively criminal, immoral behaviour that harms the many – as exemplified by the scandals in the financial services industry. Just as the cartel capitalism that characterises global finance (and indeed other sectors) reflects an egregious culture of greed, so too the only alternative is to create a new culture of virtue and ethos by linking profit to a wider social and civic purpose and thereby serving the common good – not just the short-term interests of the few.[14]

Transforming the 'economy of exclusion' requires the recognition that contemporary capitalism combines the resurgence of the importance of inherited wealth in a period of low growth with the newly excessive wages encouraged by the climate of 'meritocratic extremism'.[15] In Britain's case, this is best illustrated by the yawning gulf between executive pay and the salaries of ordinary workers (with top-to-bottom pay ratios of around 300:1 in the FTSE 100 companies) as well as the perverse 'bonus culture' that excessively rewards risky success, mere chance or even failure. In consequence, we see both nationally and internationally the emergence of a new 'aristocracy without honour'. Its continuity both with the debased aristocracies of the various *anciens régimes* and with the new moguls of nineteenth- and twentieth-century industry reveals just how little in the long term either Keynesian-style redistribution or neo-liberal trickle-down wealth have been able to temper the inegalitarian tendencies of the capitalist market.

However, contemporary capitalism is not 'the end of history'. Just as high wage demand tends to eat into profits, so, in the end, debt demand eats into the return upon capital in general. It is quite simple: someone has to pay up sometime; debts cannot be endlessly offloaded onto more and more fictional vehicles. Therefore the resort to debt by the few in terms of securitisation and hedging, in order to shore up capital returns in the face of excessively 'easy credit' to the majority (as with consumer loans, etc.) is not sustainable indefinitely or even for very long. Thus one cannot really do without the final securitisation of abstract wealth in concrete assets, i.e. real profits and real wages derived from real production and consumption of things with use-value, understood in however generous a sense. Hence our current impasse.

THE MARGINAL UTILITY OF KEYNESIAN, MONETARIST AND 'SOCIAL MARKET' MODELS

In response to the 2008 crash, there was much talk but little action about rebalancing and diversifying the British economy. Labour, the Conservatives and the Lib Dems still subscribe to a liberal economics that underpins both Keynesian and monetarist theories and also perpetuates the political pact with capitalism. Like political liberalism, economic liberalism privileges individual rights, commercial contracts and self-interest over interpersonal relationships, mutual obligations and social benefit, without which there can be neither a vibrant democracy nor a thriving market economy that benefits all.

Economic liberalism characterises not just late nineteenth-century laissez-faire but also Keynesianism and the neo-liberal combination of monetarism with fiscal austerity that has dominated politics in Britain since 1979. All three strands share a base commitment to the presuppositions of neoclassical economics that generated the theory of 'marginalism' on the basis of utilitarian ethics.[16] The quest for maximal utility is subject to the 'law of diminishing returns' because – beyond a basic subsistence level – we get progressively less satisfaction from increased consumption of the same basic item. Linking the Marginalist revolution in economics to utilitarianism is the idea of a single flattening quantitative calculus with which we can measure the 'value' of all goods and services, as they merely provide the same kind of stimulus for our soulless organism.

Thus the unnatural leaching of the economic realm can only be secured by the dominance of large primary powers that force all to think in terms of marginal quantification, and seduce the masses to consume more and more shoddy and temporary goods and processes whose appeal will indeed soon pale – causing them to seek to earn more in order to be able to buy a new variant of the same seductive sedative. Just this logic has led to the contemporary dominance of large producers and massified consumers – to the cartel capitalism of contemporary Britain with the 'big four' banks, the 'large six' energy companies, Rupert Murdoch's media empire and various conglomerates that dominate the high street in every town or city up and down the country.

The rise of 'clone towns' is directly related to the decline of independent shopkeepers, of small- and of medium-sized enterprises (SMEs), which tend to compete in terms of ethos and excellence as opposed to low prices based on poor wages and precarious employment conditions.[17] Mid-sized companies and a diversified economy were once the foundation of Britain's global success. Today family businesses and SMEs constitute the industrial and manufacturing backbone of Germany, Europe's economic powerhouse. The German model of a 'social market economy' that combines robust growth with high employment and social cohesion is now widely seen as the best alternative to Anglo-Saxon market capitalism and 'Asian-style' state capitalism.

At its best, the 'social market' model draws on a rich tradition of political economy that includes elements of Catholic Social Teaching.[18] Against both liberalism and Marxism, this tradition has sought to fuse ideas of the common good and human flourishing with new institutions and policies in order to entangle ineluctably the operations of both state and the market in the skeins of interpersonal relationships. There is much Britain can learn from the German model, especially in relation to co-determination and workers' representation on company boards, the role of regional banks in channelling capital into different sectors and providing crucial funds for SMEs, as well as the importance of vocational training and labour market entry – as Maurice Glasman has rightly argued.[19]

However, starting in the late 1970s the Germans adopted their own version of the neo-liberal settlement by reviving the post-1919 tradition of ordo-liberalism. By contrast with Anglo-Saxon capitalist anarchy that is policed by state coercion, the ordo-liberal model views the competitive market order as the best guarantor for economic efficiency and social justice.[20] For this reason, the overriding role of the state is to enforce central regulations that create the conditions (*Rahmenbedingungen*) for free and fair competition in the marketplace, on the debatable assumption that where these prevail they will automatically tend in the direction of equity and fair reward, following Wilhelm Röpke's illusory view that the grosser tendencies to inequality within a market system were but the result of a feudal hangover.[21] (In reality, capitalism relies upon, augments and de-ethicises pre-capitalist inequalities.) The ordo-liberal version of a 'social market' combines bureaucratic state control with an amoral economy that does *not* after all 'automatically' share the proceeds of export-led growth with ordinary workers, whose wages have stagnated for much of the past 15 years. These and other market failures are partially compensated by rationalised welfare and a significant role of the state in the direction of the economy.

It is nonetheless true that the German model still differs fundamentally from Anglo-Saxon capitalism that fuses a Benthamite utilitarian ethic with Rawlsian political liberalism. By contrast, ordo-liberalism weaves together a Kantian ethics of context-less duties with Weberian rationalist (and sternly amoral) statecraft and Bismarckian welfarism: strict rules, multiple layers of bureaucracy and a Prussian desire for more efficient and quasi-military management of civilian populations thereby become ever more the order of the day.

At its core, this compound combines a large measure of Kantian formalism with a dose of Schmittian decisionism. Indeed, it dictates rules to the rest of the eurozone on the heinousness of national debt based on over-consumption. Meanwhile, it regards itself as a justified exception by virtue of its effective economic sovereignty, and so as uniquely permitted to run persistent trade surpluses sustained by domestic under-consumption which is equally damaging. For these surpluses neither benefit ordinary German workers (who have seen their real incomes stagnate or even decline over the past decade), nor are they being reinvested in the peripheral countries. Thus the current version of the German social market economy runs against the interests of European workers, including those in Germany itself.

Whereas the social market economy tends to restrict the role of the state to providing a legal framework for the supposedly neutral operation of competition in pursuit of abstract wealth, the 'civil economy' alternative which I argue for in the remainder of the chapter requires that the state assist (and by no means can it perform this task alone) in crafting a different sort of market altogether. The purpose of a 'civil market' is not to engender growth as a purely quantitative sum, but the real wealth of human flourishing in every dimension – which dictates an imperative to a different sort of 'increase'. If such real wealth be pursued, then the first aim of all economic activity must be social benefit, with acceptable rates of profit related to such benefit, both in terms of proportion and rates of successful achievement. Accordingly, state promotion of economic development must naturally include as its heart an encouraging and rewarding of virtuous behaviour – understood not as a sort of moral addendum to purely economic activity but rather as a performing well of the economic more properly understood as the securing and distributing of human consumable and renewable benefit.

This encouragement would include the rewriting of company law in such a way as to foster the internal ethos of firms and professional associations and the putting in place of rewards for businesses that deliver both social benefit and a reasonable profit. In this fashion 'business ethos' and competitiveness would by no means be abandoned, but rather be more honourably and integrally redefined and then both worked-with and worked-through. This approach departs from the liberal myth of value neutrality and the ordo-liberal myth of impartiality that are both questionably ascribed to government. Thus models of 'civil economy' have a positive vision of the state as upholding the common good and popular participation in the polity in ways that involve democratic co-determination of society and the economy.

CATHOLIC SOCIAL THOUGHT AND THE 'CIVIL ECONOMY' ALTERNATIVE

In the face of the economic and ethical crisis of global capitalism, we need to learn from those traditions that always stood outside the totalising logic of modern politics and economics. It is here that Blue Labour's fusion of the 'civil economy' tradition with Catholic Social Thought (CST) can offer an altogether different story. A powerful new story that can challenge not just the stories told by the Labour Party since 1945 and by the Conservative Party since 1979, but the story told by liberalism since the late nineteenth century. A story that could propel Blue Labour's vision to the centre of Britain's polity, the economy and society. Such a vision centres on three closely connected principles: (1) defending the market economy against both capitalism and collectivism; (2) renewing cooperative competition in the face of monopolies, cartels and the bureaucratic compensation for market failure; (3) promoting the firm against capitalist corporations and national control of the economy's 'commanding heights'.

These and other paradoxical positions are not contradictory. Rather, they challenge the prevailing liberal ideology that can only think in terms of binary oppositions such as state vs market and cognate categories. This ignores the 'radical centre' – the realm of interpersonal relationships governed by the principle of reciprocity, which can variously lead either to more cooperative or more conflictual outcomes.[22] Blue Labour is pro-business *and* pro-worker precisely because it refuses to view capital and labour as inevitably opposed but instead sees them as estranged interests that can be brought together in a negotiated settlement through new civic institutions.

Common to the 'civil economy' tradition and CST is the defence of a moral market and a democratic state against both individualism and collectivism, which combine commercial commodification with central state dominance. Here it is important to explain our first argument above that both traditions insist on the fundamental difference between the market economy and capitalism.[23] The former means the division of labour, the freedom to work and to trade and the attempt to increase wealth in the real sense of trying to improve human life – make it more comfortable, exciting, various and fulfilling. By contrast, the latter denotes a permanent process of primary accumulation through dispossession and speculation linked to the concentration of wealth in the hands of the few and the double movement of abstraction and spatialisation that does not serve genuine human needs. If capitalism is about individual self-interest backed by the collectivist state, then the 'civil economy' is about the relational pursuit of both private profit and social benefit for the sake of mutual flourishing.

But how can we do that by labouring and trading in the market? The answer is that one can be both pursuing a reasonable profit for oneself, and at the same time trying to offer to other people a social benefit – in return for a social benefit that they are offering you. One can trade in real human goals as well as in hard cash. Likewise, a contract can be a reciprocal agreement about a shared goal and value, not just the joint meeting of two entirely separate individual goals.

The second element that binds together the 'civil economy' tradition with CST is the balance between competition and cooperation. Instead of the purely individualist and competitive contract that characterises capitalism, the market economy has a price mechanism that operates to a degree cooperatively as well as competitively. So, for example, it is not assumed that you would always charge the highest possible price that the market would tolerate. You might lower that price to help your neighbour because you did not want to destroy your neighbour and it would not even make *economic* sense to do so. Now even tough-minded economists are rediscovering this idea that so-called 'shared value' makes much more economic sense than maximising profit and supplementing capitalism with exercises in 'corporate social responsibility' that are little more than window-dressing.[24] As Pope Benedict XVI put it so succinctly in *Caritas in veritate*, 'in *commercial relationships* the *principle of gratuitousness* and the logic of gift as an expression of fraternity can and must *find their place within normal economic activity*. This is a human demand at the present time, but it is also demanded by economic logic'.[25]

Alongside this fusion of contract with gift, the civil economy is a vocational economy. People serve apprenticeships, and they are conditions of entry to professional associations or guilds. Adherence to vocation and the underlying ethos is also a requirement in order to be given and to retain a licence for production and trade. These guilds try to govern quality, treatment of customers and protection of workers. They confer dignity and genuinely value craft against both market commodification and state collectivisation. All this formed the operative basis for notions of just prices, just wages, just rates of interest and the restriction of usury – principles that have shaped the tradition of Catholic Social Thought since Pope Leo XIII's encyclical *Rerum Novarum* in 1891.

The third element that is common to CST and the 'civil economy' model concerns the nature of the firm and the market. If social recognition is fundamental also for the economy, then trust is basic for the economic firm. One could say (in line with the thinking of the seventeenth-century English Levellers) that it should constitute a sort of benign semi-monopoly which prevents the emergence of malign monopoly.[26] How so? Well on the basis of naked individualism, people strive for monopoly in order to produce the shoddiest possible products, buy the materials for those products as cheaply as possible and sell them as dearly as possible. In this way they undermine competitors and bad practice drives out good. But in the case of the firm that is a 'civil enterprise' or partnership between owners, managers, workers, consumers and suppliers, good practice can drive out bad in a tendency that is actually more stable and more profitable at once. One can see this for much of the history of a firm like the John Lewis partnership but also in those credit unions, mutualised banks and building societies that survived the de-mutualisation of finance as part of the 'big bang' in 1986. There are also many new examples, including social enterprises and 'fair trade' companies.

Such firms will tend to thrive in the long term, not by driving out *all* other competitors, but rather by forcing other firms to compete in terms of quality of produce, fairness of pricing and humane treatment of workers and customers. And a crucial aspect to 'quality of produce' is the fact that *real* goods (including 'relational goods' that we can only enjoy in common) are less subject to the law of diminishing returns. Habit dulls us to the appeal of the latest mutation of the chocolate bar from slender to chunky... But habituation only discovers ever *more* in the enjoyment of fine wines, beers, and ciders, and still more in the practice of fine cuisine and in all aesthetic and reciprocally enjoyed social goods in general.

Both CST and the 'civil economy' tradition insist that we can 'crowd out' bad behaviour and 'crowd in' good behaviour by creating incentives and rewards for virtue and good habits. Where might one locate such self-sustaining and intensifying good habits? One thing we ignore is that many elements of CST – opposition to usury, the just price, the just wage, guilds, corporations, distribution of assets, the primacy of land as sacred, solidarity and subsidiarity[27] – exist in certain degrees in many parts of the world where they have been tried and successfully tested, in particular Northern Italy and large parts of Germany that have adopted a form of constitutional corporatism that is neither statist nor merely propping up the neo-liberal market. Worker participation in management, control of entry conditions to labour by voluntary associations and high-status technical education are all predicated on the relative primacy of labour with respect to capital. And labour, not capital, is the dynamic factor, because it is to do with release of personal, creative human power. This is quite different from the negative freedom of the Anglo-Saxon will – for creativity goes along with the power to judge and discern the aesthetic and social value of one's product.

Other than parts of Italy and Germany, further examples for the successful operation of 'civil economy'-type models include Austria, the Basque country, as well as the new Economies of Communion.[28] The latter operate in Brazil, Portugal and elsewhere in the southern hemisphere, bringing together businesses, social enterprise and educational institutions in deprived areas so as to create a local economy that blends private profit with social purpose. Business profits are shared between three distinct kinds of purposes that are considered to be of equal importance. One purpose is to help people in need by creating jobs in neglected areas that have been abandoned by the central state and the free market. Another purpose is to institute a 'culture of giving' grounded in human relationships of mutual support. The final purpose is to sustain and expand businesses that combine efficiency with solidarity. Here the objective is to blend investment with charitable giving and to change the market from within by locating the logic of gift-exchange at the heart of ordinary economic processes. According to some estimates, some 735 businesses have joined such 'economies of communion', with a majority in Europe (notably Italy and Portugal) but also more than 245 in the Americas. Small numbers perhaps, but a concrete example of how ethical enterprise is good business.

In conceptual terms, a more moral market would also be a *more* genuinely free market: morality need not be just an external corrective to the economic sphere, as social-democratic pathos tends to assume. Another aspect of this moralisation of the market would be the genuine sharing of risk, which would remove the relative protection against risk currently enjoyed by the investor and moneylender as compared with both employees and consumers. But if the economics of egoism do not work for the firm, then it turns out that they do not work at any level whatsoever.

POLITICAL ECONOMY OF VIRTUE: SOME BLUE LABOUR POLICY IDEAS

It could be objected that in the aftermath of the crisis, no transformation is possible because of the sheer debt burden. The latter means we must ruthlessly retrench social provision, whilst withdrawing all restraints on the very market systems that created the recession. To this extent the objection is not wrong: austerity is a reality. The state of public finances and household debt is not acceptable. But this problem is precisely the opportunity to change things and to shape a new, fairer economic model. The post-crisis situation provides a space in which to transform both the operation of the global market and the central state. Blue Labour's blending of CST with the 'civil economy' tradition can offer a post-liberal political economy.

Above all, Blue Labour's 'civil economy' alternative refuses the logic of debt that characterises monetarist and Keynesian approaches, which merely differ on the relative balance of private vs public debts. Since the 1990s, Britain has witnessed a massive transfer of debt from the public sector to private households as a result of keeping wages stagnant and creating perverse incentives for ever-higher personal debts (zero-deposit mortgages, consumer loans, etc.). Neo-liberal austerity may reduce the budget deficit but it undermines the productive economy by slashing capital spending and failing to diversify away from finance – all of which actually depresses growth and thereby increases both public and private debt over time. Crucially, this treats debt as absolute and in some sense primary vis-à-vis assets, and it also privileges the interests of creditors over those of debtors. In this manner, the logic of neo-liberal austerity is of a piece with the separation of profit and risk between institutional investors and managers, on the one hand, and customers and employees, on the other hand.

By contrast, CST and the 'civil economy' model view debt in more relational terms and argue for models whereby unsustainable debt is either partially forgiven or converted into equity. In this manner, both profit and risk are shared more equitably among all the stakeholders: lenders and borrowers, investors and owners, shareholders and managers as well as employers and employees, producers and consumers and suppliers and sellers. Key to this is to create a genuine value chain with a virtuous circle of competition in both excellence and efficiency. That, in turn, also requires regional investment banks and a whole transformation of corporate governance. If implemented, we would begin to shift the economy away from an obsession with short-term results towards the securing of long-term interest and shared prosperity.

Moreover, Blue Labour's 'civil economy' alternative would address deficient demand not simply by either printing money (to offer cash handouts to the population) or by financing massive infrastructure projects from the centre. Instead, the economically more sustainable and ethically more effective option is to promote fair wages and just prices. That would include not only creating 'living wage' cities and regions, but also establishing a link between salary increases and productivity growth. That necessitates investment in vocational training and innovation, including Will Hutton's idea of a new public 'trust' for the pooling of technological knowledge to replace the current patenting system which favours large private corporations over small- and medium-sized businesses and social enterprise.[29] The argument that globalisation requires a cost 'race to the bottom' is economically and ethically non-sense, as developed economies will never be able to compete with low-wage countries such as Vietnam and Cambodia. On the contrary, the only route towards sustainable, high growth is to compete in both excellence (quality) and ethos.

As the first 'civil economist' Antonio Genovesi (a near-contemporary of Adam Smith's) showed in his seminal *Lectures on Civil Economy*, what matters is not the absolute cost of labour or the relation between foreign and domestic production of goods.[30] Rather, what matters is who you share your labour market with. Paying higher prices for locally produced goods not only encourages domestic manufacturing, industry and a greater division of labour within one's polity. Since traders are interconnected, it also raises real wages in all trades from agriculture and manufacturing upwards, promoting both higher productivity and greater justice. In this manner, we can realign fair wages with just prices and defend the interests of all stakeholders, including workers, suppliers and consumers (not just managers, shareholders and lenders) – as argued by the Catholic priest John Ryan who coined the term 'living wage'.[31]

Furthermore, the 'civil economy' alternative would break the over-reliance on unproductive finance by lining a national network of investment banks (constrained to lend within cities, regions and sectors, as Glasman has suggested) to a corresponding structure of professional associations that can offer vocational training and guarantee minimum standards of quality and ethos. Membership in sector-wide 'meta-guilds' would be a necessary condition for getting a professional licence to produce and trade, but employers and employees would be free to choose from among the various associations that make up the guild (to avoid a situation of monopoly). This would also diversify the range and kind of employers' associations and trade unions (both of which currently suffer from self-serving bosses and barons who neglect the interests of their ordinary members). The natural institution to bring together local councils, regional/sectoral banks and professional associations is the guild hall, which would represent democracy vocational at the local level in every city and every county – just like the city and the county hall would represent democracy locational (to extend Glasman's account of the two houses of Parliament).

Finally, the 'civil economy' alternative promotes virtuous businesses by rewriting company law to make social purpose and profit-sharing conditions for company licence (as John Milbank and I have suggested elsewhere)[32] and also by replacing the current incentive structure with a new system of awards and rewards. At present, we have a system that incentivises the privatisation of profit, the nationalisation of losses and the socialisation of risk. A 'virtue economy' can mutualise profit, loss and risk by fostering greater regard for shared interest, value and relational goods and also by providing proper reward for virtuous behaviour. Our current model is based on two elements: first, individual incentives that influence *ex ante* motivation – whether in the form of private sector performance-related pay and bonuses or in the form of public sector policies 'nudging' our behaviour towards greater efficiency and happiness; second, public prizes to acknowledge a specific contribution to society (including military medals and civilian awards for achievements in the arts, sciences, sport and public affairs).

The problem of the underlying logic is fivefold: (1) it sunders *ex ante* motivation from *ex post* outcomes, which leads to the perverse situation of rewarding failure (bonus payments and golden handshakes even in case of bankruptcy); (2) it privileges private self-interest and views social benefit merely in terms of indirect, unintended outcomes; (3) it designs incentives purely in extrinsic ways and reduces the question of reward to a principal–agent relation; (4) it separates monetary from non-monetary rewards, which divorces material value from symbolic worth; (5) it prioritises the individual and the collective over association, which perpetuates the primacy of states and markets over intermediary institutions.

To reward virtuous behaviour and promote an economy of both honour and regard, we need a system that breaks with the logic of private profit, national loss and socialised risk. Here the crucial point is that virtue is pursued for an intrinsic reason, and not for the sake of personal reward. Yet at the same time, virtuous behaviour may yield pleasure or even profit while also making a contribution to the common good. Thus there are good ethical *and* economic reasons for practising virtues. In turn, this means that virtue – the promotion of excellence and ethos – is part of a properly functioning market economy that produces prosperity for all. Thus, the government – in close coordination with employers' associations and trade unions – could rewrite legislation on contracts to promote virtuous behaviour by means of both awards and rewards. Awards refer to a public recognition of virtuous practices, i.e. an acknowledgement of intrinsically good activities that are *not* an expected (though hoped-for) counter-action within a contractual exchange where recompenses have been fixed beforehand. By contrast, rewards denote a public recompense for virtuous behaviour that blends self-interest with social benefit, including the possibility of a monetary recompense (e.g. tax breaks, preferential treatment in terms of government procurement or public service tenders, etc.).

Crucially, virtuous businesses could be given membership in certain professional associations that uphold more stringent standards, which could in the long term give a market advantage – thereby encouraging membership based on a competition in quality, excellence and ethos. Such a form of recognition combines immaterial awards with material rewards and overcomes the false separation of contract from gift that gave rise to the predatory economy of modern capitalism.[33] All these policy ideas reflect Blue Labour's paradoxical stance of being pro-business and pro-worker, and it charts a radically transformative middle path between the status quo, timid reform and a wholesale revolution that all go against the best English and British traditions.

NOTES

1. On the notion of 'moral economy' in English and British history, see E. P. Thompson, 'The moral economy of the English crowd in the 18th century', *Past & Present* 50 (1971), pp. 76–136; *idem*, *Customs in Common: Studies in Traditional Popular Culture* (London: Merlin Press, 1991).

2. Karl Polanyi, *The Great Transformation: The Political and Economic Origins of Our Time* (Boston: Beacon Press, 2001 [orig. pub. 1944]).

3. For the most concise statement of the 'civil economy' tradition, see Luigino Bruni and Stefano Zamagni, *Civil Economy: Efficiency, Equity, Public Happiness* (Bern: Peter Lang, 2007). On Catholic Social Thought and the 'civil economy' model, see Adrian Pabst (ed.), *The Crisis of Global Capitalism: Pope Benedict XVI's Social Encyclical and the Future of Political Economy* (Eugene, OR: Wipf & Stock, 2011).

4. Adam Smith, *Inquiry into the Nature and Causes of the Wealth of Nations* (London: Random Century, 1910 [orig. pub. 1776]), Book I, ch. 9.

5. For a vivid account, see Michael Lewis, *Flash Boys: A Wall Street Revolt* (New York: W. W. Norton & Company, 2014).

6. Maurice Glasman, 'A tale of two cities', Independent Labour Publications, 13 September 2012. Available at http://www.independen-

tlabour.org.uk/main/2012/09/13/a-tale-of-two-cities/ (accessed on 25 August 2014).

7. 'An anatomy of economic inequality in the UK', Report of the National Equality Panel (London: Centre for Analysis of Social Exclusion, London School of Economics and Political Science, 2010). Available at http://webarchive.nationalarchives.gov.uk/20100212235759/http:/www. equalities.gov.uk/pdf/NEP%20Report%20bookmarkedfinal.pdf (accessed on 25 August 2014).

8. Colin Crouch, 'Privatised Keynesianism: An unacknowledged policy regime', *The British Journal of Politics & International Relations* 11 (2009), pp. 382–99.

9. Jacob S. Hacker, *The Great Risk Shift: The New Economic Insecurity and the Decline of the American Dream*, rev. ed. (New York: Oxford University Press, 2008).

10. Massimo Florio, *The Great Divestiture: Evaluating the Welfare Impact of the British Privatizations 1979–1997*, new ed. (Cambridge, MA: MIT Press, 2006).

11. Robert Ford and Matthew J. Goodwin, *Revolt on the Right: Explaining Support for the Radical Right in Britain* (London: Routledge, 2014), pp. 143–82.

12. Thomas Piketty, *Le capital au XXIe siècle* (Paris: Ed. Seuil, 2013), translated as *Capital in the Twenty-First Century*, tr. Arthur Goldhammer (Cambridge, MA: Harvard University Press, 2014). Piketty's analysis is key, if incomplete in crucial ways, and his proposed solutions are neither realistic nor desirable. See John Milbank and Adrian Pabst 'Capitalism in question: Thomas Piketty and the crisis of inequality', *ABC Religion & Ethics*, 6 June 2014. Available at http://www. abc.net.au/religion/articles/2014/06/05/4019629.htm (accessed on 25 August 2014).

13. Pope Francis, *Evangelii Gaudium*, Rome, 24 November 2013. Available at http://w2.vatican.va/content/francesco/en/apost_exhortations/docu-ments/papa-francesco_esortazione-ap_20131124_evangelii-gaudium. html, chap. 2 (accessed on 25 August 2014).

14. For concrete policy ideas on how to transform the prevailing culture of short-term profit maximisation with a new culture of long-term prosperity, see the ResPublica report 'Virtuous banking: placing ethos and purpose at the heart of finance'. Available at http://respublica.org. uk/documents/ueq_Virtuous%20Banking%20Final%20new.pdf (accessed on 25 August 2014).

15. Piketty, *Le capital au XXIe siècle*, pp. 47–57, 206–16, 259–74, 368–70, 468–71, 500–5, 596–9, 642–65, 701–14, 740–4, 941–50.

16. Ernesto Screpanti and Stefano Zamagni, *An Outline of the History of Economic Thought* (Oxford: Oxford University Press, 2005), pp. 163–95.

17. On 'clone towns', see the work of the New Economics Foundation, in particular Andrew Simms, *Tescopoly: How One Shop Came Out on Top and Why it Matters* (London: Constable, 2007).

18. Wilhelm Röpke, *The Social Crisis of our Times*, tr. William F. Campbell (Brunswick, NJ: Transaction, 2009).

19. Maurice Glasman, *Unnecessary Suffering: Management, Markets and the Liquidation of Solidarity* (London: Verso, 1996); M. Glasman, 'Politics, employment policies and the young generation', in A. Quadrio Curzio and G. Marseguerra (eds), *Rethinking Solidarity for Employment: The Challenges of the Twenty-first Century* (Vatican City: Libreria Editrice Vaticana, 2014), pp. 255–270.

20. See, inter alia, Alan Peacock, Alan and Hans Willgerodt (eds), *Germany's Social Market Economy: Origins and Evolution* (London: Macmillan, 1989).

21. John Milbank, 'The real third way: for a new metanarrative of capital and the associationist alternative', in A. Pabst (ed.), *The Crisis of Global Capitalism*, pp. 27–70.

22. Of course to promote reciprocity and interpersonal relationships is to risk being cheated upon, ripped off, exploited or otherwise being wounded by others. See Luigino Bruni, *The Wound and the Blessing: Economics, Relationships and Happiness*, tr. N. Michael Brennan (New York: New City Press, 2007). However, the liberal claim that we can insulate ourselves from such hurt by the impersonal forces of the market and the state merely reinforces a culture of mutual suspicion in which contract and law can become instruments of injustice.

23. On the difference between capitalism and the market economy, see Polanyi, *The Great Transformation*; Fernand Braudel, *Civilisation matérielle, économie et capitalisme, XVe–XVIIIe siècle*, 3 vols (Paris: Ed. Armand Colin, 1979); Martha C. Howell, *Commerce Before Capitalism in Europe, 1300–1600* (Cambridge: Cambridge University Press, 2010).

24. Michael E. Porter and Mark R. Crane, 'Creating shared value', *Harvard Business Review*, Jan.–Feb. 2011, pp. 2–17.

25. Pope Benedict XVI, *Caritas in veritate* (Charity in Truth), 7 July 2009. Available at http://www.vatican.va/holy_father/benedict_xvi/encycli-cals/documents/hf_ben-xvi_enc_20090629_caritas-in-veritate_en.html, c. 36 (original italics) (accessed on 25 August 2014).

26. Antony Black, *Guilds and Civil Society in European Political Thought from the Twelfth Century to the Present* (London: Methuen, 1984), pp. 126–7.

27. See, inter alia, Pontifical Council for Justice and Peace, *Compendium of the Social Doctrine of the Church* (Vatican: Libreria Editrice Vaticana,

2004); Daniel K. Finn (ed.), *The True Wealth of Nations: Catholic Social Thought and Economic Life* (Oxford: Oxford University Press, 2010).

28. Lorna Gold, *New Financial Horizons: The Emergence of an Economy of Communion* (New York: New City Press, 2010).

29. Will Hutton, 'Britain's future lies in a culture of open and vigorous innovation', *The Observer*, 14 October 2012.

30. Antonio Genovesi, *Lezioni di commercio o sia di economía civile*, ed. F. Dal Degan (Milan: Vita e Pensiero, 2013); see also Adrian Pabst, 'Political economy of virtue: Genovesi's 'civil economy' alternative to modern economic thought', *International Review of Economics* 62 (2015), forthcoming.

31. John A. Ryan, *A Living Wage: Its Ethical and Economic Aspects*, rev. ed. (New York: Macmillan, 1914 [orig. pub. 1906]); and *Distributive Justice: The Right and Wrong of Our Present Distribution of Wealth*, rev. ed. (New York: Macmillan, 1927 [orig. pub. 1916]).

32. John Milbank and Adrian Pabst, 'The "Civil Economy" alternative', in *idem.*, *The Politics of Virtue: Post-liberalism and the Human Future*, chap. 4, forthcoming – on which this chapter draws.

33. See Avner Offer, 'Between the gift and the market: the economy of regard', *Economic History Review* 50/3 (1997): 450–76; Geoffrey Brennan and Philip Pettit, *The Economy of Esteem* (Oxford: Oxford University Press, 2004).

CHAPTER NINE

Globalisation, Nation States and the Economics of Migration[1]

David Goodhart

INTRODUCTION

Humanity is on the move on an unprecedented scale and the nation state is inexorably losing power. These are two of the commonplace assumptions that inform the debate in Britain about globalisation and mass immigration. And neither are true.

Human beings have not given up the largely settled life we have lived since hunter gathering gave way to the agricultural revolution 10,000 years ago. There is unprecedented movement within countries from the rural to the urban but we have not suddenly become country hoppers. The number of people living in countries other than the one they were born in is tiny. Even within the European Union in 2000, prior to the opening up towards Central and Eastern Europe, less than 0.1 per cent of the EU's population moved to live in another EU country each year. Rootedness remains a strong human impulse.

And nor is the nation state dying out. As the Soviet Empire collapsed at the end of the Cold War, there was another burst of nation creation, just as there had been in the first part of the twentieth century with the disappearance of the Ottoman and Habsburg empires and later the French and British empires.

It is true that the world is more economically interdependent than 50 years ago, and more national sovereignty is vested in international institutions such as NATO, the World Trade Organisation and the UN. Moreover, the technology of travel and media reinforces the metaphor of a 'borderless world'. But it is a metaphor. More of us than ever before are rich enough to frequently travel long distances, and sometimes work abroad for a few years, but most of us in the developed world come back to places we call home in solid nation states – we cross national borders into countries with national armies, national economies, a national language (in a few cases more than one).

Indeed, to a remarkable extent ours is still the age of the liberal democratic nation state and of liberal (or in some cases illiberal) democratic nationalism. Not all states are nation states but much conflict in the world – from Palestine to Tibet and Chechnya – involves stateless nations seeking nation states of their own. And more of the world's problems arise from too little nation state than too much: why was rapid economic development possible in the East Asian Tigers but not in Africa? A strong sense of national solidarity in the former giving elites and masses a common interest is recognised to have played a significant role.

Why is this remarkable? Only because the ideology of globalisation has told us that it isn't so. Open one of the serious newspapers any day of the week and you will read paragraphs like the one below from Philip Stephens in the *Financial Times*:

> Governments have ceded power to mobile financial capital, to cross-border supply chains and to rapid shifts in comparative advantage. Control of information now belongs to 24-hour satellite television and the cacophony that is the web [...]. Citizens expect national politicians to protect them against the insecurities – economic, social and physical – that come with global integration. Yet governments have lost much of the capacity to meet the demands.[2]

This is not completely wrong, it is just that by focusing on those many forces – trade, finance, transport and communications technology, immigrant diasporas – which flow constantly across national borders it ends up painting a distorted picture. Most of those things are, in any case, still regulated by national laws or international agreements drawn up by national governments. It also leaves out of the picture the areas – like welfare – where the nation state is more not less enmeshed in people's lives than 50 years ago. And in some versions of the ideology it is not just describing, it is advocating – it is saying that by transcending the nation state these forces are promoting the cause of peace, economic growth and human well-being.

THE ENDURING IMPORTANCE OF THE NATION STATE

But nation states still underpin the institutions that manage the greater interdependence of the modern world and only they can mobilise their publics for global collective action. Global institutions are not irrelevant but most of them are still forums where the great powers try to find common interest. Those that are more globally representative like the UN or WTO do not express a global 'demos' in any meaningful sense and seldom try to impose their will on dissenting states.

Meaningful international agreements are still notoriously difficult to reach but as global governance grows in importance *so too* will the nation state. As the centre of power close to where people live and have their attachments it is only the nation state that can confer legitimacy and accountability on global bodies and thus prevent the emergence of tyrannical global leviathans like those imagined by George Orwell.

One group of rich nation states has, of course, gone a bit further and created in the EU an institution that is partly designed to transcend national interests and identities. But most of the EU's work is just a conventional pooling of national sovereignty to achieve together what cannot be achieved by individual nation states acting alone, in global trade negotiations for example.

There is no significant 'European' interest or identity over and above the pooled, and sometimes conflicting, interests of its member states. There is a kind of European democracy in the increasingly powerful European Parliament but the elections to this body are mainly national affairs, and its deliberations are largely ignored. And there is a small degree of redistribution between richer countries (and regions) and poorer ones, but the sums involved remain trivial.

Although the EU mimics the nation state in some trivial ways, it is not a nation state and to the extent that it commands a loyalty it is at a far lower level than a national loyalty. Very few people would die for the EU and very few would make big economic sacrifices for another EU state. We have seen this clearly in the case of Germany, one of the least nationalistic and pro-EU of the big European states, which was happy to spend about $1 trillion on unification with East Germany but is very reluctant to spend far smaller sums helping to support the weaker eurozone economies and what they call a European 'transfer union'.

The modern law-bound, liberal nation state is the least threatening of political institutions. Anyone can join (if invited) and an allegiance to the liberal nation state is compatible with internationalism, with the rapid advancement of developing countries and with support for bodies like NATO and the EU. It is also compatible with a high degree of localism and devolution to regional authorities.

Indeed, after a long and often bloody pre-history the modern nation state is the only institution that can currently offer what liberals, of both right and left, want: democratic legitimacy for the exercise of power and upholding the rule of law; cross-class and generational solidarity and even, in Europe's post-religious age, a sense of collective identification that is bigger than families and neighbourhoods but more tangible than the whole world. It is possible in the future that more global or regional institutions might be able to deliver democracy and welfare; the EU is one prototype but its current difficulties underline what a slow and stuttering process this is likely to be.

So this is ultimately a pragmatic argument. The nation state is not about mystical attachments, it is not a good in itself, it is rather the institutional arrangement that can consistently deliver the democratic, welfare and perhaps psychological outcomes that most people, when given a choice, seem to want.

Yet while the mainstream political and media debate is often stridently chauvinistic in tone, in left-wing and liberal circles in the academy, business, the law, the media and politics the debate is too often the mirror image of this – positively hostile to even moderate national feeling and the idea that one might favour the interests of one's fellow citizens before others.

The progressive assumption often seems to be that it is fine to have an attachment to friends and family and perhaps a neighbourhood or a city – 'I'm proud to be a Londoner' – and, of course, humanity as a whole. But the nation state – especially a once-dominant one like Britain – is considered something old-fashioned and illiberal, an irrational group attachment that smart people transcend or ignore.

THE GLOBALISATION NARRATIVE AND THE 'UNIVERSALIST SHIFT'

One reason why modern liberals are tempted by the globalisation narrative, even those who are critics of global capitalism, is because many of the sixties generation cut their political teeth battling against the prejudices and conformism of their respective nations in the decades after the Second World War. It was a time when nationalism was tarnished by war and fascism and often resisted the idea of human equality.

The nation state has changed radically since then, especially in rich countries, both through internal liberalisation and externally through the promotion of a more equal world via aid and trade policies – albeit sometimes more in rhetoric than in reality. Yet many people on the left remain transfixed by its historic sins. If people are squeamish about the associations of the word nation they should just call it society.

There is a bigger and rather under-explored story here about Western values. In the mid-twentieth century, elites in the liberal democratic West began to embrace what Geoff Dench has called the 'universalist shift' – the belief in the moral equality of all people. This meant that differences of sex, ethnicity and, above all, race, were no longer deemed obstacles to someone's full membership in a society. Although the idea did not extend to economic inequality it was profoundly anti-hierarchical and egalitarian, and demanded that power and rewards in society be justified by performance rather than inherited characteristics (whiteness or maleness).

It now seems so banal to believe in the moral equality of all people that we have forgotten what a novel and revolutionary notion it is, and how many people around the world (even in the liberal democracies) still have traces of more racial worldviews. And in the lifetimes of many older people still alive today very different official views prevailed. As recently as the 1940s and 1950s respectable strands of British political opinion were arguing that many colonised people were not yet mature enough to govern themselves, they were like children or teenagers not yet able to join the adult community of self-governing states.

Yet because all people are in principle equal it does not mean that they are all equal to us – it does not follow from a belief in the moral equality of all people that we owe the same obligations or commitments to them all; we feel special obligations to family members but not because they are morally superior to other people. Both liberal and conservative voices in favour of globalisation and the 'universalist shift' seem to confuse the specialness of a national identity with superiority and even racism.

So ubiquitous rhetoric about globalisation and the apparent inevitability of mass migration combined with this morally appealing ideology of liberal universalism has reinforced a carelessness about national citizenship among intellectual, and business, elites in many rich countries. Britain is especially vulnerable to this carelessness, partly because of its own multinational and imperial history which has left behind a sense of ambivalence about the nation state.

THE 'IMMIGRATIONIST' IDEOLOGY

These attitudes have created a sympathetic audience for the 'immigrationist' ideology, which supports as open as possible a door to newcomers, partly on cultural grounds – Britain is dull and grey and needs leavening from outside – and partly on global economic justice grounds. Thanks to immigrationism many people on the left abandon their normal suspicion of Big Business and embrace free market assumptions – echoed in the pro-mass-immigration *Economist* and the *Wall Street Journal* – about competitive labour markets and the assumption that America, a country built on mass immigration with few collectivist checks, is the global model that the historic nations of Europe are destined to follow.

A key part of the immigrationist story is that mass immigration is an unstoppable aspect of modern life. It is said that 200 million people, and rising, are living permanently outside the country of their birth. This seems an impressively large figure but is in fact just 3 per cent of the world's population. In several European countries, including Britain, there is a greater sense of population flow because the number of immigrants in rich countries has indeed more than doubled in the past 30 years. Most forced migrants continue to live in adjacent countries in the global south but about three-quarters of all international migrants now live in 12 countries, of which half are rich (20 per cent live in the US alone).

There are reasons to believe that this trend will not continue indefinitely. The number of global refugees rose sharply in the late

1980s and early 1990s – partly prompted by the conflicts following the break-up of the Soviet Union – reaching a peak of more than 18 million in 1993, but has since fallen back. Peering into the future, global human flows will depend to a large extent on what happens to global economic growth and population increases as well as worldwide climate change. As big developing countries like China and India become richer and as the world gradually becomes more equal – at least between, if not within, states – the incentive to leave may become less pressing even as the ability to do so rises.

And population in most parts of the world is now stable or falling: Europe, China, Russia, South America, Iran. In a few places it is still rising sharply: Pakistan, parts of the greater Middle East and above all Africa. The population of Africa is now just over 1 billion; no one knows whether it will stabilise at 2 billion or 3 billion. If it is the latter there will clearly be greater pressure to migrate.

Not all developed countries have embraced mass immigration in the manner that Britain has since 1997: two very successful countries – Japan and Finland – have kept the door quite tightly closed. Neither the Japanese nor Finnish model is necessarily desirable, especially for a 'hub' economy like Britain's, but it shows if the political will is there the flows can be controlled. Those in the British debate who argue that huge immigration flows are a fact of life have short memories: as recently as the early 1990s net immigration was close to zero. Mass immigration is not a force of nature.

What's wrong with the case made for large-scale immigration to rich countries? There are two broad strands to the case. The first, more radical one takes as its perspective humanity as a whole and argues that it is a human right to emigrate and immigrate in an 'open-border' world. The second, more conventional case looks out from a rich country like Britain and says that mass immigration benefits both the immigrants and the citizens of the receiving country. It accepts that an open door is politically unrealistic but wants as much openness as reasonably possible.

The idea behind the perspective of humanity as a whole and open frontiers is, as the Dutch writer Paul Scheffer has pointed out, that native populations do not have any special rights as compared to newcomers. Why, in other words, should a country belong to its inhabitants? The liberal argument is that having a particular birthplace cannot have any moral significance and therefore should not bring with it unearned rewards. But this surely represents a thin and unhistorical understanding of people and societies, regarding society as a more or less arbitrary collection of individuals without any particular ties or allegiances to each other. This is what one might call the 'cruise liner' theory of the nation, in which people come together for a voyage but have no ongoing identity. Liberalism likes the idea of community in theory but does not see that a meaningful one must be able to exclude as well as include.

There is a genuine dilemma here, especially for the left, between the obligations of governments to prioritise the well-being of their own citizens and a more universal ethic that values the well-being of all humanity. As David Miliband has written: 'The left is torn between a commitment to individual human rights for all people, whatever their nationality, and a recognition that communities depend on deep roots'.[3] But it is also a dilemma that is relatively easily resolved. It can be resolved partly by considerations of human nature and organisation, at least at this stage of evolution, but also by considering the likely economic and social outcomes of an open-border world.

All human associations and communities need boundaries of some kind; they can be easier or harder to join but require some means of demarcating between insiders and outsiders. The modern nation state has become far more internally inclusive in recent generations – the idea of the equal status of all citizens is underpinned by historically unprecedented social provision, free to all insiders – but towards the outside world it has become, if anything, more exclusionary. There is nothing perverse or mean-spirited about this. As the value of national citizenship in rich countries has risen, and the cost of physically reaching those countries has fallen, so the bureaucracy of exclusion has had to grow. If that bureaucracy were to be abolished or even relaxed it would lead to more random and pernicious exclusions at a lower level. Michael Walzer talks about 'a thousand petty fortresses'. It is already possible to see signs of this in the growing levels of both ethnic and social class segregation in many of Britain's major towns and cities.

How many people would come to live in a rich country like Britain if border controls were abolished? No one knows for sure. But in many poor parts of the world, in Africa in particular, there has been rapid urbanisation in the absence of industrialisation or high economic growth. That has created a large surplus of urban labour well connected enough to know about the possibilities of life in the West and with a miserable enough life to want to get there. Who could say confidently that 5 million or 10 million people would not turn up in the space of a couple of years, especially to a country with the global connections that Britain already has?

This claim may appear to conflict with my earlier assumption about human rootedness. But the point is that many of the urban poor in developing countries are already recently uprooted and the promise of security and relative wealth in a diaspora community in the West can override the relatively shallow attachments of life in the slums of Lagos or Nairobi.

IS THERE A CASE FOR HIGH LEVELS OF IMMIGRATION?

What about the more conventional case for high levels of immigration: that it benefits receiving countries as well as the immigrants? No sensible person is opposed to immigration *tout court*. It is a matter of how much and how it is managed, and how it affects the national political community. For the nation state to have any meaning it must in the democratic era 'belong' to existing citizens: on important matters citizens must have special rights over non-citizens. That means immigration must be managed with the interests of existing citizens in mind. The question is: what are those interests? And what kind, and what level, of immigration should it translate into?

Looked at year on year the numbers arriving in Britain seem tiny. But according to the Office of National Statistics (ONS), persistent immigration at around the current rate sees the UK population rising from 62.3 million in 2010 to 81.5 million in 2060 – an increase of 19.2 million. In the absence of migration, the ONS projects that the population would only rise to 64 million by 2060.

In several European countries the immigrant and ethnic minority population is rising to 20 or 25 per cent in the next few years. Many large towns in Europe are already around 40 per cent minority – Birmingham, Malmö, Marseilles. In Britain, the capital city is already 'majority minority' along with three others: Slough, Leicester and Luton.

The arrival of the rich and the skilled and the inventive has long brought blessings to this land. Unskilled immigration brings its benefits too. There is no doubting the dynamism of many young migrants, and their willingness to do dirty or under-rewarded jobs (like caring for the elderly) that few natives want. But these benefits would have to be large and demonstrable to justify the cultural and social disruption caused by the rapid, large-scale immigration we have experienced in recent years. And they are not. Almost all the economic analyses of mass immigration in recent years have found that the effect on employment, wages, fiscal balance and per capita growth is small, either positively or negatively.

Moreover, existing British citizens not only have very different experiences of immigration, depending on where they live, they also have very different economic interests arising from it. Employers, big and small, and better-off people tend to benefit from imported labour that is usually relatively cheaper and higher quality than the domestic equivalent. And many millions of us as consumers have enjoyed lower prices for cleaners or for redecorating our houses in recent years.

Immigrants themselves benefit, of course. They would not endure the pain and disruption of uprooting unless there were very clear gains in security or comfort. But national social contracts still matter and low-skilled locals (often recent migrants themselves) face greater competition both in the labour market and in public services. And as they are more likely to live in areas of high immigrant settlement too, they might face a sense of displacement and competition in three different areas of life: neighbourhood, work and state services.

Moreover, professional people tend to have a sense of themselves derived from their careers, while most people in ordinary jobs draw their identity more from place and community (60 per cent of British people live within 20 miles of where they lived when they were 14). So where immigration happens most, in the poorer parts of town, is also where it has a greater psychological impact.

The pressure on public services is partly offset by the extra taxes paid by immigrants, but when the inflows are on the scale of recent years that cannot prevent acute short-term problems arising, especially in favourite 'landing' destinations such as Slough, Newham or Hounslow, but also in places farther afield such as Boston in Lincolnshire or Goole in Humberside that suddenly acquired large East European populations after 2004.

The pressure on housing is another factor. In the first wave of post-colonial immigration, immigrants were generally excluded from public housing by 'sons and daughters' policies that effectively excluded all outsiders (from other boroughs as well as countries). In the 1970s and 1980s this became the site of tense conflicts in London and other big cities as legislation shifted the balance to favour individual needs rather than community preservation, which propelled many new arrivals to the front of the housing queue.

Now there is a more general problem of the low supply of all types of housing, which is not caused by immigration but is certainly exacerbated by it. Recently household growth in England has been running at about 200,000 a year of which about 40 per cent is the result of migration – but since 2000 actual house-building has been lagging that rise in households by 40,000 a year.

THE ECONOMIC BENEFITS OF IMMIGRATION: MYTH AND REALITY

The idea that power and prosperity is driven by immigration-fuelled population growth is the wrong way round. Successful economies and open, liberal societies pull in immigrants – immigrants do not create that success, though they may help to sustain it. And here I want to drill down deeper into the economic arguments made in defence of large-scale immigration. There are three main claims. First, young immigrants help prevent our societies from ageing and generally pay in more than they take out. Second, immigrants are complementary to natives, so bring many labour market benefits for employers and do not take jobs or depress wages. Third, immigrants are a source of growth and innovation.

The first argument about ageing is a tired old cliché that has long since been refuted. It seems a common sense assumption: our society is ageing so import lots of young people and encourage them to have large families and, hey presto!, we are youthful again. But the truth is that immigrants grow old too, and usually converge quickly on native fertility rates, so for this to work it would require very high and continuing immigration. The current age structure of the UK is a result of the rapid growth of the population over the past 100 years, from about 30 million to a bit over 60 million. To keep that age structure as it is now would require another surge of population growth. But that is not a popular policy, especially in our more green-minded, congestion-conscious times.

The key formula here is the 'potential support ratio' (PSR) which indicates how many people there are of official working age potentially able to support each person of pension age. The ratio is due to fall in Britain around 2020 as the baby-boomer generation born in the 1950s and early 1960s retires. But the curious thing is how little difference a lot of immigration makes to this ratio. Assuming zero net immigration the PSR is 1.94 in 2074, but add an extra 20 million people to the population by that date and the ratio rises to just 2.11.

As Adair Turner pointed out in a lecture on demography at the London School of Economics (LSE) in 2003, arguments for high immigration to keep the PSR low are usually made on the basis of assumptions that leave the retirement age untouched.[4] He argues that if the retirement age is raised to reflect greater longevity, then half of the change to the support/dependency ratio disappears and the problem becomes more manageable. There are other things that can be done: increasing automation and productivity can play a small role as can bringing more women into the workforce (something that is happening anyway in most rich countries) and, indeed, allowing moderate levels of immigration. Britain, which has a younger population than many comparable European countries, does not face a big ageing problem, and to the extent that it does it can adjust to it without relying on enormous levels of immigration – and it can in the end grow a little bit older gracefully.

Some scepticism is also required towards the claim that immigrants pay more in than they take out. Highly educated, skilled or talented immigrants, provided they get decent jobs and do not displace native workers, normally make a positive fiscal contribution – they pay more in taxes than they absorb in government spending. Such people come disproportionately from other developed countries. Unskilled immigrants can also make a positive contribution, provided that they and their dependants do not make large demands on the welfare state.

There are many different ways in which the numbers can be drawn up, but the mainstream conclusion (shared by the Treasury and the Migration Advisory Committee) is that the overall fiscal contribution is close to neutral. This broadly neutral outcome does, of course, hide a huge variation between groups. An Institute of Public Policy Research (IPPR) report found that only 1 per cent of Poles and Filipinos claim income support, compared with 39 per cent of Somalis.

Looking beyond the most recent immigration the picture is less positive. Because of the historic legacy of unskilled labour from New Commonwealth countries in the early post-war period, and then the arrival of other large groups with low education levels such as Bangladeshis and Somalis, about 40 per cent of minority Britain is classified as poor, compared with 20 per cent of white Britons. And nearly one-third of minority Britain lives in public housing compared with about 17 per cent of white Britain. That means minority Britain is, on average, likely to be somewhat more welfare dependent than white Britain, though with large variations within both groups.

What about the immigration effect on jobs and wages? There is a broad consensus among economists that, when properly managed and at moderate levels, immigration has no noticeable negative effect on the employment prospects or wages of native workers but greases the wheels of the labour market by filling vacancies that local workers either don't want to do (at least at the wages on offer) because they are too boring or 'dirty' or can't do because they don't have the right skills.

But it is not 'economically illiterate', as free market economists often suggest, to say that immigrants can substitute for locals as well as complement them. When the recession struck, the number of UK-born workers fell by 278,000 in the year to December 2008; in the same period, employment of non-UK-born workers rose by 214,000. Or even more strikingly, between the second quarter of 1997 and the last quarter of 2011, there were almost 2.7 million extra people employed in Britain, of whom 2.1 million were born outside the country.

The issue of job displacement is a complex and controversial one. What seems to be happening is this. There is a daily churn in the labour market with about 2,000 jobs disappearing and another 2,000 being created. Of those 2,000 new jobs, most are taken by British-born workers but a disproportionate number of net new jobs on top of the reshuffling are being taken by recent immigrants. And in some sectors it seems that employers have acquired a 'foreigner bias' when it comes to new hires, finding them better motivated and with lower wage expectations.

In a huge research analysis of more than 45 studies between 1982 and 2007, Longhi (and others) found the immigration effect on employment was small; however, it uncovered evidence that immigration did discourage workless natives from entering or remaining in the labour market.[5] And a paper by Hatton and Tani found that foreign immigration into a region leads to less migration from elsewhere in the UK, so northerners are less likely to come south to take jobs.[6] The report by the Government's Migration Advisory Committee in January 2012 concluded that there has been an 'association' between an extra 100 non-EU working-age migrants arriving and 23 fewer native people being employed.

The 'illiteracy' that economists refer to is the so-called 'lump of labour' fallacy, the false idea that the demand for labour is fixed. It is true that immigrants create extra demand for labour through the incomes they spend and the taxes they pay. Polish builders create new jobs for locals – in supermarkets, at builders' merchants and for interior designers; at least they do so long as they are expanding the market for building work and not just displacing natives or sending much of their income home. But there is often a lag of some years between the jobs they take and the jobs they create, and the new jobs may also be in different places to the lost jobs. And because it is concentrated at the top and bottom, mass immigration often reinforces inequality and reduces social mobility for domestic workers. As the 2008 House of Lords report on the economics of immigration vividly puts it: 'The City of London illustrates this range of occupations, where immigrants are widely found among the staff of the restaurants serving financial executives, many of who are also immigrants'.[7]

One-third of all graduate jobs in London are taken by people born outside Britain, which is likely to be one factor behind the apparent slow-down in social mobility in recent years. There is less room at the top for people from low- and middle-income backgrounds. Indeed, if you pursue a 'global talent' policy there must be a more general crowding-out effect for the resident population – bright and inventive natives, whatever their background, are going to get somewhat less good jobs if they have to compete with the very best in the world.

So, what about wages? As with employment all the studies suggest no great effect either positively or negatively on native workers. But while wages 'overall' may not be significantly depressed by mass immigration, there is strong evidence that the bottom layer of workers are hurt. Christian Dustmann, Tommaso Frattini and Ian Preston found that immigration has led to a small reduction in the wages of the bottom 20 per cent in Britain.[8] Stephen Nickell and Jumana Saleheen found that a 10 percentage point rise in the proportion of immigrants working in semi- and unskilled sectors like care homes, bars and shops leads to a 5.2 per cent reduction in overall pay in the sector.[9] And there is a strong consensus among economists that the immigration effect on the low-paid would have been much sharper but for the introduction of the minimum wage in 1999. (The majority of Eastern Europeans who arrived after 2004 have been working for around the minimum wage.)

There is also the 'opportunity cost' for native workers, meaning the higher wages that they would almost certainly have enjoyed, at least in some sectors, if not for the big inflows in recent years. The enthusiasm of the Treasury for mass immigration in the 1990s and 2000s was partly based on the assumption that it did indeed hold down real wages. Eastern Europeans represented a bit less than 10 per cent of the unskilled workforce in 2007, higher in certain areas. Indeed according to the ONS roughly 20 per cent of all unskilled workers are born abroad, which is enough to create significant downward pressure on local wage rates.

It is often said that immigrants are needed to do the jobs that local workers won't do. That is sometimes the case but not generally so; in most parts of the country where there are not many immigrants local people will fill the vacancies. It is true that workers in welfare states usually have a strong sense of their worth – surely a welcome product of a civilised society – and will not do certain jobs *at the wage rates or conditions on offer*. Immigrants, from poorer places, will often do those jobs instead. A keen young Latvian graduate who is here for two or three years on a working holiday to improve his or her English and have some fun is almost bound to be more attractive to employ in a pub or a care home, and cheaper given lower wage expectations, than a local kid with a clutch of not very good GCSEs and a bit of attitude.

Of course workers in rich countries with welfare states can sometimes be lazy or difficult or poorly educated, and a keen, well-educated foreigner who speaks good English will usually be preferable to an individual employer. But it makes no sense from the point of the country as a whole to have millions of sullen locals sitting at home on benefit (and even during the boom years in Britain the number on out-of-work benefits never fell much below 5 million) while poorer foreigners come in and take the jobs that they should be doing.

At the more skilled end of the labour market immigrants are often helpful in plugging temporary skill shortages. But they can also discourage investment in education and training. The classic example of this was UK medicine where for many years we were over-dependent on luring doctors from Third World countries because we didn't train enough of our own.

Martin Ruhs of the Migration Advisory Committee argues that the historic institutions and policy assumptions of British economic life – low levels of labour regulation, non-existent employer collaboration on training – make this country particularly vulnerable to over-dependence on foreign labour. The construction industry, for example, is highly fragmented and does very little training, relying instead on project-based labour, informal recruitment and casualised employment. By contrast, many European countries have proper training and apprenticeship programmes, producing workers with a wide range of transferable skills. It is often these workers who are doing jobs in Britain. Most of the skilled construction jobs on large projects – for example the Olympic sites – were filled by non-British citizens. Social care is another sector that has an in-built bias towards foreign workers, in this case not so much because of their skill but because of their readiness to work long and anti-social hours for low pay in an often physically and emotionally demanding job. Because of the constraints on the local authority budgets that pay for social care, about two-thirds of care assistants in London are immigrants, though the number is much lower in some other parts of the country.

Importing cheap and motivated foreign labour in effect shelves the problem of how to get the difficult natives back into work. It has, as Fraser Nelson, the editor of *The Spectator*, argues, 'broken the link between more jobs and less dole'.[10]

Supporters of large-scale immigration will argue that immigration is not a zero-sum game; the right kind of immigrant labour is a kind of yeast that helps to swell the economic brew both for the incomer and the native. Higher growth might justify shelving the 'difficult native' problem, but growth per head has not been significantly increased by mass immigration, especially once the immigrants themselves are removed from the equation. A paper by the National Institute of Economic and Social Research published in 2006 concluded that since 1998 immigrants had added 5 per cent to the working-age population but only 3.1 per cent to GDP, meaning a fall in GDP per head.[11] And a 2007 National Institute paper found that the arrival of 700,000 Eastern Europeans since 2004 has raised output by merely 0.4 per cent, also meaning a small fall in GDP per head.[12]

So, even on wages, employment and economic growth it is a mixed picture. But what about the more generic claim about diversity and dynamism? It is a commonplace of the immigration debate to say that Britain has benefited in the past from small inflows of dynamic outsiders – perhaps most significantly the small Jewish inflow of the late nineteenth and early twentieth century and the smaller East African Asian inflow of the 1970s. Britain continues to attract creative and inventive foreigners and should, of course, go on doing so – immigrants are twice as likely to start a business as natives, both the corner shop and bigger businesses too.

The 'immigrationists' make much of how immigrants see things differently and are more determined to succeed. Without immigration Britain today would no doubt be a less dynamic place. But the idea that if we reduce net immigration to 80,000 a year (still meaning a gross inflow of around 350,000) we will become economically stagnant is absurd. Finland, one of the most prosperous and dynamic countries in Europe, has virtually no immigration. In any case we have a vast amount of diversity stored up already thanks to the immigration of the last 60 years. We need time to absorb it and make the best use of it.

CONCLUSION

The economics of immigration in a place like Britain involves complicated trade-offs. Many of us benefit as employers and consumers from certain types of immigration and, arguably, all of us benefit from the downward pressure on wage inflation. But then all of us might be said to suffer from the fact that a mass immigration policy allowed the economy to grow rapidly for 10 years without tackling the welfare ghettoes – about 1.8 million new jobs were created when Labour was in power but the number of people on out-of-work benefits of various kinds never fell below 4.5 million. The complaint that (at least from about 2002) the main beneficiaries from the boom years were bankers and immigrants has some truth.

This argument is also about divergent attitudes to national citizenship and what special protections and entitlements it should imply. Immigrationists and libertarians argue for minimal protections while social democrats and most ordinary voters – who regard labour, like capital, as a special kind of good – generally want some citizen favouritism in labour markets. The sweeping away of that historic protection in 2004 with the arrival of a large number of East Europeans was a political shock. An implicit part of the social contract had been removed by an elite that seemed to have little need for it. The common-sense communitarianism of most ordinary voters clashed with the more universalist and free market preference of the political class, and Labour paid a heavy political price for it at the 2010 election.

But how much protection is really necessary? A former Whitehall economist like Jonathan Portes, one of the most influential supporters of mass immigration in the late 1990s and early 2000s, argues that it is not an either/or question. It is possible in theory to spend billions on improving training and work incentives for the hard to employ locals, as Labour in power did, and benefit from reasonably open immigration. But the failure to make a big dent in the workless numbers in the 2000s suggests that there is a trade-off – employers, given an option, will almost always opt for the cheaper and better motivated foreigner. And he or she is better motivated partly because an unemployed East European will normally better his or her situation considerably working in a coffee shop in Croydon; an unemployed British citizen is quite likely to be worse off, or barely better off, once loss of housing and other benefits have been factored in. This is unfair competition for the domestic worker.

This is not an argument for a closed door but for relatively low and highly selective immigration, especially at the lower and middling skill levels. It is also an argument for extra protection and help for hard to employ citizens, and, of course, for further welfare reform to give people a hand back into jobs rather than trap them in dependency. There are 1 million young people who are not in employment, education or training, and 300,000 unemployed graduates. And yet in the south-east of England more than 80 per cent of staff in the hospitality sector are not British citizens. It is a similar picture among London Underground cleaning staff and more than half of those in the care sector, and on many big building sites up to 70 per cent of the skilled jobs are taken by outsiders.

Employers will have to be persuaded to change their attitudes too. It has become a cultural reflex to assume that British workers are less good than foreigners – like British cars in the 1970s. Jobs, indeed whole sectors, with low pay and status often become thought of as 'migrant jobs' by both employers and potential employees. But the status of a job is a surprisingly elastic and subjective thing, and with a little bit of imagination – some training or career development – it can be made to seem more attractive.

It was never envisaged in the late 1950s that free movement within the EU would encompass economies with hugely different wage rates or that 1.5 million people from Eastern Europe would end up coming to work in Britain between May 2004 and December 2008. The principle of free movement cannot now be undone, it is part of the EU religion, but it can surely co-exist with special protections and support for hard to employ national citizens, something currently ruled out by the EU principle of non-discrimination. Labour should be talking to its sister parties in the European socialist group about revising this rule. There is nothing in socialist internationalism or the European spirit that says you should not try to protect your most vulnerable and least successful citizens from certain kinds of labour market competition.

The evidence is now pretty clear. The economics of mass immigration is broadly neutral except for those at the bottom, but the social and cultural case has turned negative thanks to the sheer scale of the inflows since 1997. We are deep into a huge social experiment, and to give it a chance of working – and of avoiding the sort of opinion swing we have seen in the Netherlands – we need to heed the 'slow down' signs.

Indeed, Britain now requires an immigration 'pause' to absorb the large inflows of recent decades – perhaps comparable to America's immigration pause from 1920 to 1970 (only 4.7 per cent of the US population was foreign born in that year). Denmark's experience shows it is possible even in the modern world. And as the settled democratic will asserts itself it does seem that we will, albeit slowly, emerge from a period of 'irrational exuberance' over immigration. We must do so carefully; even if the last 15 years have brought few net economic gains for the resident population, untangling ourselves too fast from our immigration dependence could have damaging consequences.

And there will be some economic costs even if the disentanglement is well managed. If we reduce the supply of cheap labour from abroad we will have to pay a bit more for many services, from restaurant meals to nursing care for our ageing parents, in order to attract staff. The extra time, cost and bureaucracy required to get people into the country for long- or short-term stays means that we will lose some individuals and economic and cultural activities that we could have benefited from. This is a price that people seem happy to pay for a return to moderate levels of immigration.

NOTES

1. This chapter is an edited version of David Goodhart, *The British Dream: Successes and Failures of Post-war Immigration* (London: Atlantic Books, 2013), ch. 1.
2. Philip Stephens, 'A new age of bitter nationalism', *The Financial Times*, 28 October 2011.
3. David Miliband, 'Why is the European Left losing elections?', lecture delivered at the LSE on 8 March 2011. Available at http://www2.lse.ac.uk/assets/richmedia/channels/publicLecturesAndEvents/transcripts/20110308_1830_whyIsTheEuropeanLeftLosingElections_tr.pdf, p. 7 (accessed on 25 August 2014).
4. Adair Turner, 'Demographics, economics, and social choice', lecture at the LSE on 6 November 2003. Available at http://cep.lse.ac.uk/events/06112003.asp (accessed on 25 August 2014).
5. Simonetta Longhi, Peter Nijkamp and Jacques Poot, 'Meta-analysis of empirical evidence on the labour market impacts of immigration', Population Studies Centre Discussion Paper no. 67 (February 2008), available online at http://www.waikato.ac.nz/__data/assets/pdf_file/0003/74172/dp-67.pdf (accessed on 23 October 2014).
6. Timothy J. Hatton and Massimiliano Tani, 'Immigration and inter-regional mobility in the UK, 1982–2000', *The Economic Journal* 115 (2005), pp. 342–58.
7. House of Lords Select Committee on Economic Affairs, 'The economic impact of immigration', 1 April 2008. Available at http://www.publications.parliament.uk/pa/ld200708/ldselect/ldeconaf/82/82.pdf (accessed on 25 August 2014).
8. Christian Dustmann, Tommaso Frattini, and Ian P. Preston, 'The effect of immigration along the distribution of wages', CReAM Discussion Paper No. 03/08, Centre for Research and Analysis of Migration, Department of Economics, University College London, 2008.
9. Stephen Nickell and Jumana Salaheen, 'The impact of immigration on occupational wages: evidence from Britain', Working Paper No. 08–6, Federal Reserve Bank of Boston, Boston, 2008.
10. Fraser Nelson, 'British jobs for whom?', *The Spectator*, 28 August 2011, available online at http://blogs.spectator.co.uk/coffeehouse/2011/08/british-jobs-for-whom/ (accessed on 23 October 2014).
11. Rebecca Riley and Martin Weale, 'Commentary: immigration and its effects', *National Institute Economic Review* 198 (October 2006), pp. 4–9.
12. Ray Barrell, 'EU enlargement and migration: assessing the macro-economic impacts', NIESR Discussion Paper no. 292 (March 2007).

PART FOUR

ALTERNATIVE MODERNITY – ON
NATURE, PROGRESS AND WORK

CHAPTER TEN

Nature, Science and the Politics of the Common Good

Ruth Davis

INTRODUCTION

This essay explores some of the complementary traditions of the Labour and environment movements. It invokes shared values and experiences, but also acknowledges areas of contention and suspicion, where reconciliation is needed to establish a politics that protects and celebrates both nature and work. Its central premise is that we have a common purpose in creating an economy that nurtures meaning – in our relationships with one another and with the natural world. For this reason, I make no apologies for beginning with a story about a crisis of meaning in my own early life and how that has subsequently informed my politics.

I am the daughter of a doctor and of a writer on psychoanalysis and child development. I was brought up in an intellectual home, but also a home where the chasms that seem to exist now between different ways of knowing the world – between science, religion, the arts and politics – were largely absent. My parents seemed capable of holding these forms of knowledge in creative tension, without feeling obliged to declare exclusive allegiance to one or the other. Moreover, they found in their relationship with the natural world a source of joy, meaning and practical value, which could be known variously through the study of natural history, through gardening, through poetry, and through religion and philosophy – as well as simply through being present in nature within the moment.

In this sense, therefore, I was born lucky – born into a relative state of grace, without even being aware of it – and it wasn't until years later that I realised that such a generous approach to different forms of knowledge was not a given, but was disappearing from our shared political life. This understanding began to seep into my consciousness when I was unsettled by the events of my own life as teenager. Firstly, my family moved house – taking me away from a community and landscape that were so familiar to me and so integral to my identity, that when I left I suffered not just a moral and emotional sickness, but a physical shock that seemed to last for years. This was my first experience of exile. Then my mother became ill with the disease that was to kill her a few years later. And I realised that the relationships that were the foundation of my life and happiness were also painfully fragile.

And then somewhere along the line a third thing happened that was much more trivial – a moment in time, a few throw-away words – but which influenced me profoundly. My three elder brothers were in the habit of using their intellectual explorations to maintain the family pecking order – an order in which I (as the youngest) was generally at the bottom. And it was no doubt in this spirit that one of them sat me down to tell me that there was nothing in the world that could not be explained by science; that religion was a childish lie; that free will was an illusion; and that any romantic notions I had about a moral and spiritual life were merely a by-product of the struggle of my individual genes for their survival.

My problem with this was not the science. Then as now, I think Darwin was a towering genius, I am fascinated by natural selection, and I don't find the idea of evolution alienating – quite the reverse, I find it a source of wonder. But nonetheless, this talk left me feeling miserable and rebellious. I was not prepared to accept the use of a brutal narrative of 'hard science' to assault the possibility of meaning emerging through other ways of experiencing the world.

Of course I largely recovered, and so did my much-loved brother. But I had begun by then to know a little bit about alienation. To understand that how we choose or are allowed to 'know' the world can foster meaning or attack it. That meaning is not equally distributed, but rather that it gathers in pools and pockets – in the creases of elbows that bend in love or work, in the places where we have kissed or argued, in the highly charged spaces between objects and our desire for them; in our sense of the past and our hopes for the future. And above all, that meaning exists where it is allowed to settle and to grow strong, in conditions of safety.

All of which is why I believe that politics in its truest sense should be nothing more or less than our shared efforts to restore, protect and nurture meaningful relationships. Which in turn, means organising our economy around the kinds of jobs, homes, schools, farming and fishing that make this possible. This is a very personal introduction to a political proposition – but I hope one that is forgivable, when speaking about the politics of relationships and experience.

More important, perhaps, is the possibility that what I have said so far begs a question – what does any of this have to do with nature? How does a politics of relationships speak to a love of lakes and mountains, or bees, birds and beetles? I will try to answer this by returning to the importance of different ways of knowing the world; and by positioning the environment movement firmly within a politics which recognises and celebrates meaning and virtue, rather than merely adjudicating on utility. In doing so, I will also explore how faith traditions provide some of the foundations for this politics as it relates to the world around us.

IN PRAISE OF CREATION

So, let me call to mind the impulse of praise for creation, which runs like an emerald thread through most of the world's religions. Animist beliefs of course locate spiritual power in natural phenomena. Christian, Jewish and Islamic traditions come from a very different place – seeing the abundance and diversity of nature as evidence of the power and generosity of a single God. But in their different ways all recognise the importance of non-human life and acknowledge a specific moral responsibility towards it. What more lovely hymn to the world's creatures is there than this one, for example, from the Book of Sirach – even if its conception of an everlasting collection of species wouldn't pass the Darwin test?

> How beautiful are all God's works! Even to the spark and fleeting vision! The universe lives and abides forever; to meet each need, each creature is preserved. All of them differ, one from another, yet none of them has he made in vain, for each in turn, as it comes, is good; can one ever see enough of their splendour?[1]

But this is not just a matter of beauty, precious though that is. Our relationship with nature also prescribes the limits of our power as human beings. Much of the life around us was there before we came into being and will persist when we are gone. We are a part of it, in the sense that we share most of our history and a common origin with other forms of life on earth – but it is also separate from us, because we did not make it. The existence, diversity and complexity of non-human life grant us an intimate sense of belonging, whilst protecting us against the tyranny of the myth of perfectibility.

The existence of value in our relationship with nature is implicitly recognised by billions of people all over the world every day – in every geranium plant hanging from a balcony in a busy city street, as well as in the sacrifices of those who give up their freedom to protect the places and creatures they hold sacred. Loving creation is not, as materialists and managerialists would have us believe, an elite preoccupation. It is a human virtue, and we sacrifice it on the altar of neo-liberal materialism at our moral and emotional peril.

Finally, and crucially, this virtue is also inseparable from our relationship with place. Because where people are allowed to settle long enough to build a sense of community through shared work and institutions, this generates a profound relationship with a specific geography. As with my childhood home, people grow into an identity which is imprinted on the land around them. This is as true of the moors around Sheffield and the streets of Brixton as the rolling Downs of Sussex. We cannot resist it even if we would. Put us down, and we root. The character of the soil we root in makes us who we are.

I believe the particular tradition of Labour politics which is proud to own its values – that reveres work; that organises itself to nurture the young, look after the sick and revere the old; that passionately resists the accumulation of power in the hands of the few, but relishes excellence – this Labour tradition is one that will naturally embrace the protection of our seas, land and rivers – both as a serious duty, and as something essential to our own nourishment. This is the same Labour movement, after all, that created our national parks.

But inevitably, this also leads me to ask why, if such an alliance feels so natural, is it not central to the way in which we work? I would argue it is because we remain in conflict about our different ways of knowing the world – in particular about the role of science in understanding our surroundings; and the role of work, in defining who we are.

ENCLOSURES, ENLIGHTENMENT AND EXILE

In British poetry, the environment movement is blessed with some of the most powerful campaigning literature every produced – so I'd like to begin this next part of my essay by turning to Wordsworth, and thinking about what he was getting at in 'The Tables Turned':[2]

> One impulse from a vernal wood
> May teach you more of man,
> Of moral evil and of good,
> Than all the sages can.
>
> Sweet is the lore which Nature brings;
> Our meddling intellect
> Mis-shapes the beauteous forms of things:—
> We murder to dissect.
>
> Enough of Science and of Art;
> Close up those barren leaves;
> Come forth, and bring with you a heart
> That watches and receives.

This is a complicated poem and any thread I pull on is likely to get me into trouble with literary scholars, but still – I think it's fair to say that it contains a warning, that if we are not careful about the way in which we deploy certain forms of knowledge, we risk them destroying rather than enhancing our relationship with nature and through this our understanding of ourselves. And I might also say that this was prescient, given the consequences of the unfolding of the Enlightenment for rural England, played out through the Enclosures and the impacts of agricultural intensification. In a great wave of displacement and alienation from nature, work and home, much of what Wordsworth might have recognised in the English countryside was swept away.

It was left to John Clare, a Midlands man and an agricultural labourer, to memorialise the loss. Between 1809 and 1820, Acts of Enclosure granted landowners the right to fence off and appropriate common land in the area surrounding Clare's village of Helpston in Northamptonshire. The public policy argument for this action was that improvements in the way in which food could be produced needed to be applied across the agricultural system, and that this could not happen as long as large areas of the countryside were managed as commons. The wreckage of Clare's working life and his childhood landscape brought forth some of the most touching poetry of loss and memory in the English language.

Here, in this poem 'The Mores',[3] Clare describes the home that he loved:

> Each little path that led its pleasant way
> As sweet as morning leading night astray
> Where little flowers bloomed round a varied host
> That travel felt delighted to be lost

And here its subsequent fate:

> These paths are stopt - the rude philistine's thrall
> Is laid upon them and destroyed them all
> Each little tyrant with his little sign
> Shows where man claims earth glows no more divine
> But paths to freedom and to childhood dear
> A board sticks up to notice 'no road here'

John Clare never recovered from this rupture of his bonds with nature, home and work. I am convinced that it contributed to his later mental collapse and alcoholism. After one terrible spell in an asylum in Essex, he almost crawled back to his village, so strong was his attachment, so devastating his experience of exile.

THE ENCLOSURE OF THE SEAS

More than a hundred years later, the echo of his loss is being heard in communities up and down the country. One modern-day example can be found in Britain's fishing industry. Here are the words of fishermen from coastal towns in England, faced with the decimation of their fishing grounds:[4]

> 'This is a way of life that has gone on around the shores of the UK for generation after generation and at the moment it's in more danger than it's ever been. We're living on a knife edge.'
> 'Fishing has been turned into a commodity – privatisation, so that the Government can wipe their hands of us.'
> 'I'm sorry for the youngsters – I know they're not getting enough to live on.'

'I feel like the sea is my garden. I do respect her, and I tell her so. I talk to her.'

'This is an island, surrounded by sea, with one of the biggest maritime histories in the world, and unless we keep things under control, we're going to lose it all.'

'We'll lose all the knowledge that's been handed down. We'll never get that back.'

'When it's too late, people will think we should have helped them, but it is too bloody late then. Now we've got the chance to do something, and we have to take that chance, otherwise it will be gone.'

These men's livelihoods are threatened by an enclosure of the seas – the privatisation and marketing of the historic right to fish in local waters, much of which has passed into the hands of highly 'efficient' and environmentally destructive factory fishing enterprises. One such factory boat off our coasts has now accumulated 17 per cent of our entire national fishing quota. This single boat has more fishing rights available to it than the entire Cornish coastal fishing fleet. The consolidation of quotas has been accompanied by an increase in the use of very low-paid overseas labour, and in some cases, slaves – as emerged recently, when Filipino workers were rescued from ships off the coast of the UK, having been captured and imprisoned for months.[5]

Different forms of this story are being played out too in the 'post-industrial' communities of our cities where skilled work has disappeared and been replaced by low-paid and temporary jobs. It is also quietly eating away at the lives and identities of hill farmers, who struggle to get a decent price from supermarkets for the food they grow. In fact, it is a story that would be recognised by communities all over the world, who are fighting a mostly losing battle to protect their sanity and livelihoods against the impacts of restless global capital, aligned with a centralising and de-humanising state.

Forms of knowledge applied without reference to tradition, meaning, value or virtue, bring in their wake the destruction of nature, loss of identity, alienation from place and cultural ruin. From Clare to *The Last Fishermen*, the cry is loud and getting louder; and the common cause between Labour and the environment movement in responding to it is clear enough, too, if we have the courage to listen. So what would need to change, for us to meet that cry together – to unite to protect what we love – and beyond that, to build new forms of economic and cultural association, which offer what Jon Cruddas describes, after Jonathan Lear, as 'radical hope'[6]?

I believe such a common response is possible; but that it will not happen whilst we remain divided over the place of expert knowledge in informing our actions; and whilst we position ourselves, however unwittingly, on either side of a cultural gulf around the value of work. Moreover, it will not happen at all, if too many of us abandon the field to neo-liberalism – as Churchill said, feeding the crocodile in the hope that it will eat us last.

CLIMATE CHANGE AND A MEANINGFUL RELATIONSHIP WITH SCIENCE

As an example of an area where we urgently need a better shared understanding, let's consider the challenge of climate change. It has become the badge of a kind of self-proclaimed popularism to dismiss climate science as a conspiracy promoted by liberal elites, for the various purposes of suborning national sovereignty; taxing the poor; lining the pockets of the renewable energy industry; and ensuring scientists get access to government grants. Many of those who cite this imagined conspiracy are mounting a proxy defence of the free market, or have specific financial interests at stake. Yet this theory would have less traction, if many more people did not share a deep mistrust of 'experts', feeling that expert knowledge is often used to erode agency and attack standards of living. How has our relationship with expertise become so problematised? And how can we achieve a meaningful reconciliation with science and scientists?

Perhaps if we return to Wordsworth, we can find the beginnings of an answer in his phrase 'we murder to dissect'. For as the nineteenth century advanced, the technological and industrial revolution was accompanied by a remarkable project of classification, measurement and codification. It was the age of the spinning jenny; but it was also the age of the amateur botanist, the list maker, the mapper and the measurer. Of course much of what we learned from this project was awe-inspiring and life-changing for those who came afterwards. But the urge to measure and codify also helped facilitate a new relationship between politics, science and economics, which began to jostle out other forms of understanding. As codification took hold in our political economy, our sense of what was valuable became reduced to what could be audited. And that did not include our relationships with one another, the beauty of nature, the ties that bind us to place or even (ironically) the value of science for the sake of science itself.

As a result, those who relied upon other forms of knowledge – on faith, on a sense of reverence and virtue, on experience, on tradition – found themselves in retreat and have never recovered their political confidence. Many continue to feel humiliated and neglected, including many in the environment and Labour movements. Others have attempted to secure a place in the new order by feeding the crocodile. Such accommodations come in many forms, but my least favourite is that of 'biodiversity offsetting' – a trade in creation which, if taken to its logical conclusion, is both farcical and terrifying. Surely no sane man or woman truly thinks we should employ accountants to consider how many ancient oaks are worth a single aspen copse, or how many slow-worms we should trade for a medium-sized adder? And yet that is the logic we pursue.

So, like many others (including educationalists and psychiatrists), environmentalists have allowed our relationship with science to become debased, putting measuring skills at the disposal of a particular kind of reductive materialism which we now recognise as the enemy – and which has in turn allowed the concentration of power in the hands of state and market elites. So far, so bad.

But for anyone concerned with the common good, a frustration with the misuses of expert knowledge cannot be allowed to lead to the wholesale rejection of scientific understanding. This remains not only a legitimate, but an essential, means of engaging with the world. Or to put it more bluntly – an eager critique of the economic and social impacts of the Enlightenment must also consider the forms of tyranny that ride on the back of anti-intellectualism and philosophical idealism. Only the mad, the bad or the silly truly believe that 'we make our own reality'. Taken to its extremes, such a belief leads to the propagandising of Stalin. It can never form part of the disposition of a democratic movement such as ours.

Instead, we need to acknowledge that science is one of the ways in which we remain in an open relationship with the truth. And that it is in this spirit that we should address the science of climate change. Because scientific enquiry is leading us to the conclusion that we are creating a climate unlike any we have known in our long walk through history and pre-history. This is the best information we have right now. Acting upon it to reduce the risks is not a matter of ideology, but rather doing what human beings have done since the dawn of time, in order to survive: adjusting our behaviour, based on the insights provided by reasoning, to the conditions we find in the outside world.

We need to act, because as far as we are able to understand, climate change threatens the very things that our politics is committed to defend – the homes and jobs we love, the peace we need to enjoy them, the natural world for which we have an intimate love; the land upon which we stand. But the need to act does not in itself make all forms of action equally useful, or equally moral. The kinds of things we choose to do are as important as the choice to do them.

We should not (for example) tackle the problem by worsening the problems of alienation and economic disempowerment which are already hitting our communities. We need responses that are collaborative rather than punitive; which put the potential to solve the problem (and to benefit from the solutions) into the hands of working people. If we ask people to trust in the science, after all, we must be prepared to trust them.

NATURE AND WORK

This brings me to my last point, which is about nature and work. It is no secret that the environment movement has too often been perceived as anti-industry, anti-work, anti-livelihood. It has been seen as narrow-minded and mean-spirited – ironically, it has been accused of failing to recognise the importance to working people of community, tradition and place.

This has generated a hostility which is anything but inevitable, and which we can ill afford. Healing actions in this context are not just practical, but essential. This is why it is so important that Greenpeace and coastal fishermen have found a way to work together to demand fishing quota reform. And why steps to mend relationships with indigenous peoples in the Arctic, damaged by anti-hunting campaigns in the 1980s, must continue – including by building on a recent public apology.

We need such points of reconciliation, hope and shared purpose, not least because the way out of our current crisis is not to do less work, but to do more – more productive, skilled and well-paid work, requiring a greater reliance on the knowledge of working people. Because whoever imagined that tackling climate change was about turning out the lights and shutting down the factories could not have been more wrong. In fact, for millions of people around the world, it is about turning the lights on for the first time – using new forms of power that are cheap, easy to transport and install – but which also require ingenuity and hard work to test and manufacture.

Mending our climate is about harnessing the potential of the digital age to use energy more intelligently. In fact, it is about the radical hope of a post-industrial revolution – one in which power generation is not controlled by a few big companies, but by a plethora of businesses, farms, schools and town halls across our country and around the world.

I am sincerely convinced that a meaningful relationship with nature is not hostile to work, but rather is forged by it. It lies with engineers, proud of the application of their expert knowledge to help solve the problem of climate pollution. It lies in the determination of coastal fishermen to protect their fish stocks and fishing grounds. It lies in farmers working to restore hedgerows, copses and ponds, to bring back birdsong to our countryside but also to protect the soils that provide their living. Making, growing, catching, mending – these are the jobs that we can do together – building on common traditions and memories, and working with the grain of nature.

This is my hope, and perhaps can become our shared hope. And so I would like to conclude this essay with a last poem, which is also a gift; a love poem – a beautiful evocation of all that we hold dear on the earth. 'And You, Helen' by Edward Thomas.[7]

And you, Helen, what should I give you?
So many things I would give you
Had I an infinite great store
Offered me and I stood before
To choose. I would give you youth,
All kinds of loveliness and truth,
A clear eye as good as mine,
Lands, waters, flowers, wine,
As many children as your heart
Might wish for, a far better art
Than mine can be, all you have lost
Upon the travelling waters tossed,

Or given to me. If I could choose
Freely in that great treasure-house
Anything from any shelf,
I would give you back yourself,
And power to discriminate
What you want and want it not too late,
Many fair days free from care
And heart to enjoy both foul and fair,
And myself, too, if I could find
Where it lay hidden and it proved kind.

NOTES

1. Sirach, ch. 42, verses 22–7.
2. William Wordsworth, *The Complete Poetical Works* (London: Macmillan and Co., 1888).
3. John Clare, *Selected Poems* (London: J Dent &Sons Ltd, 1965).
4. From the film *The Last Fishermen*. Available at http://www.greenpeace. org.uk/last-fishermen-film (accessed on 25 August 2014).
5. Available at http://www.express.co.uk/news/uk/456085/Boat-slave- shame-of-fishing-industry (accessed on 25 August 2014).
6. Jonathan Lear, *Radical Hope: Ethics in the Face of Cultural Devastation* (Cambridge, MA: Harvard University Press, 2008).
7. Edward Thomas, *Selected Poems* (London: Faber and Faber, 2011).

CHAPTER ELEVEN

The Problem with Progress

Dave Landrum

ONWARDS AND UPWARDS

'Things can only get better,' resounded the song in May 1997 as a youthful Tony Blair made his way to the door of No. 10 through a sea of delirious party staff and members. Things were looking good – very good indeed. This was a new day, and the Labour Party was high on the intoxicating air of progress. A couple of years later Blair would confirm the new mission of the left with a battle cry for 'the forces of progress' to defeat the 'forces of conservatism'. Seeking a 'progressive consensus' for 'our progressive future', the slogan was 'forward, not back'. We even had a 'progressive manifesto'.[1] For many in the Labour Party who would self-identify as progressive, this was radicalism reborn (or at least repackaged), and to quote Wordsworth: 'Bliss was it in that dawn to be alive'.

Fast-forward to 2008. When we survey the 13 years of Labour government from 1997 to 2010, what 'progress' can we discern? Over a decade of unprecedented spending on public infrastructure had brought real benefits to many more people through better schools, hospitals and public services. Our long-blighted urban areas received vast amounts of regeneration funding and government attention through a myriad of schemes and initiatives. The introduction of the minimum wage, working tax credits and pension credits even meant that some wealth was redistributed. Public transport was improved, and there were important policy developments in criminal justice and the environment. Smoking in public places was banned, and so was cigarette advertising. A Freedom of Information Act was passed, and perhaps most significantly, peace was established in Northern Ireland. All of these changes can be said to represent 'progress' as we have come to understand it. Yet, despite our unprecedented long boom of low unemployment and high disposable income, even Blair had to acknowledge that something was amiss, observing:

> My generation enjoy a thousand material advantages over any previous generation. And yet we suffer a depth of insecurity and spiritual doubt they never knew... Mine is the generation with more freedom than any other but less certainty in how to exercise it responsibly.

In the final analysis, Tony Blair was just another neo-liberal, championing both economic and social liberalism with equal vigour. Far removed from its classical roots, this new form of liberalism was geared to support omni-individualism – the rapacious, unaccountable self. With a naked focus on status and wealth, this liberalism sustained elites at all levels of society, and helps explain Peter Mandelson's acknowledgement that he (and by implication the Labour government) was 'intensely relaxed about people getting filthy rich as long as they pay their taxes'.

By promoting individual wealth so long as it could be taxed *ex post facto*, this attitude failed to recognise two things: the impact of individualism on the 'social cohesion' of poor people; and the lack of social responsibility felt on the part of wealthy individuals when they are encouraged to see taxation as a substitution for consciousness. David McLellan predicted this would be a problem in 1996. He foresaw that Tony Blair's emphasis on community (often to avoid talking about the family) was doomed to break down into instrumental factors since in order for a community to behave as a community it needs to stress a vision beyond itself: 'Tony Blair's Fabian pamphlet on Socialism talks of social justice, equality and community – but these ideas are left floating in a way that suggests they could be blown in almost any direction'.[2] And blown in many directions they surely were.

At the end of it all, we have crises of leadership in politics, the city and in the media. Amid an epidemic of debt, we have over a million people dependent upon prescription tranquillisers, and our cities have been torched by a vast new consumer-led underclass[3] who, en masse, seized an opportunity to go 'shopping with violence'.[4] While 'middle England' has secured numerous comforts, generally income inequality has soared, trust has decreased and we are less civil. In the multiple deprivation areas where populations are most concentrated in the UK, ordinary family life is more difficult to sustain and solidarity amongst the poor is rapidly depleting. Here, the daily reality is of crime, drug addiction, illiteracy, mental illness, juvenile delinquency, illegitimacy and welfare dependency – and unemployment is back with a vengeance. On every level and in every way, we live in a society that looks and feels like it is being ethically eviscerated.[5]

As for the Labour Party, it was like a microcosm of British society: deeply divided, lacking in vision, haemorrhaging membership and pretty much bankrupt. And, being dominated by liberal elites, it had very little to say to its much abused and lately abandoned core constituency – working people and their families.

Things can only get better? Well, so much for progress!

QUALIFYING PROGRESS

Progress conveys a general sense of forward movement, and it retains a cachet in politics, with many on the left comfortable describing themselves as 'progressives'. Common parlance in political discourse, its political appeal seems to rest upon its ambiguity. 'Devoid of real meaning, capable of adoption to any cause, but conveying a fuzzy sense of well-being, like a mug of hot tea: you can see why politicians use it so much'.[6]

On the face of it progress seems a perfectly reasonable, even noble idea. Defined as being forward or onward movement toward a destination, it is a positive word suggesting good things in a good future. Full of optimistic connotations, it is about growth, development and 'getting on'. In 1968, the historian Sidney Pollard described it as: 'the assumption that a pattern of change exists in the history of mankind [...] that it consists of irreversible changes in one direction only, and that this direction is towards improvement'.[7]

Crucially, progress retains great power over contemporary imaginations because it has made the journey from an idea to a myth – and along the way collected some features of the religion that it mimics. Ronald Wright explains this historical circular reasoning:

> Our practical faith in progress has ramified and hardened into an ideology – a secular religion which, like the religions that progress has challenged, is blind to certain flaws in its

credentials. Progress, therefore, has become 'myth' in the anthropological sense [...] an arrangement of the past, whether real or imagined, in patterns that reinforce a culture's deepest values and aspirations.[8]

Myths in this sense are 'maps by which cultures navigate through time'.[9] And they are so fraught with meaning that we live and die by them.

The great promise of modernity was progress without limit. In politics, this means promising far more than can ever be delivered. To be sure, all democratic governments are doomed to fall short of their plans. The dilemma for politicians is that solutions are mundane, and it is ideas and vision that excite people. Ideas are heroic and grandiose, while practical solutions and improvements based on negotiation, tradition and consent are really quite boring. For example, 'Make Poverty History' is a far more appealing slogan than 'Let's help some people who really need our help'.

Either consciously or unconsciously the language of our politicians reflects this dilemma. But, in the end, when the sandy foundations of political thinking are exposed by the storms of reality, things begin to fall apart. As they do, it is the trauma of broken promises and unrealised dreams that is most harmful to the public psyche.

To qualify, the term 'progress' as ideologically applied in the way that people self-identify as 'progressives' and policy is subjected to 'progressivism' is different from improvement – in intentions, actions and outcomes. Moral and social improvements of the human condition through sustained benefits in living standards are historical and contemporary realities that, given what we know about human nature and history, we can all be thankful for. It is clear that even piecemeal political changes can bring about genuine, trans-generational enhancements in working conditions, social relations, security, housing, education, health, and well-being. In turn, such practical *improvements* in quality of life, as measured against previous generations and other cultures, often provide inspiration and aspiration for more of the same. All of which is very welcome, but none of which is ultimately guaranteed, and therefore does not constitute progress.

Progress is also different from amelioration – the reduction of suffering or the bringing of aid and relief in order to make a bad or unpleasant situation better. This has immediate and temporary connotations, unlike progress which assumes eventual and perpetual betterment. And progress is not the same as growth – a natural maturation or increase in the size or the importance of something. Our understanding of growth tends to derive from interaction with ecology, biology and the natural order. As such, growth infers that abilities and characteristics have models into which and from which they will gradually develop. Progress, on the other hand, has historically been more associated with human control of the environment rather than cooperation with a natural order which is far more cyclical than expansive.

Although progress fundamentally differs from improvement, amelioration and growth, it does co-opt and subvert such terms. Consequently, it needs to be acknowledged that, whether through explicit, implicit or complicit usage, the idea of progress has contributed to numerous substantive and lasting improvements in human conditions. As an intentional engineering of conditions, despite killing and immiserating more people than any other idea in history,[10] it has also produced lasting benefits – think of the scientific advances from the space race. As an assumed ontology it has induced demands for improvement, many of which have been realised – think of the extension of women's rights or democracy. As a co-opted ideology it has helped to gain freedoms and security for many – think of the Universal Declaration of Human Rights.

Globally, many are now benefiting from a plethora of projects to improve the human condition. For millennia people lived to the age of just 25 or 30, with most parents mourning the death of at least one of their children. People live much longer today, often beyond 65 and, in some countries, past 80. Across the world average income is far higher than it has ever been. With a few exceptions, the global rate of literacy is now above eight out of ten. Also, ordinary men and women can vote and find work, regardless of their race. In large parts of the world they can believe, think and say what they choose. If they fall ill, they will be treated. If they are innocent, they will generally walk free.[11]

Even so, outside of warfare, twentieth-century governments murdered 7.3 per cent of their people, through needless famine, labour camps, genocide and other crimes. That compares with 3.7 per cent in the nineteenth century.[12]

Culturally, the error of progress is not the idea that human life can improve, but the assumption that such achievements are cumulative rather than recurrent. Neglecting or wilfully denying the truth that what has been gained 'civilisationally' can also be lost, the philosophy of human progress is: today is better than yesterday just because it's today; and that human nature is essentially good and even perfectible.

Although history can be rewritten or ignored, for a while, the 'anxious certainty' of contemporary progressives often betrays the real doubts that exist about this secular creed. Yet, as 'the Prozac of the thinking classes',[13] it remains a dominant feature of Western philosophy and politics.

PROGRESSING FROM THEOLOGY TO IDEOLOGY

The story that has shaped Western culture for centuries is a narrative of progress that speaks of humanly driven movement towards ever-greater freedom and material prosperity, especially through science embodied in technology, and in the application of scientific principles to our social life, in economics, in politics, and in education. Beyond the cult of French Positivism,[14] this evolution of progress as an ideology occurred through the Enlightenment gift of boundless confidence in scientific rationalism. With humanity free from the oppressive superstitions of the past,[15] the unpredictability and chaos of the natural order could be replaced with a relentless, irrepressible and inevitable journey to utopia. The credo that humanity advances towards a historic terminus through a growth in knowledge points towards the deeper, religious roots of progress.

The liberal humanist driver for the idea of progress may well be a 'shoddy replica of Christian faith markedly more irrational than the original article, and in recent years more harmful',[16] but it is hard to deny that it has a great deal in common with the belief it was meant to supplant. By aping the Christian idea of history as a universal narrative of salvation, progressivism has mutated into a militant political religion that promises paradise on earth. As John Gray has observed:

> The trouble with secular myths is that they are frequently more harmful than the real thing. In traditional Christianity, the apocalyptic impulse was restrained by the insight that human beings are ineradicably flawed. In the secular religions that flowed from Christianity, this insight was lost. The result has

been a form of tyranny, new in history that commits vast crimes in pursuit of heaven on earth.[17]

As a copy of the teleology of the Christian doctrine of the Kingdom of God, the secularist narrative of progress historically drew much of its language and legitimacy from faith itself.[18]

However, the confident pursuit of harmony, nirvana or heaven on earth was arrested by the fact that 'utopias are dreams of collective deliverance that in waking life are found to be nightmares'.[19] This is because the totalising logic of a desacralised idea of progress works against ideas of difference, dissent or plurality. History shows that when subordination and assimilation become priorities, the legal and coercive power of the state is increasingly used to affirm that what is not forbidden is compulsory, and what is not heretical is orthodoxy.

As with all flawed political ideas, the flowering of progressivism was accompanied by its unravelling. Beyond factors such as urban blight, social anomie or environmental degradation, the idea of progress as a credible guiding motif for human history was above all else shattered by the First World War, and its continuance in the Second World War and the Holocaust. During the twentieth century, communism, fascism and neo-liberalism (socially and economically) were in John Gray's words: 'messianic movements, using the language of reason and science, but actually driven by faith'.[20] Embracing the cold logic of evolutionary biology that only the fittest will (or should) survive, Stalin, Hitler, Mussolini, Mao, Pol Pot and Kim Jong Il all had two things in common. They were all mass murderers and they were all self-avowed progressives.[21]

Orwell's identification of the self-deceit that accompanies the ideal was summed up in his statement that: 'All progress is seen to be a frantic struggle towards an objective which you hope and pray will never be reached'. Including the term in his list of 'meaningless words', he saw how the 'variable meanings' of it meant that it could be used in a 'consciously dishonest way'. At source, this often painful cognitive dissonance is related to the more iniquitous features of human nature that progress itself denies. As Voight observes, 'secular eschatology is always caught in its own contradiction. It projects into the *past* a vision of what *never was*, it conceives what *is* in terms of what *is not*, and the *future* in terms of what can *never be*'.[22]

Analysing the roots of this delusion, Gray cites how many of the philosophers of the Enlightenment – the architects and engineers of progress – could not admit what pre-Christian thinkers took for granted – that human history has no overall meaning. With existence perceived as endless, cyclical and bounded, a worldview for avoiding despair and enabling hope is required – an idea that conveys a de-sacralised vision for humanity. That idea is progress, and without it there remains only a comfortless nihilism and a Nietzschean 'will to power'. Not many are willing to venture out beyond the proxy Christian narrative to the desert of reality, so a mirage is sustained whereby '[s]ecular societies are ruled by repressed religion. Screened off from conscious awareness, the religious impulse has mutated, returning as the fantasy of salvation through politics'.[23]

MEANS AND ENDS

You can't make an omelette without breaking eggs, and the historical tendency of progress towards totalitarianism reflects a recurring, in-built logic in which the ends justify the means. This is because, once an inevitable utopia is even vaguely envisioned, all the energies and resources that pre-exist are considered of lesser value than that of the ultimate goal. Indeed, they are strategically subordinated to the project. It doesn't matter how it is achieved as long as you get the desired result. More often this 'progress' takes a milder form of pursuing 'the dream society' across generations through a variety of benign steps and measures – and often the dream fades from view as new horizons open up. However, occasionally (and with a guaranteed recurrence) our fascistic tendencies seek to speed things up.[24] When this happens, it is clear that freedom, security, nature, truth, justice and people are all expendable.

This is not new. History is replete with examples of people investing perfectly reasonable ideas with ontological ultimacy – making them both the means and the ends of life. However, it is the idea of progress, what Baudelaire called 'this great heresy of decay', that provides the common link. In social, economic or political application, for sheer destructive power it is unmatched.

Sociologically, the idea of progress trumps all organic, traditional, and normative structures that may be required to temper human nature and to encourage human flourishing. Achieving the dream society is increasingly described in 'laboratorial' terms, and the deliberate engineering of social relations and identities is encour-aged. In mass societies, this means that life itself is effectively instrumentalised. The traditioned familial and communal bonds that form civil society are relegated below the aspirations of ideology, status, wealth or advantage. Here, the role of government is to realise progress, and it expands inexorably to manage the process – often in cooperation with the market – ergo our imperial regulatory state.

In economics, progress is the supreme driver. Although history shows that markets operate in cycles of profitability, when imbued with the idea of progress, they are beset by delusions of ever-expanding prosperity. Adam Smith called this trope of capitalism 'the natural progress of things towards improvement'.[25] Karl Marx admiringly described the systemic effect as 'a machine for demolishing limits'.[26] Both, in different ways and to varying degrees, invested our processes of material value and exchange with an ontological ultimacy. Consequently, whether the economic model is laissez-faire, communist or Keynesian, with 'development' as a primary objective and 'growth' as something to be maintained at all costs, the faith in progress is the same. The difference now is that the progress narrative has globalised as a belief system:

> Detached from religion and at the same time purged from the doubts that haunted its classical exponents, the belief in the market as a divine ordinance became a secular ideology of universal progress that in the late twentieth century was embraced by international institutions.[27]

With most people now seeing affluence as a normative condition (even as an aspiration), growing the economy depends on consumption and creating demands for new things. Competition for profits and market share fuels this insatiable consumerism and demands an incessant proliferation of new products, commodities and lifestyle experiences.

To sustain this situation the aim is no longer wisdom, but control. If human history is the sole vehicle of salvation, the principal means of this salvation is the technological domination of nature. This progressive liberation of ourselves from nature entails a refashioning of nature into a world we have made to serve our ends. But 'if we redesign nature to fit human wishes, we risk making a mirror of our own pathologies'.[28] So, if industrialisation and consumerism (producing more goods and services) represent progress, then the degradation of our natural environment can continue until all finite resources are expended. Progressive thinking about our planet may provide some short-term solutions, but trans-generationally it is delivering a depletion of natural resources, scarcity, and inequality of wealth on a hitherto unimagined scale. This is because once we are 'possessed by an end' our progress towards it becomes a modern form of idolatry in which anything and everything can be sacrificed[29] – including people.

Historically, progressivism has always been the principle driving force behind the eugenics movement[30] because 'Technology is addictive [and...] Material progress creates problems that are – or seem to be – soluble by further progress'. The newfound ability to manipulate DNA will have profound, and potentially terrible, consequences for our political order, even if undertaken with the best of intentions.[31] In our embrace of progress, with most lacking the wealth to access new technologies, it is likely that a new genetic underclass will develop.[32] And although genetic technologies promise a better future, we should be in no doubt that their development and use will be governed by war, profit and ideology.

CHANGE FOR THE SAKE OF CHANGE

The 'means justify the ends' logic of progressivism has sustained a handy denial of the historical fact that ethics and politics do not advance in line with the growth of knowledge, even scientific knowledge.[33] This thinking helps to avoid anything seen as a moral (or 'conservative') constraint, and in turn fuels the modern (and post-modern) proclivity for change for the sake of change.

Forcefully divorced from its own roots, progressivism was quick to develop a disdain for history, for what went before. This neglect or wilful denial of the roots of the fruits in culture is an Enlightenment psychology. As John Locke observed,

> He that travels that road now, applauds his own strength and legs that have carried him so far in such a scantling of time; and ascribes all to his own vigour; little considering how much he owes to their pains, who cleared the woods, drained the bogs, built the bridges, and made the ways possible.[34]

In politics, the persistence of this kind of cultural amnesia helps to explain the 'initiativitis', policy plethora and campaign rhetoric that characterised New Labour – and the 'New' motif itself.[35] This disdain for the past and a preoccupation with novelty can be traced directly to a fundamental contradiction at the heart of the idea of progress – the impossibility of empirical reckoning. Because the real goal for humanity cannot be determined (in a secular sense), progress cannot be measured. All that can be measured is change itself. So change itself becomes the metric for progress. The newest is the truest, the latest is the greatest – and as that great progressive Henry Ford declared, 'all history is bunk'.

From the Enlightenment onward, this mindset may well have challenged numerous oppressive social relations, but it has also had a devastating effect on the beliefs and customs that gave meaning and identity to poor people and communities. With tradition trumped by all things 'radical' (a word that is literally derived from the Latin 'to uproot'), those who look to the past for something to build their lives and societies on are derided as 'nostalgic' (a word that has a Greek root meaning of 'homesickness'). Severely limiting the possibilities for building upon the gains of the past in any meaningful way or maintaining strong links between generations, this de-conservatising agenda has had the effect of disrupting and fragmenting working-class identity. In *Utopian Dreams* Tobias Jones explains the cultural impact of this tyranny of innovation on the ancient social value of regard for the aged:

> The cult of the youth has reached iconographic invincibility [...] Technology, sport and personal beauty have become obsessive themes of our times [...] Innovation and change are central rather than peripheral [...] When society's most important value is function, a thing's utility, old people are deemed irrelevant [...] Now the value of everything is instrumental instead of intrinsic. Tradition is a synonym for detritus. Age has lost the cache of sagacity.[36]

The political ideology of the left has, in the words of Christopher Lasch, 'come to regard common sense – the traditional wisdom and folkways of the community – as an obstacle to progress and enlightenment'. This compulsion for perpetual change and constant critique has rooted itself on the left through two dominant theories. The first is Leon Trotsky's theory of permanent revolution, whereby all existing institutions must be demolished in order to create a world without oppression. The second is Antonio Gramsci's theory of cultural hegemony, whereby all existing institutions that cannot be captured for the 'revolution' must be degraded to the point that they need to be replaced. Both endorse the use of violence and subversion as conditions of progress, and both insist on total dominance. Generally, centre-left politics has provided a reality check against this kind of unfettered futurology, but it has evidently not done nearly enough to stem the tide. Indeed, it was the lure of progress that drew Philip Gould to hail the twenty-first century as 'an age of permanent revolutions' and 'unceasing modernisation'.[37] Jon Cruddas explains the consequences for the Labour Party:

> We see everything through the binary terms of forward or back, future or past, new or old, and eventually good or bad. The good 'Progressive Tradition' has always won and the bad 'Romantic Tradition' always lost. New Labour was all about the 'radical new' rather than the past. The project was always defined as one of 'modernisation' – a modernisation that embraced the uncontrollable forces of globalisation. By the end, it embraced a dystopian, destructive neo-liberalism. It cut loose from the traditions and history of Labour. 'Leave the past to those who live in it,' said Tony Blair. It is a short step to associate hope with change – and despair with the past. But what about the victims of change? Who speaks for them?[38]

PROGRESS WITHOUT A COMPASS

To appreciate the scale of the corrupting effect of liberalism upon centre-left politics, we need to see how the idea of progress is connected to the way in which the post-modern turn is shaping liberal politics. Ideologically much of this connection is related to the large-scale conversion of 1960s-inspired leftist academics to social constructivism in the wake of the intellectual collapse of Marxism in the 1970s and 1980s. In their journey from Engels to Foucault these new (or 'neo-') liberals carried much of the intellectual baggage of progress with them. The confluence may be philosophically vacuous, and even nonsensical, but it has enabled a hybridisation of progressivism with liberalism and relativism. The result has been to reduce politics to a smash and grab for power between competing identity groups – most notably in relation to the sectionalism of special interest groups and issues of sexual 'emancipation' (or consumer choice).

All of this has been made possible by the fact that morality is to all intents and purposes subjectivised to the project of progress. This is because the inconvenient, yet rather obvious flaw of 'progress' is that it is lacking a 'compass' (yes, this is a think-tank joke). The ideal is incapable of discerning what is better or worse because it cannot measure the distance travelled toward its destination. It cannot chart the distance because it cannot define the destination.

This is because if we try and move beyond the abstract and establish whether humanity is in a better state than formerly, we are philosophically stuck. Does our metric involve happiness, knowledge, less suffering, artistic expression, altruism, wealth, longevity? Or what about morality, which seems to cover a multitude of such aspirations? No. The fact is that, without reference to an objective anchor, all our virtues are relegated to a subjective calculus. Lacking a definitive knowledge of the goal of universal history, progress is sheer delusion.[39]

As a consequence of this disorientation, truth becomes less important than freedom and the post-modern turn is taken – usually at breakneck speed. The tragedy is that: 'Truth was once the guarantor of freedom; now with truth announced as extinct, freedom is promoted as the cornerstone of tolerance'.[40] Traditionally freedom is defined by and centripetal to duty or responsibility. On its own all that matters is individual choice. We simply drift 'towards a dictatorship of relativism which does not recognise anything as certain and which has as its highest goal one's own ego and one's own end'.[41]

> The point is that without the notion that some choices are wrong, no choice that we eventually make will ever seem consequential or correct. The actual criteria by which we make choices have become themselves subject to choice: anything goes which means nothing stays. There's no permanence. The tyranny of relativism has replaced the tyranny of orthodoxy.[42]

In late modernity, the logic of liberalism became that of: if progress is assured and automatic, why suffer, toil or make sacrifices? Now, despite the progress narrative peddling the 'jam tomorrow' line to avoid solving problems today,[43] the paradox is that it 'celebrates impermanence and living for the moment, a wilful detachment from ethical and political concerns, and the cultivated display of provocative individuality'.[44] This illusion of individuation is necessary to camouflage the new modes of conformism that progress inevitably engenders.

In politics, the subjectivising effect of progress has meant that what is good is usually eclipsed by the need to gain power to achieve it. Now in tandem with the new tyranny of relativism it produces a kind of crusading amorality. On the right this is usually about legitimising forms of economic natural selection, sugar-coating Nozickian libertarianism[45] with an often very thin veneer of 'social justice'.[46] On the left and in the Labour Party the liberalism-cum-relativism that now masquerades as the defender of the vulnerable is most visible through the defunct multiculturalism and human rights discourses. Here, with all lifestyles being considered to be of equal value, the very notion of normative behaviour becomes suspect as oppressive – and moral judgements are simply prejudices. The result is that the interests and agendas of 'oppressed minorities' must always trump the will or identity of the majority.[47] The values of any dominant culture are replaced by self-designated victim groups – and anti-discrimination becomes *the* political cause. Evermore deconstructive of a sense of normativity or a common 'way of life' this senseless non-judgementalism sees traditional family structure as oppressive and the idea of cultivating a national identity as an anathema.[48]

Very different from classical liberalism,[49] the neo-liberal agenda on the left displays an ironic harmony with the libertarianism of the right in as much as it tends towards state control over all aspects of public life, while paradoxically proposing total liberation in the private sphere[50] yet invading privacy by increasing legislating about marriage, sex, education, etc. Its existence helps explain why a Labour government can propose policies such as the legalisation of drugs, the legalisation of prostitution, legalisation of euthanasia and liberalisation of gambling to allow super-casinos to be built in areas of social deprivation. All prescribed to help the poor by conferring more liberty. All destined to make the poor poorer and the rich richer.

Affirming of the maxim that 'nothing stands in the way of progress', this kind of liberalism unites 'must-have' choice and 'must-have' change and invests it all with an air of inevitability. But the elephant in the room is power. Now, those who lack the wealth or education to enjoy such freedoms are simply left behind. As Zygmunt Bauman has observed:

The post-modern era is perhaps the first not to allocate a function to its poor – not a single redeeming feature which could prompt solidarity with the poor. Post-modern society produces its members first and foremost as consumers – and the poor are singularly unfit for that role; by no stretch of imagination can one hope that they would contribute to a 'consumer-led recovery'. For the first time in history the poor are totally un-functional and wholly useless; as such they are, for all practical intents and purposes, 'outside society'.[51]

With social relations thus fragmented, the post-war residues of solidarity amongst working people simply dissolved into a consumer wasteland of individual choice. Anaesthetised by the state and incentivised by the market, much of what remains of the working class after the *faux embourgeoisement* of Thatcherism is now a vast *lumpenproletariat*. Relieved by liberal progressivism of the normative securities and resources provided by things like religion, family and nation, the inhabitants of this brave new world, though numerous, are very much alone. Disenfranchised by liberalism and alienated by metropolitan political elites, they are reminded daily through television and advertising of the blessings of progress and their utter inability to attain them. So they simply float way from politics. Here,

> There is no lighthouse keeper. There is no lighthouse. There is no dry land. There are only people living on rafts made from their own imaginations. And there is the sea.[52]

BLUE LABOUR AND EARTHED POLITICS

In light of the many problems of progress, where now for the left? And, where now for the Labour Party? Or more precisely, what's new after 'New' Labour? What are the prospects for the party to regain its role as a voice for working people and their families – and to therein gain an authentic mandate to govern for justice and mercy?

Political history, as Blair (progressively) noted, is more sequential than cyclical, with successive governments building what they inherit. Fusing the immediacy of *realpolitik* with an indefinable 'project' of transformation, it is this pragmatic progressivism that enabled New Labour to propose reform rather than revolution in social and economic policy. In many ways such an approach can be justified.

Indeed, given the political context at the time, much of the Third-Way thinking about reviving public services while debunking the myths of the left[53] can be seen as being quite dynamic, even heroic.

However, the liberal obsession with promoting rights-claiming individualism (what I want) at the expense of normativity, solidarity and social institutions that support them (what we need), coupled with the progressive preoccupation with radical change, are having a devastating effect on our human ecology.

The malignancy of the liberal intelligentsia is not confined to the left. Now conjoined with Cameron's 'progressive conservatives', Nick Clegg has recently talked about developing this marriage of convenience to forge a 'new progressivism'. Although the ideological partnership is clearly more akin to 'traditional liberal conservatism', because Clegg chose to reframe it in progressive terms it is seen by political historian Emily Robinson as being indicative of 'the extent that British political discourse has coalesced around the ideas of progress and progressivism as seemingly uncontroversial, positive values'.[54] The fact that Clegg also coined the phrase 'progressive austerity' is a sign that the political morphology of the term is far from exhausted. Indeed, a survey for the Centre for British Politics on public understandings of the word 'progressive' has shown that, although most people don't understand what it actually means, and don't associate it with the left, they do think that it's a good thing.[55] This suggests that, unless directly and consistently challenged, it will continue to have a catastrophic cachet in political economy.

But something needs to happen. If the global financial meltdown in 2008 represented the myth of progress exploding in the economic sphere, we can be sure that a similar 'credit crunch' is upon us in the social sphere. Blue Labour is about meeting this challenge. It is not an ideology – or a political movement. As a space for debate on the left, it represents the most significant modus to challenge the liberalism-cum-relativism of progress. Against the backdrop of the monumental collapse of thinking on the left,[56] and in the absence of any clarity of political purpose,[57] it is the only viable direction of travel for the Labour Party. Although in many ways a kaleidoscope of various narratives and ideas, Blue Labour does cohere both philosophically and politically as a distinctive politics of reciprocity, mutuality and solidarity. It is also profoundly practical in its policy orientation.

Unlike rich societies which place the needs of the individual first, most traditional societies are 'sociocentric' – meaning that they place the needs of groups and institutions first.[58] With their focus on localism, subsidiarity and renewing the associational bonds that are essential in civil society, the ideas being generated by the Blue Labour debate offer an opportunity for centre-left politics to once again provide real-time solutions for real people experiencing real problems. Moving beyond the 'pie in the sky' folly of progressivism, Blue Labour redresses the damaging obsession with all things shiny and new. By retrieving tradition to generate greater solidarity and inclusion, it offers the possibility for people to build lives on the more solid ground of social normativity and inherited identities.

Affirming of the traditions and histories that forged the working-class identity which gave birth to the Labour movement in the UK, it looks to restore civic pride to many of our long-devastated communities. The experiences of London Citizens attest to this and give hope for a more earthed form of politics in which people gain a voice against those who seek to exploit, demean and patronise them.

This narrative is not revisionist, in the sense of seeking a return to 'Old Labour' in the negative, extremist sense of the term. Revalorising the sacred in public life, it acknowledges the vital role of religion in poor communities and in national life, helping to locate people in a historical narrative that has lasting value. By exploring reasonable, practical and grassroots policy solutions which can take account of the obligations that we owe to those who have gone before – while being mindful of the responsibilities we have to future generations – it discards the amoral project of progress and embraces a moral project of civil renewal based on empowerment with responsibilities. This is not a reformulation of Burkean conservatism, it is a human response to large groups of people that change has progressively rendered mute.

In the context of a rapidly de-secularising world,[59] Blue Labour offers the opportunity for people of religion (many of whom are also poor) to be better recognised and represented. This reconnection to Labour's historic roots[60] is essential for the realisation of the hitherto elusive, authentically plural public square that our political classes feign to desire. It directly challenges the alienating atheism of liberal elites:

Contemporary atheism is a Christian heresy that differs from earlier heresies chiefly in its intellectual crudity [...] The Chief

significance of evangelical atheism is in demonstrating the
unreality of secularisation [...] for it is defined by what it
excludes [...] Those who demand that religion be exorcised
from politics thinks this can be achieved by excluding
traditional faiths from public institutions; but secular creeds
are formed from religious concepts, and suppressing religion
does not mean it ceases to control thinking and behaviour. Like
suppressed sexual desire, faith returns, often in grotesque
forms, to govern the lives of those who deny it.[61]

This 'grotesque governing' entails the proliferation of experts to
deliver progress. Progress proposes or imposes solutions to social
problems primarily or exclusively through politics and technocratic
elites. Such a Hegelian approach, whereby charity is subsumed by law,
inevitably empties society and fills the state with authority,
responsibility and action. All the evidence suggests that this
command and control social engineering simply does not work. In
reality, people need to feel that they have something valuable to
contribute, and their stories need to be relayed from the micro to the
macro through politics. This used to be what the Labour Party did –
indeed it was why it was created.

On the left, and in the Labour Party, the presence of Christian
Socialism has traditionally provided a valuable buffer to the secularist
politics of paradise.[62] Today, it has a new and exciting role to play in
the process of reconnecting politics to people. As Blue Labour
compels the party to take more seriously its relationships with
different communities across the nation, it will allow for a much-
needed reinvigoration of thinking (and membership) in local and
national politics. Indeed, by drawing upon the Christianly inspired
ideas about human dignity, community, hospitality, cooperation and
solidarity, and in seeking a more inclusive future for people of religion
in politics, Blue Labour offers a salient alternative to the culture war
scenario that liberalism has been fuelling.

Eschewing the primacy of both the state and the market, it is about
strengthening the associational bonds that provide collective
identities in the space between the state and the family. It is also
about recognising the indispensable role that marriage and family life
play in providing the raw material or social capital necessary for
renewing civil society. This is because it accepts Alexis de
Tocqueville's analysis that civil society cannot be instituted by legal

diktat. It requires civility – and as the primary socialiser, the family is critical for its cultivation. Consequently, at the heart of Blue Labour is a restoration of family life. This is particularly important in relation to the normative familial structures and processes that those living in disadvantaged communities rely upon daily for security, identity and purpose. It is a long overdue riposte to the progressive devastation that John Stuart Mill's 'experiments in living' have visited upon family life.

If the errors of progressivism have taught us anything, it is that a silver bullet solution in politics does not exist. In the debates generated by the Blue Labour motif, for the first time in many years there are opportunities to reconnect politics with people who need a voice. This is an exciting and quite daunting prospect for the left and the Labour Party. But seizing the day involves accepting a number of key truths.

We need to accept that there are serious problems with progress, and that we should be careful to qualify what we mean when we use the term. We should accept the sociologist Faguet's unsensational doctrine that in certain directions improvements and ameliorations are possible,[63] but be mindful of the fact that we can surely lose whatever we think we have gained. We should accept that the idols of the state and the market have thoroughly failed us, and that the renewal of civil society is an urgent priority. We should accept that enlightened self-interest and expediency are insufficient as drivers for political economy, and that the neo-conservative right is incapable of addressing the problems that beset poor communities. We should accept that social and economic neo-liberalism has decimated the lives of people who lacked the means to 'get on' or progress, and that liberalism-cum-relativism is offensive to centre-left politics.

We should accept that radicalism has become a dangerous euphemism for elite control through perpetual, disorienting change, and that working people have traditions that they can be proud of and can build communities on. Moving from social contract to social covenant, we should accept that an idea of a common good which is primarily, but not exclusively, informed by religious ethics is an essential prerequisite for helping the poor.

And as the left seeks to recover from its ideological illness, we should also accept that the last thing we want to hear are the words: 'It's progressive'.

Blue Labour

NOTES

1. Anthony Giddens, *The Progressive Manifesto* (London: Polity Press, 2003).
2. David McLellan, 'A Catholic basis for socialism', in *Restoring Faith in Politics* (London: CSM Press, 1996), p. 45.
3. The popular analysis of Owen Jones, *Chavs: The Demonization of the Working Class* (London, Verso, 2011) provides some good insights into the persistence of class as an issue and the shifting identities of the much-maligned 'emerging underclass'. However, it does disservice to the ideal (and the reality) of working-class identity as a moral construct by basing much of the analysis on the liberal presuppositions that undermined it in the first place – and that continue to undermine it today.
4. See Luke Bretherton, 'Shopping with violence: riots and the responsible society'. Available at http://www.fulcrum-anglican.org.uk/page.cfm?ID=654 (accessed on 25 August 2014).
5. For an understanding of the philosophical roots of this new public 'non-ethic' in the West, see Gertrude Himmelfarb, *The De-Moralisation of Society: From Victorian Virtues to Modern Values* (New York: Knopf, 1994).
6. Paul Richards, 'Is "progressive" a meaningless term?', LabourList, 5 July 2012. Available at http://labourlist.org/2012/07/is-progressive-a-meaningless-term/ (accessed on 25 August 2014).
7. Sydney Pollard, *The Idea of Progress: History and Society* (London: C. A. Watts, 1968), p. 90, quoted in R. Wright, *A Short History of Progress* (Edinburgh: Canongate Books, 2005).
8. Wright, *A Short History of Progress*, p. 4.
9. *Ibid.*
10. See John Gray, *Black Mass: Apocalyptic Religion and the Death of Utopia* (London: Allen Lane, 2007).
11. See 'Onwards and upwards: why is the modern view of progress so impoverished?', *The Economist*, 17 December 2009. Available at http://www.economist.com/node/15108593 (accessed on 25 August 2014).
12. *Ibid.*
13. Gray, *Black Mass*, p. 3.
14. Victor S. Yarros, 'Human progress: the idea and the reality', *American Journal of Sociology* 21 (July 1915), pp. 15–29.
15. Alister McGrath, *The Twilight of Atheism: The Rise and Fall of Disbelief in the Modern World* (London: Random House, 2004).
16. Gray, *Black Mass*, p. 41.
17. John Gray, *Heresies: Against Progress and Other Illusions* (London: Granta, 2004), p. 44.

18. See Michael Burleigh, *Earthly Powers: The Conflict between Religion and Politics from the French Revolution to the Great War* (London: Harper Perennial, 2006).

19. Gray, *Black Mass*, p. 17.

20. Gray, *Heresies*.

21. In our own day it is North Korea that describes itself as the most progressive country on earth.

22. F. A. Voight, *Unto Caesar* (London: Constable, 1938), pp. 49–50, re-quoted in Gray, *Black Mass*, p. 65.

23. Gray, *Heresies*, p. 2.

24. This includes seemingly democratic fascisms. See J. Goldberg, *Liberal Fascism: The Secret History of the Left from Mussolini to the Politics of Meaning* (New York: Penguin, 2009).

25. Adam Smith, *The Wealth of Nations* (New York: Random House, 1937), p. 326.

26. The relationship between the idea of progress and the Marxist dialectic are historically and philosophically obvious. Indeed, they are complementary and inseparable, and vastly more could be written about the relationship than this essay allows.

27. Gray, *Black Mass*, p. 75.

28. Gray, *Heresies*, p. 19.

29. See Bob Goudzwaard, *Idols of our Time* (Nottingham: Inter Varsity Press, 1994).

30. Michael Freeden, 'Eugenics and progressive thought: a study in ideological affinity', *The Historical Journal* 22 (September 1979), pp. 645–71.

31. Wright, *A Short History of Progress*, p. 7.

32. Francis Fukuyama, *Our Posthuman Future: Consequences of the Biotechnology Revolution* (London: Picador, 2003).

33. As David Bowie has observed, 'The humanists' replacement for religion: work really hard and somehow you'll either save yourself or you'll be immoral. Of course that's a total joke, and our progress is nothing. There may be progress in technology but there's no ethical progress whatsoever'.

34. John Locke, *The Reasonableness of Christianity*.

35. See Tony Blair, *New Britain: My Vision for A Young Country* (London: Fourth Estate, 1996); Neil Fairclough, *New Labour, New Language?* (London: Routledge, 2000); and Mike Powell (ed.), *New Labour, New Welfare State?* (Bristol: Policy Press, 1999).

36. Tobias Jones, *Utopian Dreams: In Search of A Good Life* (London: Faber & Faber, 2007), p. 123.

37. See Paul Richards, 'The permanent revolution of New Labour', in A. Coddington and M. Perryman (eds), *The Moderniser's Dilemma:*

Radical Politics in the Age of Blair (London: Lawrence & Wishart, 1998), pp. 32–46 and also Alan Finlayson, 'Forward not back: the Labour Party manifesto', *Renewal* 13, 2/3 (2005).

38. An excerpt from the Liverpool John Moores University lecture, 'Robert Tressell – The ragged trousered philanthropist' given by Jon Cruddas MP on Thursday 3 March 2011.
39. As Simone Weil noted: 'Nothing can have as its destination anything other than its origin. The contrary idea, the idea of progress, is poison'.
40. Jones, *Utopian Dreams*, p. 131.
41. Pope Benedict XVI (when Cardinal Ratzinger).
42. Jones, *Utopian Dreams*, p. 48.
43. After all, if progress is assured, and automatic, why suffer, toil or make sacrifices?
44. Gray, *Heresies*, p. 206.
45. See Robert Nozick, *Anarchy, State and Utopia* (New York: Basic Books, 1977).
46. This is in reference to the oft-deployed and now largely emptied term 'social justice' – which has been contorted beyond recognition from its original Rawlsian conception. The libertarian co-optation of the term by neo-liberals and neo-conservatives is also far removed from the often valuable work of the Centre for Social Justice – which if anything provides a helpful 'Red Tory' check on the Darwinian inclinations of many on the right.
47. This is with the notable exception of the majoritarian faux tribalism of popular culture in which all things important are rendered trivial and all things trivial are rendered important. Here, despite the pretensions of social solidarity all that matters is the consumption of entertainment.
48. All of which denies legitimate expressions of patriotism, and allows for the emergence of forms of reactionary nationalism such as the British National Party and the English Defence League.
49. This is liberalism that conforms to the view of Strauss and Heidegger, in as much as it is divorced from virtue and results in nihilism – which in turn undermines liberalism itself. Ultimately, the purest expression of this modern nihilism is Nietzsche's cult of the will.
50. See Roger Scruton, *The Uses of Pessimism and the Danger of False Hope* (London: Atlantic Books, 2010), ch. 8 – 'The Aggregation Fallacy'.
51. Zygmunt Bauman, in D. Smith, *Zygmunt Bauman: Prophet of Postmodernity* (Cambridge: Polity Press, 1999), p. 193.
52. An excerpt of the poetry of John Dominic Crossen, quoted in B. Walsh and R. Middleton, *Truth is Stranger Than it Used to be: Biblical Faith in a Post-modern Age* (London: SPCK, 1995).
53. See Anthony Giddens, *Where Now for New Labour?* (Cambridge: Polity Press, 2002).

54. See Emily Robinson, 'What's new about Clegg's "new progressivism"?'. Available at http://www.historyandpolicy.org/opinion/opinion_59.html (accessed on 25 August 2014).

55. See the survey conducted and produced on behalf of the Centre for British Politics. Available at http://d25d2506sfb94s.cloudfront.net/ cumulus_uploads/document/c5fsvqgba9/ progressive_conference_sendout_WithResults_HT.pdf (accessed on 25 August 2014).

56. See Deborah Orr, 'The monumental collapse of the left', *The Guardian*, 17 September 2009.

57. For an excellent review of the confusion that now characterises the left see Nick Cohen, *What's Left: How Liberals Lost their Way* (London: Fourth Estate, 2007).

58. See David Goodhart, 'Last hope for the left', *Prospect*, 19 March 2012.

59. John Micklethwait and Adrian Wooldridge, *God is Back: How the Global Rise of Faith is Changing the World* (London: Allen Lane, 2009).

60. See Paul Bickley, *Rebuilding Jerusalem? Christianity and the Labour Party* (Swindon: Bible Society, 2010).

61. Gray, *Black Mass*, pp. 189–190.

62. See Frank Field, *The Politics of Paradise* (London: Fount, 1987).

63. See Emile Faguet, *The Cult of Incompetence*, Classic Reprint (Charleston: Forgotten Books, 2012).

CHAPTER TWELVE

Meaningful Work: A Philosophy of Work and a Politics of Meaningfulness[1]

Ruth Yeoman

THE PROBLEM OF MEANINGLESSNESS

One consequence of the present economic crisis has been to heighten anxiety that we lack a social bond resilient enough to secure the trust between groups and individuals upon which the long-term stability of our political and economic institutions depends. Yet at the same time as we mourn the weakening of traditional sources of solidarity, such as community, religion and family, we fail to appreciate a fountainhead of everyday interactions involving at least 70 per cent of the population – that of the work we do together to sustain a system of social cooperation. Such neglect is short-sighted because, in work, we are required to relate to one another across lines of difference in order to maintain the social and technical complex upon which we all depend for our survival and flourishing. Through acting together to get the work done we form understandings of self and others, in the process forging social bonds which spill over into other areas of life. In other words, when we work together, we make meanings and create values in order to make sense of the world, and of our place within it. Because cohesive social bonds are created and sustained through collective meaning-making, then how we make meanings, and what we do with them, is not simply of interest because it is a dimension of personal psychological development: it is also, and vitally, of *public* interest. Positive values in work, such as usefulness, contributing, providing or achieving, are goods we share, because each one of us draws upon them to construct practical identities which give our lives a sense of purpose and meaning.[2]

Conversely, negative values which foster a sense of meaninglessness generate social ills, such as physical and mental ill-health, increased risk of poverty, stunted life trajectories and social unrest. Because these social ills affect us all, then what happens inside the experience of work is of public concern, transcending neo-liberal claims that all we need to be worried about with respect to a just organisation of work is to guarantee the personal freedom to choose one's occupation, to create fair competition for the scarce resource of good-quality jobs, or to alleviate unemployment by providing any kind of job, no matter how precarious or exploitative. Instead, proper public concern for how people experience their work will pay attention to the ways in which the content and quality of work enriches or impoverishes the common stock of positive meanings and values, and, specifically, will seek to enable everyone to develop their meaning-making capabilities through meaningful work, organised by a system of workplace democracy. This essay concludes that themes of Blue Labour – community, solidarity and mutual interdependence – provide a particularly productive intellectual space for reflecting upon the character of work, and for generating a distinctive politics of meaningful work through the institution of workplace democracy.

THE MEANING POTENTIAL OF ALL WORK

All work, even the most unpromising, contains positive meanings and values. These meanings, however, are not given automatically: instead, they arise out of interrelations between self, others and the material world.[3] As we interact with people and things in order to get the work done, then we find ourselves struggling with resistances and differences – struggles which give rise to new understandings of the work we do, and of the people we do it with and for. For example, a study of hospital cleaners found that, despite the low social valuation of their work, some cleaners sought to positively revalue their work as skilled and worthwhile by actively engaging in tasks which supported patient recovery, including interacting with patients, visitors and nurses.[4]

But in power-laden hierarchies where the organisation of work is seen as a management prerogative, such differing interpretations of meaning and value often remain as pre-political potentials, unless they are brought into public evaluation through democratic deliberation. When interpretive differences become subject to public evaluation and judgement through a system of workplace democracy in which workers are co-decision-makers, then they have the potential to generate a public resource of positive values, from which we can draw to create meaningful self-identities. Thus, the organisation of work is an important political project because, not only do we make work, but to the extent that we diminish or enhance work as a source of positive values, work makes us, giving narrative shape to our lives by grounding our identities and forming our capabilities.

The creation and promotion of meanings in work, however, is riven by the uses and abuses of power; in other words, work is replete with politics and difficult choices, demanding that we *work out* what justice demands with respect to what kind of work is made available to whom, how it is to be organised, and how we are to determine what it means to us. Therefore, deliberative engagement with interpretive differences requires a politics of meaningfulness, instituted by a system of workplace democracy, where economic citizenship is rooted not only in paid employment, but in all the work – paid and unpaid – we do together to sustain a complex system of social cooperation.

POLITICAL NEGLECT OF THE ORGANISATION AND CONTENT OF WORK

Serious political attention to the organisation of work is lacking. One reason for this neglect is the peculiarly ambivalent position which work occupies in advanced post-industrial societies – simultaneously valued for providing the means for self-realisation and disvalued for being burdensome and compulsory. Work is either a source of expressive human action, one of 'the hopes of civilisation',[5] fulfilled in a correctly ordered society which enables all persons to do decent, humane and dignified work; or it is an experience of oppressive degradation, from which we must escape, since the worker deprived of worthwhile activities 'generally becomes as stupid and ignorant as it is possible for a human creature to become',[6] resulting in him or her becoming 'a crippled monstrosity'.[7] Even though our survival, and our capacity to flourish, depends upon our being able to work together, the work itself often fails to meet vital human aspirations for expressive self-determination, non-dominated relations to others and stable identities.

But although changes in the nature and organisation of work appear to have diminished work as a site of worthwhile human action, the meaning of work as compulsion has not entirely crowded out the meaning of work as free, expressive and creative action.[8] The ideal of meaningful work, of activity which aims at worthwhile purposes, uses the full range of a person's distinctive capabilities, and commands our emotional engagement retains a strong hold upon our imagination, motivating us to seek work which adds to the personal meaning of our lives – and even to aspire to a society transformed by each person being able to do work which he or she finds to be worth doing. And no work is so objectively degraded that it cannot be revitalised through forms of democratic participation in meaning-making with others.

Another reason for political neglect is the assumption that work is best organised by management experts, according to technical reasoning which needs no deliberative evaluation. Or, in other words, the political has no place in the economic. But the work we do together is a social institution, which we can arrange either to enable or disable a person's capabilities for meaning-making; capabilities which we need to create and sustain the stock of positive values from which we forge a sense that our lives have meaning. Kovacs describes work as 'a basic mode of being in the world', where 'to work means to humanise the world and to produce something'.[9] In this sense, work is a site of human action which produces values and meanings beyond the realm of its economic productivity. It is a mode of being in the world which exceeds the employment relation to include all the activities which contribute to producing and reproducing a complex system of social cooperation.

But, if work is to humanise the world, it must at the same time humanise the one through whom the work takes place; in Morris' terms: 'Nothing should be made by man's labour which is not worth doing; or which must be made by labour degrading to the makers'.[10] Work cannot be meaningful if it requires the enslavement of the worker, the deformation of her human capabilities, or the misrecognition of her vital commitments. This means that some work is morally desirable, and some work is not, requiring that the improvement of individuals and of society depends upon work having a certain interior content, given by the structure of meaningfulness. And we should seek to give to all work the structure for meaningfulness, because being able to experience our lives as meaningful – that is, containing worthwhile purposes and projects which are able to command our emotional attachment – is a fundamental human need which, in contemporary societies, is very difficult to realise if our work lacks the requisite structure.

THE FUNDAMENTAL HUMAN NEED FOR MEANINGFULNESS

Engaging with positive meaning by creating, nurturing and promoting the values embodied in worthy objects such as persons, animals, material things or institutions is something we all do: indeed, we *must* do, if we are to be human.[11] Frankl identified the 'will to meaning' to be a fundamental human drive, compelling us to engage in a search for the positive values which give us a sense that our lives are worth living.[12] For Holbrook, the harms of a frustrated will to meaning, manifested in dysfunctions such as compulsive consumerism, are of such public concern that he proposes a fundamental question for politics: 'what opportunities do societies provide for the satisfaction of the human need for meaning, and how should societies be organised in order to provide those opportunities?'[13]

This question is directly relevant to the sphere of working. When we work, we are not motivated purely by external goods, such as pay or profit – we act also out of a fundamental need for living a worthwhile life. In the absence of a politics of meaningfulness, people will seek some outlet for their frustrated will to meaning; for example, denied the experience of autonomy, workers will invent simulations of self-determination in the form of games, or even make deliberate mistakes, which Burawoy describes as the art of 'making out'.[14] Amongst numerous testimonies to such practices, is that of the worker who said: 'Yes, I want my signature on 'em too. Sometimes, out of pure meanness, when I make something, I put a little dent in it. I like to do something to make it really unique. Hit it with a hammer. I deliberately [...] it up to see if it'll get by, just so I can say I did it'.[15] In a liberal democratic society, the need for expressive self-determination ought to be satisfied in a politics of meaningfulness which seeks to ensure that people are not prevented from experiencing their lives as meaningful because of the work they do. Having an equal share of decision-making power, instituted by a system of workplace democracy, not only supports the emergence of such a politics, but is part of what realises the meaningfulness potential of work.

Whilst it is necessary for us to make a living, it is needful also for us to satisfy our interests in having something worthwhile to do which is constituted by the goods of autonomy, freedom and social recognition. The importance of such goods for shaping a person's life as a whole makes meaningful work a fundamental human need; that is, a need which is not to be met in any way whatsoever, but in a manner consistent with the kinds of creatures we are – beings who have unavoidable interests in being able to express free, autonomous action in association with others. Providing a person with any kind of work which simply sustains human existence is not sufficient for satisfying the need for meaningful work, since a person who has become inured to non-meaningful work will still have inescapable interests in the goods of autonomy, freedom and social recognition, and therefore possess an unmet need for meaningful work. A study of mid-life Australians suggests, for example, that poor-quality work involving job strain and insecurity may be as bad for health outcomes as unemployment,[16] and evidence from the Whitehall Studies links poor health outcomes for civil servants with low control over their work.[17]

Furthermore, poor-quality, non-meaningful work impacts a person's sense of self-worth and self-efficacy, damaging their sense that they have a life of their own to live, which is not subject to the arbitrary control of others. Simone Weil in her philosophical reflections upon factory work suggests that some work is subject to such arbitrary relations of power between managers and workers that, in order to protect themself from the harms of domination, the worker will avoid imagining the possibility of personal change and development; their 'thought draws back from the future' so that 'this perpetual recoil upon the present produces a kind of brutish stupor'.[18] In such a condition, a person is unable to plan for the future; their capabilities for meaning-making are stunted, therefore radically reducing their chances of being able to find positive values in their work which can form the basis of a stable self-identity.

In no small way the work we do determines 'the distribution of lives':[19] work provides access to the roles, practices and social institutions of society which allocate resources for the development of the capabilities we require to secure our social position and economic participation over the course of life. Furthermore, such social structures embody the values we can potentially incorporate into our practical identities, grounding the sense that our lives have meaning. This makes being able to experience work with the relevant structure for meaningfulness of such importance that it is a fundamental human need, requiring the organisation of society to eliminate non-meaningful work from the work of social cooperation. Meaningful work has always been available to the few who occupy social roles allowing them to exercise complex capabilities, such as expressive freedom and personal autonomy, through activities which aim at a worthwhile purpose and affective engagement. But a just social order will be concerned to mitigate the harms of an uneven distribution of meaningfulness in work, and will seek to ensure that all work provides for the development and exercise of complex capabilities.[20] This does not imply that society must be organised so that each person can access an elite ideal of exceptional meaning, or even that the state should guarantee that all persons actually find their work to be meaningful, but suggests instead the more modest and practical aim that everyday work is structured to ensure that it contains objects which are worth pursuing, and is organised to develop our human capabilities for meaning-making with others by instituting democratic practices in work.

DESCRIBING THE VALUE OF MEANINGFULNESS

Meaningfulness is not anything we want it to be: not any activity or attachment is meaningful just because it makes us happy, or even if it fulfils a duty. Moral philosopher Susan Wolf specifies a value of meaningfulness distinct from welfare and universal duty, where meaningfulness is 'a category of value that is not reducible to happiness or morality, and that is realised by loving objects worthy of love and engaging with them in a positive way'.[21] For Wolf, the value of meaningfulness is described by bringing together subjectivity and objectivity into a 'bipartite value' of meaningfulness in which 'meaning arises when subjective attraction meets objective attractiveness'.[22]

Such an experience of meaningfulness is more likely to occur when a person becomes connected to a worthy object – something or someone of value – such that they are actively 'gripped, excited, involved by it'.[23] Thus, meaningfulness consists of uniting objectivity and subjectivity in activities which contain worthy objects we can publicly agree have positive value, and which enable emotional attachments signalling our personal endorsement of their importance in our lives. In this way, the bipartite value of meaningfulness explains the special ties we feel towards our 'ground projects'[24] – projects which help us to answer the question, 'what reasons do we have for living?'[25] And it is this interior structure at which a politics of meaningfulness in work should aim.

For a person to experience the bipartite value of meaningfulness, their work must be structured to enable objectively attractive values to be actively incorporated, via subjective attachment, into their practical identity, or their self-conception of what makes their life worth living. This is a process in which we already participate on a daily basis, since it is in ordinary human living that the need for meaning is satisfied: 'Life ultimately means taking the responsibility to find the right answer to its problems and to fulfil the tasks which it constantly sets for each individual'.[26] As we grapple with the everyday tasks of living, then, as far as our situation allows, we develop capabilities for meaning-making, and participate with others in creating, promoting and appreciating positive values. These capabilities are more securely developed in contexts of autonomy, freedom and social recognition – and a system of workplace democracy is an especially fruitful context because such a system establishes our equal status as co-authorities in the public creation and maintenance of values.

But being responsive to, and engaging with, the particular value of worthy objects does not mean that we can have any kind of orientation we want towards them, just in case such orientations generate strong affective attachments. What is required also is that our appropriation of worthy objects to the meaning content of our lives gives rise to *legitimate* involvement, where legitimacy means promoting the *good for* the worthy objects; in other words, that we have a care for how well they are doing. This suggests that an ethic of care, not technical-economic reasoning, forms the standard against which we judge the good for worthy objects, and therefore the quality of our actions towards those objects.

EXPERIENCING THE VALUE OF MEANINGFULNESS AND AN ETHIC OF CARE

Since meaningfulness is not anything we want it to be, nor is it any kind of action with respect to others which satisfies our preferences or increases our personal utility, then an ethic of care provides a standpoint from which to evaluate our actions towards worthy objects. Fisher and Tronto define taking care as including 'everything that we do to maintain, continue and repair our world, so that we can live in it as well as possible'.[27] Caring for something implies taking up responsibilities to secure the good for the object of our caring activities. The numerous social roles which make up the work of social cooperation are a source of active relations to worthy objects which present us with innumerable opportunities to take up responsibilities, and thus to learn to become practitioners of caring. Being able to fulfil our responsibilities is closely tied to our membership of practices and institutions, and the social roles we inhabit. And discharging our responsibilities requires a 'proneness', or a readiness to have our actions guided by reasons of love, which ensures that we are 'acting in a way that positively engages with a worthy object of love [...] even if it does not maximally promote either the agent's welfare or the good of the world, impartially assessed'.[28]

Becoming susceptible to reasons of love means putting ourselves into an active relationship with objects of value, where we develop the capabilities for recognising what is of value and for acting appropriately towards worthy objects. Held distinguishes an ethics of care from an ethics of justice in what is morally relevant for 'attending to and meeting the needs of the particular others for whom we take responsibility'.[29] For Held, care is both a value and a practice, where care is a *practice* because it involves 'the work of care-giving and the standards by which the practices of care can be evaluated'.[30] Held points out that activities can be performed without adhering to the values relevant to the practice: 'An activity must be purposive to count as work or labor, but it need not incorporate any values, even efficiency, in the doing of it. Chopping at a tree, however clumsily, to fell it, could be work'.[31] The implication of Held's observation is that positive values are realised not in just any kind of work, but in work of specific character: that is, meaningful work in which practising care towards worthy objects enables the practitioner to experience the goods of autonomy, freedom and social recognition.

Thus, being able to ascribe the positive values inherent in social roles, practices and institutions to the meaningfulness of our lives depends upon our accepting the relevant responsibilities, where consenting to take on responsibilities for worthy objects often requires us to expend discretionary, as well as remunerated, time and effort. Each day, people willingly take up responsibilities in the work they do: cleaners, call centre operatives and carers (to name but a few vital occupations) clean, make calls, and care for the sick and elderly – and they do not take up these responsibilities simply because they are paid to do so, but because they want to do good work. Indeed, many seek to extend their roles, excavating positive meanings from their work, meanings which motivate them to expend discretionary effort in order to meet the needs of fellow human beings.

It is, of course, possible for people to train, to take up responsibilities, and to engage in complex, cooperative activities without those activities having the relevant structure for meaningfulness, but this is to instrumentalise people with no regard for their fundamental human need for meaning. One of the injustices of the modern organisation of work is the way in which organisations aim to increase workers' responsibilities, without a commensurate increase in control over the resources and decision-making necessary to fulfil their responsibilities.[32] Frequently, work is organised to extract discretionary effort from workers to the benefit of organisations, and fails to address normative concerns for asymmetrical power relations which exploit effort without instituting voice as co-decision. And whilst the responsibility/control gap does not eliminate all positive meanings from those activities, it does severely inhibit a person's ability to engage with others in meaning-making, and to find those positive meanings affectively attractive.

Work incorporating positive values of care is meaningful work, and is susceptible to being evaluated against an ethic of care when we ask what constitutes caring in relation to the particular worthy objects at which the actions aim. This is a profoundly political question, because what we mean by good care involves disagreement, deliberation and judgement, demanding an ethico-political understanding of care as the basis for deliberating over the values and standards necessary to the work we do together. Developing such an understanding requires the practice of 'democratic caring'[33] in which all citizens have access to structures of social belonging allowing them to make their contribution to the work of social cooperation, and to participate in the interpretation of values inherent to their work. Tronto, for example, argues that 'creating caring institutions' is an unavoidably political process requiring us to evaluate power relations, to ensure that care remains both particular to the worthy objects at which our actions aim and pluralist in the range of caring values, and to ensure 'care has a clear, legitimate purpose'.[34]

To enable us to orientate ourselves to the needs of worthy objects, caring institutions must provide public space for needs-interpretation, in which both workers and the cared-for can engage with values, finding them worthy or unworthy, attractive or unattractive, as they seek to satisfy the human need for meaningfulness. This requires democratic deliberation, and in the work of social cooperation, a system of workplace democracy sufficiently extensive to institute a politics of meaningfulness which allows for public evaluation of the values upon which we draw to give our lives purpose and meaning. Furthermore, it implies a public policy suite designed to secure meaningful work for all, including: a good work index; a guarantee of individual capability development through institutional belonging; a framework establishing direct and representative employee voice, which includes the collective voice of union representation; an equal playing field for different organisational forms, such as mutuals, cooperatives and employee-owned enterprises – and a general dismantling of hierarchies or networks which foster the arbitrary use of power through non-democratic authority.

BLUE LABOUR AND A NEW POLITICS OF MEANINGFULNESS

If the Labour movement is about anything, then it is about the lives of ordinary people, their experiences of working and of not working, and of how those experiences shape their practical identities. Specifically, Blue Labour is about designing the political, social and economic institutions which allow for expressive modes of being beyond the commodification of the self, and the expropriation of human capabilities to a rent-seeking financial elite. One route to realising the values of Blue Labour is to revive and enrich the public good of meaningfulness, by enabling everyone to engage in the co-production of our common stock of positive values. The themes of Blue Labour are particularly valuable in this endeavour because, in the political economy of Blue Labour, the individual is not cast out to create meaning alone, but neither is she subsumed into pre-given meanings; instead, the individual, as an equal co-authority, is interrelated to others through the co-creation of positive values.

This requires the establishment of a deliberative society, including widespread workplace democracy, in order to draw people into meaningful encounter across social and economic divisions. Mary Parker Follett characterised the process of group decision-making as 'the inner workshop of democracy',[35] because it is in the direct experience of deliberating with others that we form the virtues, attitudes and habits of citizenship. Thus, the promise of a Blue Labour political economy is that citizenship becomes grounded in the joining of personal meaning-making to public deliberation, supported by an economic architecture in which structures of ownership and control provide everyone with a share of decision-making power.

In sum, the concept of meaningful work deserves wider intellectual and political attention. Although we are now exhorted to find satisfaction and self-fulfilment in consumption, Morris' call for dignified and humane labour retains a toehold in our imaginings of what a flourishing human life ought to look like. Indeed, Morris' comment upon the purchase of goods, 'Tis the lives of men you buy',[36] indicates how we might link the moral and political dimensions of consumption and production.

This is because if we acquire goods from the oppressions of others then we compromise the possibilities for our own life – if one life can be made vulnerable because of the work he or she does, then so can the life of any man or woman. Consumers can be satisfied even where producers are exploited, alienated or otherwise harmed, but consumers are also producers with interests in not being exploited, alienated, or subjected to undignified work. This provides us with common cause in ensuring that all work is meaningful work, constituted by the goods of autonomy, freedom and social recognition, thereby increasing the likelihood of it being the source of social bonds essential to stitching together the institutional fabric upon which we all depend.

NOTES

1. Ruth Yeoman, *Meaningful Work and Workplace Democracy: A Philosophy of Work and a Politics of Meaningfulness* (New York and Basingstoke, UK: Palgrave Macmillan, 2014).
2. B. Roessler, 'Meaningful work: arguments from autonomy', *Journal of Political Philosophy* 20 (2012), pp. 71–93. See C. Korsegaard,

Self-Constitution: Agency, Identity and Integrity (Oxford: Oxford University Press, 2009).

3. C. Dejours, 'Subjectivity, work and action', *Critical Horizons* 7 (2006), pp. 45–62.

4. A. Wrzesniewski and J. Dutton, 'Crafting a job: revisioning employees as active crafters of their work', *Academy of Management Review* 26 (2001), pp. 179–201.

5. William Morris, *News From Nowhere and Other Writings* (London: Penguin Books, 1993).

6. Adam Smith, *The Wealth of Nations* (London: Penguin Books, 1999 [1776]).

7. K. Marx, 'Capital, vol. 1: the process of production of capital', in *The Marx-Engels Reader*, ed. R. Tucker (New York & London: W. W. Norton & Company, 1978).

8. See D. A. Spencer, 'The 'Work as Bad' Thesis in Economics: Origins, Evolution, and Challenges', *Labor History* 50 (2009), pp. 39–57.

9. G. Kovacs, 'Phenomenology of work and self-transcendence', *The Journal of Value Inquiry* 20 (1986), pp. 195–207, quote at p. 198.

10. W. Morris, *Art and Socialism* (1884).

11. Ruth Yeoman, 'Conceptualising meaningful work as a fundamental human need', *Journal of Business Ethics* 125/2 (2014), pp. 235–51.

12. V. Frankl, *The Will to Meaning* (New American Library: New York, 1988).

13. D. Holbrook, 'Politics and the need for meaning', in R. Fitzgerald (ed.), *Human Needs and Politics* (Oxford: Pergamon Press, 1977).

14. M. Burawoy, *Manufacturing Consent: Changes in the Labor Process under Monopoly Capitalism* (London: University of Chicago Press, 1979).

15. See S. Terkel, *Working* (Wildwood House: London, 1975), p. 22.

16. D. H. Broom, R. M. D'Souza, L. Strazdius, P. Butterworth, P. Paslow, B. Rodgers, 'The lesser evil: bad jobs or unemployment? A survey of mid-aged Australians', *Social Sciences & Medicine* 63 (2006), pp. 575–86.

17. H. Bosma, M. G. Marmot, H. Hemingway, A. C. Nicholson, E. Brunner, S. Stansfeld, 'Low Job Control and Risk of Coronary Heart Disease in Whitehall II (Prospective Cohort) Study', *British Medical Journal* (1997), p. 314.

18. S. Weil, 'Factory work', in G. A. Panichas (ed.), *The Simone Weil Reader* (New York: David McKay Company, 1997), p. 57.

19. M. Walzer, *Thick and Thin* (Paris: University of Notre Dame Press, 1994).

20. Cf. P. Gomberg, *How to Make Opportunity Equal: Race and Contributive Justice* (Malden, MA: Blackwell Publishing, 2007).

21. S. Wolf, *Meaning in Life and Why It Matters* (Princeton, NJ: Princeton University Press, 2010), p. 13.
22. Wolf, *Meaning in Life and Why It Matters*, p. 9.
23. *Ibid.*
24. Bernard Williams, *Persons, Character and Morality*, in B. Williams (ed.), *Moral Luck* (Cambridge: Cambridge University Press, 1981).
25. Wolf, *Meaning in Life and Why It Matters*, p. 56.
26. V. E. Frankl, *Man's Search for Meaning* (New York: Washington Square Press, 1984), p. 98.
27. B. Fisher and J. Tronto, 'Toward a feminist theory of caring', in E. K. Abel and M. K. Nelson (eds), *Circles of Care: Work and Identity in Women's Lives* (Albany: State University of New York Press, 1990), p. 40.
28. Fisher and Tronto, 'Toward a feminist theory of caring', p. 33.
29. V. Held, *The Ethics of Care: Personal, Political and Global* (Oxford: Oxford University Press, 2006), p. 10.
30. *Ibid.*, p. 36.
31. *Ibid.*, p. 37.
32. F. D. Pot and E. Koningsveld, 'Quality of Working Life and Organizational Performance – Two Sides of the Same Coin?', *Scandinavian Journal of Work and Environmental Health* (2009). Available at http://www.rower-eu.eu:8080/rower/conferences/1stWorkshop/pot.pdf (accessed on 25 August 2014).
33. S. Sevenhuijsen, 'Caring in the Third Way: the relation between obligation, responsibility and care in Third Way discourse', *Critical Social Policy* 20 (2000), pp. 5–37, at p. 22.
34. J. Tronto, 'Creating caring institutions: politics, plurality, and purpose', *Ethics and Social Welfare* 4 (2010), pp. 158–71, at p. 162.
35. M. P. Follett, *The New State: Group Organization the Solution of Popular Government* (Pennsylvania: The Pennsylvania State University Press, 1998).
36. W. Morris, *Art and Socialism* (1884).

PART FIVE

LABOUR'S RADICAL 'CONSERVATISM'

CHAPTER THIRTEEN

Labour's 'Conservative' Tradition[1]

Rowenna Davis

INTRODUCTION

Our country is conservative, and that is beautiful. Beyond Westminster and Victoria Street, the British people have a desire for order, strength, stability and community. People feel shaken by the downturn, and they are silently haunted by the perceived inevitability of national decline. They feel let down by the state, and humiliated by unemployment. Rows of terraced houses and tower blocks crave meaning, and fear a loss of identity. Managerialism doesn't speak to them. Human rights legislation doesn't feel like it belongs to them. People crave the products of the market, but hate the debt, doubt and disappointment that it breeds. As a country we've confused aspiration with consumerism and we loathe ourselves for it. We don't just regret that we could be better; we suffer a burning anger that we should be.

Ed Miliband is beginning to get this, but 'conservative' is not a word that our party likes. The word of the opposition, it makes us feel threatened. It is an unsettling word for a party that profited from a socially and economically liberal sense of progress in the heady 1990s. Tradition has become associated with a lack of reason, with an oppression that holds back rather than a source of radicalism that inspires new direction. We fear conservatism as a roadblock against women, diversity, liberty and internationalism. It pricks our anxieties about immigration and crime. We see it as a politics of polls that abandons conviction to the swing voter. It is associated with selling out.

It would be complacent to deny that liberalism has given this country huge benefits. It has helped us challenge domestic violence, homophobia, racism. As a feminist, I have personally gained from liberalism and I'm under no illusion that our battles are far from done. But the left has always been better at knowing what it wants to reform rather than what it wants to protect. If Labour wants to win the next election, it needs to understand what it wants to preserve as well as what it wants to transform. To tell a story about where we're going, we need to know who we are and where we've been. The challenge is to harmonise them both. To find a way of being conservative that is true to Labour.

If what we mean by 'conservative' is a politics that wants to safeguard the values and institutions that this country can be proud of, then this is perfectly possible. Family, neighbourliness, hard work and place are part of it. Dedication, honesty and compassion speak to it. This agenda is consistent with Ed's central theme of responsibility. It chimes with Rachel Reeves' call for fiscal discipline, Kitty Ussher's call for a more empowering form of welfare and a renewed emphasis on localism. David Cameron might be Conservative by name, but he doesn't offer anything like this agenda. He is old money with new markets, pragmatism and power. He is tearing up honoured institutions and the fabric of civil society without regard. We have to offer people something genuine, a better way of being conservative. This isn't just consistent with what people tell us in polls, pubs and high streets, it is also true to our values, and our tradition as one of the greatest grassroots organisations in this country.

Blue Labour reminds us that our history is at once more radical and more conservative than anything many of us dare to imagine. The official Labour Party website says we started as a 'parliamentary pressure group' whose chief achievement was to establish the welfare state. The truth is so much richer than that. Forged by workers who came together in representation committees, our earliest advocates were united by a desire to improve themselves and their families through collective action like the famous Dockers' Strike of 1889. This tradition of self-organisation weaves its way through our history of cooperatives, mutuals, civic groups and unions, enriching our actions, building our leaders and strengthening our friendships. We saw it in the work of George Lansbury in the East End, in Bermondsey through Alfred Salter and the work of the great Keir Hardie. It continues to this day through organisations like Hope Not Hate and London

Citizens. 'Small c' conservatism is not about blocking all change, but honouring the civic institutions, the localities, stories and relationships that allow us to build it together.

In recent times this tradition has been uprooted, and it's been painful. The Labour Party that lost power in 2010 sounded hollow and technocratic. In its eagerness to help, it forgot that the market can leave us vulnerable as well as rich, that the state can leave us dependent as well as protected. The British people are now more than aware of these dangers. Ed Miliband knows he cannot ignore the poll data. He does not sign up to all of Blue Labour's agenda, but he drew from it throughout his leadership campaign, and some of his most distinctive contributions continue to be inspired by it.

THE ECONOMY

When Lehman Brothers came crashing down in 2008, it brought the party's political economic model down with it. For years Labour had let the City grow with the best of intentions – to fund our high ideals delivered through public services – but we didn't stop to think enough about how dependent this left us on the banks. We let the financial bubble grow unregulated, and used the profits to hand out benefits and public services. Now we are bankrupt, and the ugly asymmetries in our economy have been exposed. We know that our financial sector benefited at the expense of manufacturing, that our southern tip grew rich at the expense of the Midlands and the North and that academic education benefited at the expense of vocation. We spent too much and it disempowered us because we became dependent. The people grew needy, and Labour politicians became beholden.

Failing to challenge the market was one reason why the last Labour government put so much emphasis on the state, as other contributors have already pointed out. When you can't challenge free market orthodoxy, the state becomes your only lever for change, so you overuse it. In the wake of the crash of 2008, markets have rightly lost their untouchable status. We now want to talk about reforming the economy so that the state has to do less work. If you can build an economy that offers good jobs, decent pay and a sense of meaning, the argument goes, then you need to offer fewer tax credits and benefits via the state. It means you achieve social aims by reforming the supply side of the economy rather than just spending on the demand side. The New Labour pressure group Progress refers to this as 'predistribution'. Ed Miliband calls it 'responsible capitalism'. Either way, we should get behind it.

So yes, 'small c' conservatism does call for fiscal prudence, it does get angry at waste and it does believe that Labour thinks too much about public sector workers at the expense of their brothers and sisters in the private sector. But it also wants an alternative that the Conservative Party cannot understand. It wants a living wage, an end to corporate monopolies, and growth that delivers increased wages as well as increased profits. Putting in a hard day's work is a conservative value, but the Conservative Party doesn't honour that. You do not respect work when you threaten to cut back on the minimum wage, make it easier to fire people and refuse to give labour any say over capital. This cannot be the only supply side policy that the country is left with. Blue Labour calls for something better.

Germany offers living, breathing examples that we can learn from. A deep emphasis on vocational education and apprenticeships combined with a refusal to cut down wages mean that the country has become an industrial powerhouse whilst Britain has become a home for call centres. Regional balance is another important part of the German story. It is simply not affordable to have talent wasting in huge parts of the country that are abandoned by a free market or propped up only by public sector employment. One way of delivering sustainable growth might be regional banks, which again have helped develop more balanced growth in Germany by forcing capital to look for local opportunities. What is lost in flexibility is gained through balance, decreased risk and self-sufficiency. Finally, Germany also teaches us something about worker representation. Even if you work in a low-skilled role, you should be given a genuine stake in the bigger picture. There must be investment in you, and mentoring, and the chance to move up the ladder. Ed Miliband has repeatedly said 'there is more to life than the bottom line'. These policies are fitting examples of what he means.

THE STATE

Ed Miliband's recent speeches have acknowledged the politics of austerity, making it an inevitable part of Labour's future vision. But we should be honest and admit that the problem with Labour's state went beyond its price tag. A purely economic explanation cannot explain why people receiving the highest benefits often hate the system most. A meagre transfer of financial resources cannot transform lives. At best it can carve out a space against material poverty, but in that space we were guilty of leaving people terrifyingly lonely. We have to fill the black hole of unemployment with relationships and experiences that give back power. Signing on once a week doesn't count. Too often people are treated like a number to be processed rather than a fellow human being to be empowered.

This is not to say that Labour didn't try to get people off benefits. But we didn't do enough. The right understood that it was criminal to leave people financially better off staying at home rather than putting in a hard day's work. It understood that a level of conditionality was essential not just for economic sustainability or a populist headline, but for a claimant's self-respect. It's true that some people are too vulnerable to contribute, and of course we must honour our obligations to them, but we shouldn't be afraid to acknowledge that many people out there can offer more than we ask from them, and it's depressing for all sides not to make the most of that potential.

James Purnell has already offered one suggestion. The former Secretary for Work and Pensions has outlined a guaranteed job scheme through his work at IPPR. This would offer anyone capable of working a job after one year on benefits, but if they refused to take it, their welfare would be withdrawn. Ed Miliband recently took up this idea with his proposal for a guaranteed job for young people, paid by a bankers' bonus tax, after one year out of work. Refusal to take the job would result in the withdrawal of benefits. Ed Miliband has taken a lot of flack from the left for talking about responsibility at the bottom as well as the top, but he is right. Responsibility is a human need. To give someone responsibility presumes dignity. Offering benefits without conditionality implies dependence.

London Citizens offers another example of good practice. An alliance of faith, community, union and civic groups, they managed to place over 1,000 people in jobs at the Olympic site in Stratford at a fraction of the cost of most corporate workfare giants. Job vacancies were advertised through their member institutions, allowing job seekers to receive interviews and training in their local schools and churches with people they already knew. These relationships were built on pre-existing trust and confidence, and in the end some 1,280 people got jobs out of 1,747 who participated. Many were in the 'hard to reach' category and London Citizens said it cost them an average of just £60 to place each claimant. More welfare should be conducted this way. The job centre employee who spends all day in front of a computer should go out and meet every nearby businessperson, church, school, union and university to bring people together. They should be paid to match up local skills with local needs.

This shift in the way that the state is conducted must also be accompanied by a wider cultural shift in our party, called for by MPs like Jon Cruddas who acknowledge that many of our politicians have become too abstract and professional. Even our local branch meetings are dominated by bureaucracy and procedure. In his Bradford West victory, George Galloway has shown us what is possible when you have a genuinely emotive vision for a local area and some meaningful relationships with faith and community groups. That is true, traditional Labour Party politics. Ed Miliband understands this. It's why he has backed the Movement for Change, London Citizens and the reforms proposed by Refounding Labour.

Of course we must also realise that there is a responsibility on the public to meet us half way. Some cynicism might be justified, but we shouldn't pander to the voter or indulge in an introverted self-hatred. We shouldn't be afraid to say that it is wrong to give up on voting or shrug off politics. We should frown on those who do not vote. If there aren't enough choices for people, they should join a party and change it or stand for themselves. The obligation is on us all, the voter as well as the candidate, the cynic as well as the optimist, the reader as well as the writer.

CONCLUSION

All of these arguments are being heard in Ed Miliband's office in Portcullis House. Throughout his leadership campaign he repeatedly said he wanted to be both a reformer of the market and a reformer of the state. The shift to a vocational economy and a more relational system of welfare should be a central part of that change. Let us be under no illusion that this is also what the public wants. It's the parliamentary party that is less convinced. It might help to point out that when we call on the party to become more conservative, we are not submitting to a right-wing presence, but reclaiming the celebrated traditions of our past. We are reinvigorating our future not through cynical poll data and the empty coldness of the swing voter, but with the warmth and soul of our experience. That is conservative, it is radical and it is Labour.

NOTE

1. An earlier version of this essay was published in John Denham MP (ed.), *The Shape of Things to Come* (London: Fabian Society, 2012).

CHAPTER FOURTEEN

The Gentle Society: What Blue Labour Can Offer Conservatives

Ed West

The short twentieth century and the great era of ideological conflict ended in August 1991 when a tipsy Communist Party maverick called Boris Yeltsin stood on a tank in front of Moscow's White House and brought a surprisingly speedy end to the Soviet Union. Like with many patients, the USSR had been obviously sick for some time but its demise was still rather sudden and shocking.

Communism's fall came after a decade in which the economic philosophy of Milton Friedman had proved triumphant in the West, a decade of Reaganomics and Thatcherism. Later Labour would vote away Clause 4, replacing socialism with a not particularly social or democratic social democracy. Looking back, few could doubt that the right had won all the economic arguments at the end of the twentieth century, with even Labour cabinet minister Peter Mandelson suggesting in 1998 that they were 'intensely relaxed about people getting filthy rich' (as long as they paid their taxes).

Yet when historian Niall Ferguson declared in early 2011 that the right had won both the important issues of the 1980s, 'the economy and the Cold War', the economically left-wing, socially conservative journalist Rod Liddle was left to remark: 'What Niall didn't say, however, was that the left – and particularly the bits of it which I do not like – won on every other issue'.[1]

Indeed. There can be few doubts that since the huge social changes of the late 1960s liberals have been victorious in the social arena. The so-called culture wars in Britain were wars only in the sense that late nineteenth-century skirmishes between European armies with machine guns and African tribesman were wars. On this side of the Atlantic cultural conservatives lost everything. To be right-wing in post-war academia, as philosopher Roger Scruton once pointed out, 'was the preserve of half-mad recluses'[2] (and when he joined Birkbeck he noted that the only other conservative in the entire building was the Neapolitan cleaner), but in the 20 years leading up to Tony Blair's victory virtually every other institution, with the exception of the Army, had become, to use a popular word, institutionally left-wing. In the universities, the BBC, the churches and even the police the centre-left view became the default one, around which was an increasingly narrow range of acceptable opinions. When the University of Virginia's Jonathan Haidt recently polled 1,000 prominent American academics about their political leanings, he found just three who identified themselves as conservatives.

Labour's 1997 triumph was more than just a political victory, then; it was the culmination of an overwhelming cultural victory over what Blair would later call the 'forces of conservatism'. And yet, some might wonder, what sort of left won? Is it a left that Cardinal Manning or Keir Hardie would recognise? It is not so clear.

It was not so much the 'rich' part of Mandelson's phrase that grated, but the 'filthy'. For there was a growing sense that the privileged felt no obligation to use their wealth to help their compatriots; tax evasion by the rich dwarfed benefit fraud by the poor, and still does, but tax evaders were still knighted and feted. But then again, why shouldn't they be? British society had come to worship conspicuous wealth, a truth illustrated by the fashion trends of the late 1990s and 2000s, and the fondness for bling, gold and champagne. Rappers who flaunted their (ill-gotten) gains were worshipped as heroes, footballers behaved like mini Roman emperors and were paid more in a day than some watching them would earn in a year, yet were continually rewarded by the people who walked through the turnstiles.

Labour ministers did not seem to exactly shy away from the company of rich men. It was not just that the super-rich were no longer considered class enemies or morally dubious, but almost as if the wealthy were actually social heroes, the Stakhanovs of capitalism. While the City of London kept on filling the Treasury's coffers no one objected, yet one could sense, in what alcoholics call a moment of clarity, that there was a serious social malaise underneath. And as it turned out the nation's institutions, most spectacularly its politics, were more rotten than anyone could have imagined.

The wealth gap continued to rise despite increased government spending on benefits; several million people festered in unemployment or disguised unemployment, and many felt not enough was done to bring work back to the areas ravaged under Thatcher. The *Evening Standard*, during its most depressing phase at the turn of the century, seemed to largely report on two aspects of London life – rich people spending a fortune on drinks, clothes and holidays, and poor people murdering each other.

The lack of shame about excess wealth went hand in hand with the hyper-sexualisation of society; sex seemed to become more than ever a commodity to sell or shock, while judgementalism replaced sexual immorality as a cardinal sin. The new government liberalised laws governing pornography and alcohol; open borders allowed the shocking proliferation of trafficked sex slaves in British cities. Pornographers and pimps alike were able to benefit from a huge cultural shift, whereby even visiting prostitutes had lost much social stigma, and bankers from respectable firms would bring clients to strip bars. The sexual revolution, once framed in terms of liberation, had long since entered the ugly phase of revolution, marred by exploitation, crudeness and violence. There were even popular dating websites that excluded poor men and women not deemed attractive enough, while others helped husbands and wives to enjoy extra-marital affairs.

The two trends are not entirely unconnected; sexual liberalisation, like economic liberalisation, frees some people to realise their dreams but ruins others. It also vastly increases inequality, for the weakening of monogamous social norms has led to a society where sexual competition has become stressfully high and where sexual, social and economic failure is rubbed in the face of low-achieving men. As French novelist Michel Houellebecq wrote in *Whatever*, 'a world where sexual pleasure is made a pre-eminent good is one where the gap between haves and have-nots is magnified along new dimensions'.[3]

This is one of the many paradoxes of the New Left movement – marriage, and monogamy generally, is a great equaliser. Indeed, long before *The Spirit Level* pointed to the link between inequality and crime, anthropologists have noted that monogamous societies tend to be less violent and more stable than ones where sexual success is unevenly distributed. Weakening marriage did not just liberate women; it also liberated womanisers. But it is a part of the wider paradox that almost every tenet of the modern liberal orthodoxy harms the poor and vulnerable the most.

The links between sexual and financial revolutions have been noted before. In *Crunchy Cons*, his ode to Chestertonian conservatism, American author Rod Dreher argued that the Democrats had become the party of lust, and the Republicans the party of greed.[4] Phillip Blond, author of *Red Tory*, sees 1968 and 1979 as essentially part of the same process that led to the broken society of today.[5] New Labour married the two philosophies into one, but long before Tony Blair's rebranding, Labour had evolved from being a largely working-class, socialist party into a predominantly middle-class, liberal one. Faced with the economic failures of Marxist economics, and the increasing unpopularity of socialism, the New Left drifted to the social sphere, turning their attention to the new movements of feminism, gay rights and racial minorities. These were righteous and noble causes, but inevitably they would conflict with the interests of Labour's traditional supporters, and with the institutions that knitted the social fabric together.

The right, meanwhile, defeatist on social issues, and fearing its association with the likes of Enoch Powell or Mary Whitehouse and various other lower-middle-class provincials, made a god of the market instead, confident it was the one subject they could dare to defend at dinner parties without looking ugly (greedy, perhaps, but not old-fashioned or, worse still, low-class). The right could also be quite confident that the confrontational economics adopted by the British trade unions and their supporters were politically self-defeating.

Yet these two philosophies, left-wing social views and right-wing economics, or social and economic liberalism, are hardly opposed. The New Left's orthodoxies are personally very inexpensive; while high tax rates and stronger unions entail financial sacrifices, supporting gay marriage or straight divorce costs nothing. In the case of immigration, holding progressive left-wing views is actually financially beneficial to wealthy liberals. Mass immigration, and the later rationale of multiculturalism and diversity, was the most crucial bell-weather issue of the New Left, influenced as it was by the civil rights movement, colonialism and the shock of the Holocaust. Today it is the issue that most divides along class lines, illustrated by the now-famous Rochdale grandmother Gillian Duffy's comments to Gordon Brown during the 2010 election; more than anything, attitudes to immigration and diversity are the biggest signifier of class and status in Britain.

Immigration has, broadly but unquestionably, made life more pleasant for the wealthy, and harder for the poor, both economically and socially. When Karl Marx wrote that 'The main purpose of the bourgeois in relation to the worker is, of course, to have the commodity labour as cheaply as possible, which is only possible when the supply of this commodity is as large as possible in relation to the demand for it', he was writing a warning for left-wing politicians, not an instruction manual. Marx's analysis would be recognisable to many people in Britain today. As Dagenham MP Jon Cruddas noted in 2005,

> immigration has been used as an informal reserve army of cheap labour. People see this at their workplace, feel it in their pocket and see it in their community – and therefore perceive it as a critical component of their own relative impoverishment. Objectively, the social wage of many of my constituents is in decline. House prices rise inexorably, and public service improvements fail to match local population expansion. At work, their conditions, in real terms, are in decline through the unregulated use of cheap migrant labour.[6]

The strange thing is that this policy is now considered 'left-wing', yet to most people it was always understood that left-wing politics were about creating a more egalitarian society and caring for the disadvantaged and weak.

The House of Lords' 2008 report, 'The Economic Impact of Immigration', concluded that unskilled immigration drove down the wages of the poor, and especially harmed young people and ethnic minorities.[7] On the other hand it kept inflation down, pushed up house prices, increased the wages of the highest earners, and drove the profits that allow major corporations to pay their directors increasingly surreal salaries. Little wonder that major American corporations spent US $345 million lobbying for just three pro-immigration bills between 2006 and 2008, or that CEOs are happy to 'embrace diversity'. And in the longer term the cultural, racial and religious diversity that results from mass immigration creates a population less inclined towards socialism and redistribution, as various studies of American society have shown. Again, one has to wonder why this policy of globalism in one country became 'left-wing'.

Indeed, many of the socially liberal reforms of the last 40 years have ended up harming the most vulnerable members of society. Who, for instance, benefited from changes in the education system, the weakening of teacher authority and the move towards more child-centred education, or the abandonment of established canons towards a view that Shakespeare is no better than dub poets? When cultural norms are vague and the route to the top becomes more cryptic, who loses out? Those who are dealt the worst cards in life to start with. Likewise our changing attitudes to marriage and illegitimacy, although directed by compassionate motives, have widened the gap between the rich and poor, as the wealthy, educated middle classes can weather the storm far easier. Even the decline of church attendances, heralded by many as a sign of social maturity, may have removed the one institution where people of different classes and backgrounds met and sat down together voluntarily.

Most controversially of all, the changing role of women has brought some unevenly distributed social costs. Women's right to work and enjoy equal opportunity was a core area of twentieth-century reform and one accepted almost universally (and rightly), yet the old, full-employment working-class communities that those on the left now lament would not have been 'communities' without their central figures – stay-at-home mothers. Can one achieve full gender and social equality? Probably not, and some cost must be suffered in some areas, but since equality and diversity policy is largely directed by people with nannies, the cost is likely to be borne by people without them.

So who has benefited from the left's turn from economic to cultural radicalism? Heavyweight sociologists from different ends of the political spectrums, Robert Putnam and Charles Murray, both argued in books published in 2012 that the gulf between America's rich and poor has become a chasm in recent years. The same is certainly true in Britain, and both economic and social liberalism have played a part. Both left and right have made Britain a far less pleasant place to be struggling, and it is hard to find a single great liberal reform of recent years that has not, in fact, expanded the gap between the haves and have-nots (one could be seriously controversial and throw in abortion, which brings about the greatest inequality of all, between life and death).

One could even argue that the revolution of 1968 made working-class communities more vulnerable after 1979, removing a layer of social protection so that when Thatcherism hit them the effects were more devastating than the Depression of the 1930s. Normalisation of illegitimacy broke down the defences of families; reform of the social housing system broke up communities; mass immigration weakened them further; while even the comfort of nationhood was officially disapproved of by an intellectual elite who despised their country as much as they did in George Orwell's day. Memories tint the bleakest of times but statistics paint a truer picture, and the incredibly low, and declining, crime levels of the 1930s say much about the strength of working-class communities during that hard decade.

The left won the culture wars, the right the economic wars? Perhaps the rich won both.

And yet the interest attracted by Phillip Blond's Red Toryism and Maurice Glasman's socially conservative Blue Labour suggest that many feel the wrong sides won the wrong arguments. The economic policies of the past three decades have seen inequality levels that continue to rise and rise. As Blond points out, this is not just morally dubious, and possibly linked to levels of social disorder, but unsustainable, leading to ever more unfathomable levels of personal debt. Capitalism, as it currently functions, is not working for enough people, and the ordinary, suburban Tory voters who kept the party in power have never had less in common with the David Camerons of this world.

It is because of housing, in particular, that those natural supporters of right-wing economic liberalism feel disenchanted. While the salaries of the super-rich have grown ever more alien to mere mortals, ordinary middle-class families find themselves unable to live within miles of Westminster, and those in the squeezed middle seem little better off than they were a generation ago, if not worse. They might have smaller gadgets, but they also have smaller homes. Even former *Daily Telegraph* editor Charles Moore was left to lament in 2011 that he had lost his faith in Thatcherism, writing:

> A society in which credit is very restricted is one in which new people cannot rise. How many small businesses could start or first homes be bought without a loan? But when loans become

the means by which millions finance mere consumption – that
is different. And when the banks that look after our money take
it away, lose it and then, because of government guarantee, are
not punished themselves, something much worse happens. It
turns out – as the Left always claims – that a system purporting
to advance the many has been perverted in order to enrich the
few.[8]

Moore is one of many conservative thinkers who have suggested that,
obsessed with economic liberalism, conservatism had lost its moral
bearings. He was writing in response to the closure of the *News of the
World*, a paper that had enjoyed a long and mutually beneficial
relationship with the Conservative Party. And yet this organ of
working-class Toryism published inconsequential rubbish and
borderline porn, spreading poison and sleaze, so that, in Moore's
words, 'much of what he chose to print on those presses has been a
great disappointment to those of us who believe in free markets
because they emancipate people. The right has done itself harm by
covering up for so much brutality'.[9]
    It is not the only area where the right has done itself harm. Rod
Dreher noted that he had witnessed local government meetings in
America's heartlands where Republican officials voted through big
business-sponsored plans to destroy local high streets, a familiar story
for British readers.[10] Yet how can so-called conservatives wish to
dismantle small, family-run shops? Likewise Peter Hitchens wonders
why the Tories have been so hostile to the railways, from the shameful
Beeching Axe to the botched privatisation, all out of some perverted
ideological attachment to cars.[11] Cars represent freedom and
independence, yet this is a restricted, adolescent interpretation of
conservatism epitomised by a disdain for fellow human beings and
the environment. As Hitchens points out, railways are beautiful,
civilised and traditional, the very epitome of conservative values (and
give us an appreciation of the landscape which cars will never
manage). Where are today's equivalent of the nineteenth-century
philanthropists and reformers, the Tories who argued against
rapacious capitalism?
    Individualist conservatism, like capitalism, values freedom, yet it
was always dependent on firmly established moral codes, and in
particular Christianity, to (gently) enforce behaviour; just as
capitalism cannot survive without trust and honesty, so individual

freedom cannot last without some internalised moral order. Modern conservatism's failure is reflected in the popularity of atheistic libertarianism, a philosophy that proposes a moral bubble which they expect nothing but self-interest to fill; instead, as we have seen in recent years, once the church is undermined, the state soon becomes the church.

Yet the British left is unable to exploit this weakness because where it was once 'civic and religious', in Cruddas' analysis, it is now 'statist and atheistic', and sees the state as the only vehicle for social change. Indeed to some almost every institution outside the state is viewed with great suspicion; the family, nation and church might promote sexism, racism and homophobia, but on top of this the countless smaller institutions that comprise this thing we call society are all viewed as suspicious and liable to encourage inequality or discrimination. By this logic almost every area of social activism that does not bridge every possible social divide can be suspect.

The left's statism has bequeathed us a strange political amnesia. The British cultural miracle of 1850–1950, when a country with a growing population and in the process of industrialisation managed to largely overcome poverty, crime, disease, illiteracy and social pathology, is presented as an almost entirely state-led enterprise, rather than a collective partnership between various individuals and groups, governmental and private, Liberal, Tory and Labour alike. Most of all the central part that Anglican, Methodist, Quaker, Catholic, Jewish and other religious groups played in bettering the lives of their fellow citizens, and of promoting what would now be called 'social justice', is forgotten. (I recall once meeting a fairly high-ranking New Labour think-tanker who had never even heard of Cardinal Manning.)

Part of the Blue Labour attraction is that it offers the possibility of much-needed social improvement outside of the state, especially the central state. This is in tune with current thinking. One of the most influential books of recent years, Robert Putnam's *Bowling Alone*, popularised the concept of social capital, a view that sees relationships, trust and civic virtue as a capital like any other form.[12] Social capital is heavily linked to a society's ability to reduce inequality and fight poverty. So while many people would agree that Britain's high inequality levels are a bad thing, both morally and practically, the state alone cannot reduce them. Unless there is an increase in Britain's social capital, in the levels of community involvement, in social trust, in virtuous, selfless behaviour, in short in relationships, inequality will continue to remain high. As Britain has become more individual-obsessed, as institutions such as the family, the church, the nation and, though conservatives are reluctant to include them, trade unions, have become weaker, this reduction in social capital has disproportionately harmed the poor.

David Cameron was elected as Conservative leader in 2005 with the aim of detoxifying the brand, and to do that he has adopted New Labour's social liberalism on certain issues. The Tory front bench mostly voted into oblivion Catholic adoption agencies, so that children dealt with the cruellest start in life were condemned to grow up in care so that rich men in London would not have to be accused of homophobia at dinner parties. Yet how large is this socially liberal constituency really? (And how likely are they to vote Conservative?) Both major parties are now chasing a metropolitan minority, at the expense of a socially conservative and economically egalitarian majority. For all the talk of detoxifying the Conservatives' brand, Labour is in danger of becoming toxically progressive to the majority of people who do not identify with 1968-derived politics. 'Left-wing' is already a derogatory term in many working-class areas of south-east England, not because people oppose the idea of greater equality, or fairness, helping the weak or protecting workers' rights, but because the left has become associated with obscure and intolerant sexual politics, utopian universalism, nonsensical doctrinal purity and state-enforced equality of outcomes.

So what does Blue Labour offer? It is of course easier to diagnose a problem than to treat it; in politics there is the further complication that there generally exists a gap between the time when most sensible people recognise that something is a failure and when it is politically possible to do something about it (Le Corbusier-inspired brutalist council housing being a great example). Some Blue Labour ideas are also politically complex to sell, being counter-intuitive and based on paradox; there will be ferocious opposition to some aspects, both from vested interests and idealists. But we are well on our way from that first moment of initial realisation to general acceptance on many social issues, not the least on the most pressing one – the family. It is vital that the message is put across, that using government policy to encourage stable two-parent families is not about moralising or punishing or even 'social engineering', but a matter of social justice, and of giving children better, safer childhoods (and, for that matter, making men behave better towards women).

So far conservative analysis of social problems has done much to expose the damage wrought by fatherlessness, but fails to acknowledge the converse – that Britain's economy makes it increasingly difficult for a 'working man', to use such an archaic term, to support a family. Both left and right carry a flame of nostalgia for the three decades after the Second World War, and much of that derives from the social stability that came from this historically unique situation. Since then rising house prices have combined with growing wage inequality (not to mention the pressures and temptations of a consumerist, credit-based economy) to make it increasingly difficult for men on low incomes to do the right thing. Neither does the right acknowledge the huge damage done by the housing bubble, a grotesque conspiracy against the poor; to 'small-c' conservatives priced out of the London housing market, hopelessly indebted and alienated from the super-rich, Blue Labour represents something different.

Ultimately many ideas now being thrown up will fall on rocky ground, but many others will almost certainly become accepted. The key attraction of Blue Labour, however, is that it remains open to new ideas, rather than shouting them down and strangling them at birth. For that reason the traditionalist Blue Labour is – suitably paradoxically because the world seems full of paradoxes right now – the most progressive wing of the movement, and the best hope of promising a fairer, more equal and gentler society.

NOTES

1. Rod Liddle, 'Even Conservative councils now think like the left', *The Spectator*, 16 April 2011. Available at http://www.spectator.co.uk/features/6864458/even-conservative-councils-now-think-like-the-left/ (accessed 23 October 2014).

2. Roger Scruton, 'Why I became a conservative', *The New Criterion* (February 2003), available online at http://newcriterion.com:81/archive/21/feb03/burke.htm (accessed 23 October 2014).

3. Michel Houellebecq, *Whatever* (London: Serpent's Tail, 2011).

4. Rod Dreher, *Crunchy Cons: The New Conservative Counterculture and Its Return to Roots* (New York: Crown Forum, 2006).

5. Phillip Blond, *Red Tory: How Left and Right Have Broken Britain and How We Can Fix it* (London: Faber and Faber, 2010).
6. Jon Cruddas, 'Long march against the BNP: Labour's obsession with middle England has made some working-class voters look to the far right. Now the fightback is beginning', *The Guardian*, 20 May 2005, available online at http://www.theguardian.com/politics/2005/may/20/labour.immigration (accessed 23 October 2014).
7. House of Lords, 'The economic impact of immigration', 1 April 2008, available online at http://www.publications.parliament.uk/pa/ld200708/ldselect/ldeconaf/82/82.pdf (accessed 23 October 2014).
8. Charles Moore, 'I'm starting to think that the Left might actually be right', *Daily Telegraph*, 22 July 2011, available online at http://www.telegraph.co.uk/news/politics/8655106/Im-starting-to-think-that-the-Left-might-actually-be-right.html (accessed 23 October 2014).
9. *Ibid.*
10. See again Dreher, *Crunchy Cons*.
11. Peter Hitchens, *The Broken Compass: How British Politics Lost its Way* (London: Continuum, 2009), pp. 163–72.
12. Robert D. Putnam, *Bowling Alone: The Collapse and Revival of American Community* (New York: Schuster & Schuster, 2000).

PART SIX

FAITH AND FAMILY

CHAPTER FIFTEEN

Vision, Virtue and Vocation: Notes on Blue Labour as a Practice of Politics

Luke Bretherton

INTRODUCTION

Blue Labour is not a political philosophy. It is born out of reflection on the practice of politics and revulsion at the way procedure – whether legal, economic or bureaucratic – suppresses and stifles building a common life. It is committed to democratic politics understood as the negotiation of a shared life among diverse and often competing interests. This kind of politics does not demand that those with different interests, loyalties or views leave the room before the negotiations begin. It involves building relationships with people you disagree with and don't like. As a politics of the common good it is built on the experience and trust that people you disagree with and don't like can show you kindness beyond what you expect or deserve, and that people who share your views can do great harm to you, to themselves and to others. In short, Blue Labour is built on the recognition that love and sin are political realities.

What follows are a series of interlinked reflections that give the background to how one can only understand Blue Labour's vision of a non-statist, democratic and pluralist politics of the common good by understanding first how Blue Labour is a vision of politics as a practice.[1]

PRACTICE BEFORE THEORY

Overly theoretical accounts of politics fail to reckon with the nature of politics itself. Politics is, as Machiavelli discerned, about action in time and as such it involves questions of power (the ability to act), historicity (the temporal and temporary nature of action) and wily wisdom (the local knowledge, cunning intelligence and practical skills necessary to respond appropriately to a constantly changing and ambiguous environment).[2] The ideal ruler is not a philosopher king, but a ship's captain who is able to safely navigate the tumultuous and mercurial sea by means of craft and quick-wittedness. The unpredictable and unstable nature of political life directs attention away from universal principles towards particular historical settings.[3] There is a need to act in a way appropriate to the time/*kairos*, and hence the need for judgements about what is best for these people, in this place, at this time. As action in time, politics requires a means of coming to judgement suited to putting people, place and history before any particular theory or programme. Practical reason (*phronesis/mētis*) is that means. It is the contention of Blue Labour that when it comes to politics, practical reason comes before theoretical reason. This should not be read as setting up a dichotomy between theory and practice. When I say practice comes 'before' theory it does not mean 'instead of', 'as an alternative to', 'a substitute for' or 'rather than'. It means putting 'first things first', 'giving priority to' or 'ordering things rightly'. The same goes for other prescriptions set out here, such as society before state, people before programme and politics before procedure.

What is often missing in modern accounts of politics is any account of how we come to learn how to make appropriate and contingent political judgements based on practical reason. Instead, politics is either about the application of universally valid principles, or it is reduced to legal, technocratic or bureaucratic considerations. By contrast, Blue Labour, as a practice-driven politics, does not work from first principles but reflects on already established practices, traditions and customs, and the presuppositions and histories that inform them, in order to generate wider prescriptions and criteria of evaluation. Thus it is rightly accused of being 'conservative' but such conservatism, by dint of the traditions, customs and practices it pays attention to, can and does generate radical proposals.[4] Against modern denunciations of tradition as inherently reactionary and the enemy of an emancipatory politics, Blue Labour is tutored not by acts of revolutionary self-assertion and their totalitarian debacle, but by forebears who appealed to and upheld common laws, common lands and a common life as a basis for liberty and rights. Moreover, it is the contention of Blue Labour that it is not an Oxbridge degree, an MA from the Kennedy School of Government or work experience in a think-tank that equips you to make good and, when necessary, radical political judgements. It is apprenticeship in particular kinds of practice that enable you to learn the craft of politics and therefore be the kind of person who is able to make good judgements. This apprenticeship is experienced in forms of self-organised institutions and mutual associations such as unions, churches, residents associations, small businesses and disability-support groups.

As already noted, political life always involves questions of power, and because it involves power, the process of decision-making and what gets to count as common sense are affected. So we are hopelessly naïve if we think that by getting the form, procedure or theory right the practice can be made good. An account of sin contends that not only is our ability to do the right thing impaired but so is our ability to think rightly about the good. Any analysis needs to face the reality of power relations and how certain forms of knowledge are legitimised and others marginalised to the benefit of some and the detriment of others. But the lesson to be learned from taking sin seriously as a political reality – whether we draw on Marx, Foucault or Augustine to develop such an account – is not that all moral claims in politics are hypocrisy but that the first step to a more moral politics is realising we are not. The next step is to take responsibility for our own complicity in structures of domination and establish the representation of other interests and voices in the decision-making process in order to reflect the contested nature of knowledge and judgement. It also involves having the humility to recognise that, despite our expertise and experience, we do not possess a monopoly on wisdom. However, this does not of necessity warrant either a species of liberal interest group politics or some form of subcultural micro-politics that eschews all claims to power. It can undergird a politics of the common good where, paradoxically, goods in common and the mutual interests they fulfil are realised through the contest of interests. This conflict involves destabilising and disrupting the selfish interests of the one, the few or the many in order to identify genuine goods in common. This is as true for the negotiation of pension remuneration rates in a company as it is for the negotiation of education provision in a borough.

In order to avoid abstract analysis of power and open spaces for politics as the negotiation of a common life between diverse and often estranged interests, there is a need to focus on how people can and do act together to make life better. Without attention to concrete issues and the ways people are able to act in concert and form a common life through public practices of speech and action, we have little to say other than wolves eat sheep, power corrupts and the strong triumph over the weak. Moreover, to only focus on a critique of power in the abstract or to make critique an end in itself results in ever-diminishing returns: critique is no substitute for a constructive alternative. While power and sin must be accounted for, not all power is bad and David (possessor of dexterity, sureness of eye and sharp-wittedness) sometimes beats Goliath (possessor of overwhelming force).

Through acting in concert the weak can resist the unilateral actions of money power and state power in order to establish goods in common. The early Labour, civil rights, women's and environmental movements are all examples of such relational power in action. The pursuit of goods in common – better working conditions or cleaner air – are the basis of a genuinely public political life as against a practice of politics as based on the individual pursuit of private interests. As Hannah Arendt puts it: 'The political realm rises directly out of acting together, the "sharing of words and deeds". Thus action not only has the most intimate relationship to the public part of the world common to us all, but is the one activity which constitutes it'.[5] Overly deterministic accounts of unilateral power and the domination of structural forces such as capitalism do not allow for the reality of the kinds of agency constituted by relational power and wily wisdom, which in turn can form the basis of a truly common life.

PEOPLE BEFORE PROGRAMME

If we are to attend to the actual practices through which people negotiate a common life then we must put people before programme. Rather than beginning with an abstract theory or programme to which it demands everyone to conform, Blue Labour contends you must begin with what people are already doing, where they are already gathered and what they hold dear. This means listening first and then deriving policies and programmes. Meaningful listening entails building relationships with people rather than relying on a listening process mediated through focus groups or polling.

In listening we have to take seriously who is before us and attend to the situation rather than predetermine what to do in accord with some prior agenda, ideology or strategy of control. Against interest-group and identity politics and their agonistic rivalry, political action born out of listening acts in trust that others not like me and with whom I disagree may well have something to teach me. Listening is vital to deepening one's ability to reason rightly about what is the right or just judgement to be made with these people, at this time, in this place.

INSTITUTIONS AND INDIVIDUALS

We cannot attentively listen at a distance or if constantly mobile. The promiscuity of capital as it moves from place to place in search of a return leads to certain social effects, one of which is population churn. Where mobility and distance (be it cultural, physical or economic) undermines the ability to listen, politics is replaced by the kinds of proceduralism and technocratic paternalism that claim to know better how others should live. Instead, listening requires active involvement and commitment to a particular place and the formation of relationships in that place because building stable and trusting relationships takes time and personal presence. Hence there is the vexed question of the relationship between incessant, large-scale migration and the ability to sustain a place-based, relational and democratic politics. This is a question that is both masked and exacerbated by making politics solely about individuals and their freedoms and ignoring the related issue of how to sustain institutions and their practices of association. Yet it is anchor institutions like schools, universities, small businesses and hospitals that are tied to place that are becoming increasingly important as arenas of common life amid the disaggregating churn of economic globalisation. It is institutions that are key to generating a listening, place-based politics of the common good rather than the individual who is often mobile and insecure. Within anchor institutions (such as religious institutions, schools, football clubs, universities, workplaces and community centres, etc.) a mobile population can be anchored, however temporarily. The negotiation of a common life between such *institutions*, and the gathered people who constitute them, rather than between individuals, allows for a listening, place-based politics of the common good to emerge.

Yet within the institutions through which we mediate and sustain a common life – schools, hospitals, universities, etc. – what is under threat is the notion of what it means to pursue a substantive good such as 'education' or 'health'. For example, much policy and practice in relation to universities does not view them as arenas of common life in which the individual good of each participant (whether student, academic or administrator) is dependent on the prior and organising good of education. Nor are they seen as having a duty of care and active interest in building up the common life of the places in which they are located. Rather, universities are increasingly subject to instrumentalising logics of the state and education itself is becoming commodified. Education is increasingly viewed as the aggregation of individual interests (in which case there is no such thing as education as a substantive good, only individual choices and careers which make use of the university for a time); and universities are run according to the dominant interest of either managers, academics or students (understood as clients or customers) rather than as a negotiation of a common life between people with different interests who share a mutual interest in the pursuit of their good in common – education – and promoting the virtues and disciplines required to fulfil this good. The result is that forms of market, legal and bureaucratic proceduralism replace trust, loyalty and reciprocity as ways of organising the institution.

Non-pecuniary institutions and forms of mutual association that are not wholly subject to logics of instrumentalisation or commodification are key for creating spaces amid political, economic, social and technological pressures that militate against developing such relationships. These institutions represent a legal, organisational, financial, and physical place to stand. For example, congregations represent institutions of this kind and are places constituted by gathered and organised people who do not come together primarily for either commercial or state-directed transactions, but who instead come together to worship and care for each other. Without such spaces there are few real places through which to resist the processes of commodification by the market and the processes of instrumentalisation by the state. In short, if we have nowhere to sit together free from governmental or commercial imperatives we have no public spaces in which to take the time to listen to each other and develop mutual trust. This is not to deny that building or strengthening such institutions and forms of mutual association is extremely difficult, and there is a constant need to innovate and imagine new kinds of institutional and associational life.

POLITICS BEFORE PROCEDURE

Without listening there can be no politics and politics is a condition of any moderately peaceable order, one derived from the pursuit of goods in common and not the exclusion or oppression of others, particularly the weak and vulnerable. As Aristotle noted, politics, as that which entails self-restraint and the conciliation of different interests, is not the only way to provide order. Tyranny, oligarchy, plutocracy, totalitarianism and what Tocqueville called 'democratic despotism' are more common ways to rule. These impose order by subverting or repressing all other interests under the interest of the one, the few or the mob. By contrast, as Bernard Crick notes:

> The political method of rule is to listen to [...] other groups so as to conciliate them as far as possible, and to give them legal position, a sense of security, some clear and reasonable safe means of articulation, by which these other groups can and will speak freely. Ideally politics draws all these groups into each other so that they each and together can make a positive contribution towards the general business of government and maintaining order.[6]

Under the pressure of processes of commodification, rights-based proceduralism and technocratic administration, the possibility of politics, especially in poor communities most intensely affected by these processes, is under threat.

Some will retort that listening is central to the politics of liberal democracies and takes the form of voting and elections. But this is to conflate two different moments in the democratic political process: election and consultation. Collapsing the process of consultation into the process of electoral legitimacy closes down any real moment of listening and divorces politicians from engaging in real consultation and shared deliberation with those they govern. The emphasis on procedures of legitimation in democracy focuses on the formal relationship between rulers and ruled and leaves out any concern about substantive political relations. Such an emphasis is in effect another way in which politics is replaced by procedures: this time, electoral procedures. Part of the reason that Blue Labour grew out of reflection on the practice of community organising is that community organising is one way of reinserting meaningful consultation into democratic politics: it is a means by which to regenerate the ability to make judgements together with others about the goods held in common on which all our flourishing depends.

As should be clear, the kind of conception of politics envisaged here is very different to that which tends to equate politics with changing legislation and administrative protocols. Such a proceduralist vision restricts politics to pressure upon and action by state agencies rather than the negotiation of a common life between multiple actors of which the state is but one player. The political vision Blue Labour encapsulates holds that if a group is directly contributing to the common work of defending, tending and creating the commonweal then they deserve recognition as a vital part and co-labourer within the broader body politic. Paradoxically, it is the very emphasis on participation and contribution to the building up of a common life that allows for a greater plurality and affirmation of distinct identities and traditions, as each is able to play a part in this common work. This is distinct from an identity politics or multicultural approaches because recognition and respect is not given simply by dint of having a different culture or identity: recognition is conditional upon contributing to and participation in shared, reciprocal, common work. London Citizens, who take this approach, find that it is often those political elites judged as anti-democratic – notably, Catholics, evangelicals and Muslims – who contribute most in terms of turnout, funds and sending people on training, and that those groups who proclaim themselves progressive bulwarks of democracy – notably, union branches and NGOs – contribute least. If the experience of community organising over 20 years is anything to go on, then involvement in a placed-based, listening politics creates space for the emergence of a shared civic story and a context for real relationship where all participants – however unsavoury their views to each other – can begin to touch on difficult issues in a place of trust.

Sheldon Wolin developed one of the fullest articulations of the contrast between politics and proceduralism. He gives an account of the centralisation of sovereignty in the nation state and the subsequent attempt to overcome political conflict within liberal nation states through a combination of rational administration, use of technology and the demarcation of the economy as the sphere of free, uncoerced relations.[7] On Wolin's account, liberalism identifies freedom with private interest rather than the pursuit of common action and shared advantage. The corollary of this is to grant the economy – the sphere of private interest and uncoerced relations – maximal scope and priority over the requirements of good government or the goods of any institution, whether it is a family, a farm or a factory.[8] Economics becomes the queen of the sciences that can best tell us about how to order our common life. As a result social harmony is no longer seen to issue from a prior set of institutional and political arrangements, but is understood to flow from the spontaneous equilibrium of economic forces. Within such a vision the status of the citizen becomes absorbed into that of the producer or consumer or, we might add, volunteer. For Wolin, the vital task in the contemporary context is the recovery of what he calls 'politicalness': the 'capacity for developing into beings who know and value what it means to participate in and be responsible for the care and improvement of our common and collective life'.[9] In Wolin's analysis the recovery of politicalness depends in part on local patterns of association born out of corporative and cooperative institutions and what he calls 'archaic', and in many cases, very 'conservative' traditions such as Christianity, Judaism and Islam. These provide the means for the recreation of political experience and extending to a wider circle the benefits of social cooperation and achievements made possible by previous generations.[10]

NEITHER SPONTANEOUS ORDER NOR RATIONAL ADMINISTRATION BUT POLITICAL JUDGEMENT

The emphasis on listening should not be understood as excluding the need for political judgement. To make a judgement about what to do with these people at this time and in this place, requires in the first instance an act of listening. Yet the modern state, in attempting to overcome politics and by resorting to various forms of legal, bureaucratic and market procedures, closes down the spaces for listening, judgement and responsibility both by the rulers and the ruled. For Hannah Arendt, a pointed example of exactly this was the Nazi, Adolf Eichmann, who refused to exercise judgement in the name of conforming to legal and bureaucratic regulations and so aided and abetted the Holocaust.

Eichmann may seem like an extreme example but what he points to is how the procedural state is congenitally incapable of seeing and acting politically. The state acting through law rather than politics cannot take account of interests, passions or meaningful relationships. These are irrelevant to neutral procedures and their operations. Such things may make moral claims upon the state but given how state actors see the world such moral claims framed in terms of narratives, passions and virtues are amoral. They simply do not exist as relevant claims for the rational administrator. The police are a good example. It is irrelevant to them whether you are speeding in order to reach a hospital to save a life or whether you are speeding for the hell of it – all there is is the sovereignty of the law and whether it is being broken. That is the only judgement to be made. It is not a political judgement but a bureaucratic one about what rules apply and when. The more procedural and rational the state the less discretion is allowed. Notions of loyalty, trust, reciprocity and thence meaningful human relationships fall completely outside the purview of the procedural state – something its social democratic advocates often fail to notice.

Listening enables genuine dispute and deliberation about what is the shared good in this place for these people at this time. Its opposite involves either the predetermination of what that good might consist of via some theoretical construction; the refusal of the possibility of such a shared good within the individualistic interest-based politics of liberalism and neo-liberalism; or the refusal of a common world of meaning and action in the identity politics of multiculturalism. Common goods discerned through a process of relational listening are neither the aggregation of individual self-interests nor the defence of vested interests but goods in which the flourishing of each is dependent on the flourishing of all. Pursuit of common goods requires political judgement rather than letting a market mechanism, electoral process or some technocratic procedure determine the good by a system of aggregation. Such proceduralism constitutes a refusal to make political judgements.

COMMUNITY AND CITIZENSHIP

To be a good citizen we need the experience and ability of ruling and being ruled. It is this experience that forms the basis of our ability to make good political judgements. As Tocqueville notes:

It is, indeed, difficult to conceive how men who have entirely given up the habit of self-government should succeed in making a proper choice of those by whom they are to be governed; and no one will ever believe that a liberal, wise, and energetic government can spring from the suffrages of a subservient people.[11]

The kind of arenas through which we gain the experience of ruling and being ruled are schools, forms of vocational, professional and craft production, congregations or any form of semi-independent, self-organised practice of cooperative association. But while such experience of self-rule is a necessary condition, it is not a sufficient one to make wise citizens capable of good political judgements. The likes of Robert Putnam hail the importance of associations for the health of democracy, but the mere fact of associating does not determine whether a group will be civil or uncivil, democratic or anti-democratic. The crucial factor is whether an association is prepared to contribute to and communicate with others in order to build a common life. This is the key to determining whether it is democratic or not.

The experience and ability of common work between different associations and their particular interests is vital for a genuinely democratic politics. Herein lies the vocation of a political party. The point of a political party is not only to provide experience and training in ruling and being ruled but also to mediate relationships between different forms of association and interests in the pursuit of goods in common. Without this kind of cross-institutional experience, institutions are vulnerable to being co-opted by the state, subordinating that which gives them purpose and meaning to the logic of capitalism (and thereby becoming commodified), or turning against each other in competitive and inter-communal rivalry. Democratic citizenship is constituted by those practices that enable us to pursue a common life between multiple loyalties while at the same time honouring our non-civic, familial, communal and institutional loyalties as having worth and value.

RELIGIOUS AND SECULAR

It is the insight of Blue Labour that the problem of religion in modernity and the problem of how to limit the overweening power of the state and the market are interrelated. The disenchanted or 'secular' modern world struggles to recognise the vital role of corporate and associational life in politics. We give legal personality and priority to corporations in the market sphere, but refuse that same recognition and priority to both religious and political forms of corporate life. Unlike its relationship to market-based corporations, the nation state constructs citizens as individual voters and religious observers as volunteers who choose to be part of a congregation but whose beliefs and practices are private. Yet neither the demos nor the congregation is a crowd in which each member does his or her own bidding. Rather, both the ability to act together either as democratic citizens or as congregants requires common action in pursuit of shared goods.

For those without power and who cannot deploy either the resources of the state or the power of money to achieve their ends, democratic citizenship opens up the possibility of relational power: one can act together to defend or pursue mutual interests. As in a congregation, associational forms of common action to generate change demand discipline and loyalty. Loyalty or faithfulness is vital for developing any kind of common life. Without it, promises are broken, commitments are not kept, trust cannot develop and so the possibility of long-term reciprocal relations is dissolved. Such loyal and loving and thence hopeful relations are the only kind that can hold in check the over-concentration of either economic or political power and the monopolisation of resources by a narrow range of interests.

In the American and British contexts, forms of popular, local self-organisation and common action emerge within such movements as the anti-slavery and abolitionist movements, the Chartists, the Suffragists, and the temperance and the civil rights movements. These were aligned and had a symbiotic relationship with popular religion. Another good example is the nineteenth-century Populists whose critique of monopolistic forms of power was combined with the language of the Methodist camp meetings and Baptist revivals in order to generate a powerful rhetoric with which to challenge the status quo. What these movements represent, and what they feed into a notion of Blue Labour's conception of democratic citizenship, is the assertion of the priority of corporate forms of social relationships in the upholding of common values and a common life over and against their instrumentalisation and commodification through political and economic processes. That is, society comes before state or market.

In terms of the relationship between organised religion and democratic citizenship Blue Labour contends that the best way to prevent the subordination of human flourishing and mutually responsible social relationships to the demands of capitalist market and the state is not law or some other procedure but through power born out of associating for common action. As already noted, the congregation and the demos are echoes of each other and neither is a crowd or multitude whose disassociated and disorganised form leaves the individual utterly vulnerable to concerted action upon her by state or market processes. Moreover, it is a partnership that can bring a mutual discipline to both the congregation and the demos. In joint action in pursuit of common goods, the congregation has to listen to and learn from its neighbours. Conversely, the congregation, as a moral tradition with a transcendent, universalistic vision of the good brings a wider horizon of reference and relationship to bear upon the immediate needs and demands of the demos. This mutual disciplining helps ensure both congregations and democratic politics (as a vehicle for the encounter with difference) remain directed towards political rather than authoritarian and anti-democratic ends.

LOCAL BEFORE NATIONAL

As well as family and faith the other left-wing 'F' word Blue Labour addresses is 'flag'. Patriotism may be broadly equated with the notion that there is a duty or reverence due from each person to the civic community, the land and the cultural environment to which one owes the condition and possibility of one's own development and future prospects. The Roman term for this, found particularly in Virgil and Cicero, was the virtue of *pietas*. I did not create the language, values and legal system or the environmental, economic and political context on which I depend and so I owe the people and place which made it possible a duty of care and respect. This is as true for the refugee and economic migrant as it is for the native. The patriot – one possessing the virtue of *pietas* – recognises the need to value his or her civic life and identity. However, that life should not be over-valued or sacralised and is not determinative of all relations; for example, one's religious, familial or professional duties may stand over and against or place limits on one's civic obligations. Patriotism

grows out of both a need for others – living in the same place one
depends on them for one's flourishing – but also friendship and
affection for those one lives amongst. Relationship with one's
neighbours is based first on utility and mutual dependence but can –
through familiarity, shared practices and customs – develop into
civic friendship which gives rise to a sense of *pietas* for one's city or
commonwealth. Thus patriotism has both an instrumental and an
affective aspect: mutual need gives rise to mutual aid that in turn
fosters public friendship. Public friendship forms the basis of *pietas*
or civic patriotism. In pointing to the symbiosis of mutual interest
and public friendship in the formation of *pietas* for a particular place
we can see that this place-based *pietas* is simply the analogue of
instances of work-based *pietas* such as is found in a guild, trade
union, or professional association, all of which integrate utility and
solidarity.

A place-based or municipal vision of *pietas* contrasts sharply with
universalist and nationalist forms. A universalist liberal cosmopolitan
conception of *pietas*, as found in Bentham and Kant, is one where
pietas to humanity is understood as overriding and prior to the *pietas*
owed to one's particular locality and community. The liberal
cosmopolitan view is best summarised by Liebniz's statement that:
'I am indifferent to that which constitutes a German or a Frenchman
because I will only the good of all mankind'.[12] Such a universalistic
conception of *pietas* fosters the Mrs Jellyby syndrome that devalues
and undermines local patterns of association and public friendship in
the name of some abstract ideal or distant programme.[13] What is
proposed here contrasts also with nationalist forms of *pietas*. While
operating on a more intermediary scale, reverence for the imagined
community of the nation is still working at a high level of abstraction
and subordinates the local to the national interest. Moreover, its all-
encompassing nature has too often led *pietas* for the nation to become
a pietistic nationalism that shows no pity for those identified as
enemies and sacralises and makes an idol of a contingent political
formation. What is proposed here is a municipal *pietas*, so that being
from London, Leeds or Loughborough (or more broadly, from city,
town or shire) becomes the basis for a shared identity story and sense
of loyalty that can sit alongside, interrupt and contest either national
or universal commitments (whether religious, philosophical or
economic) and their oftentimes abstracting and depoliticising
orientation.

The municipal vision of patriotism sketched here points to a way to rethink questions of union and federalism. Rather than focus on how to create an English parliament or how to rethink the relationship between England, Scotland, Wales and Northern Ireland conceived of as national units, what is needed is genuinely political federalism that starts with population density. London, Glasgow and Cardiff are perhaps more salient units of governance that England, Wales or Scotland. A genuinely federal system of governance for the British Isles that retains Westminster as its point of national government could devolve more power to urban mayoralties and to more ancient forms of rural governance – the county hundred, the division and the shire – calculated on the basis of households within an area (albeit a calculation modulated through the lens of historic, affective ties). These would form the basis of a less centralised, more genuinely democratic and socially federated form of government.[14]

CONCLUDING REFLECTIONS

Nurturing and sustaining political relationships requires virtue, vocation and moral vision. However good its intentions, a politics without such pieties is pitiless and alienating. Although conversely, attention to virtue, vocation and vision without any broader conception and engagement in politics is pitiful, as it has no means to challenge, protect and pursue the very relationships it loves and values most in the face of their erosion and co-option by the market and the state. A politics that fails to pay heed to the health of the moral vision, virtue and associational life of the people it claims to represent will leave untended not only the basis of its political vision, but also the basis of its ability to make good political judgements. This applies to Blue Labour as much as to any other political vision.

NOTES

1. Many of these reflections grew out of work Maurice Glasman and I did together with London Citizens and draw on a more systematic account of this given in Luke Bretherton, *Resurrecting Democracy: Faith, Citizenship and the Politics of a Common Life* (Cambridge: Cambridge University Press, 2015).
2. 'In my view, he who conforms his course of action to the quality of the times will fare well, and conversely he whose course of action clashes

with the times will fare badly', in Niccolo Machiavelli, *The Prince*, tr. P. Constantine (New York: Modern Library, 2008), p. 116.

3. The recognition of the unpredictable nature of political life is not to assert it is a realm of total chaos. It is simply to recognise that political judgements address modes of action different from those of the chemist or engineer and no amount of 'evidence-based policy' can circumvent this.

4. Arguably this has been a feature of key streams of radical politics in the modern period. On this see Craig Calhoun, *The Roots of Radicalism: Tradition, The Public Sphere and the Early Nineteenth-Century Social Movements* (Chicago: Chicago University Press, 2012).

5. Hannah Arendt, *The Human Condition*, 2nd ed. (Chicago: University of Chicago Press, 1958), p. 198.

6. Bernard Crick, *In Defence of Politics*, 5th ed. (London: Continuum, 2005), p. 4.

7. Sheldon Wolin, *Politics and Vision: Continuity and Innovation in Western Political Thought* (Princeton, N.J.: Princeton University Press, 2004), p. 261. See also James C. Scott, *Seeing Like a State: How Certain Schemes to Improve the Human Condition Have Failed* (New Haven: Yale University Press, 1998).

8. Wolin states: 'The free politics of a liberal society allows, indeed presumes, that those who control economic power are naturally entitled and expected to promote corporate or self-interest through the political process', in Wolin, *Politics and Vision*, p. 526.

9. Sheldon Wolin, *The Presence of the Past: Essays on the State and the Constitution* (Baltimore: Johns Hopkins University Press, 1989), p. 139.

10. Craig Calhoun clarifies the sociological relationship between 'archaic' traditions and the rejuvenation of a 'radical' politics that challenges the status quo. Against Marx, Weber and most other modern social theory, he contends there is no inherent incompatibility between tradition and rationality and that political thinkers from left and right have failed to understand the 'paradoxical conservatism' in revolution and the radicalism of tradition. He argues that traditional modes of corporatism provide the social foundations and means of organisation for widespread popular mobilisations and that traditional values, particularly when these are threatened by rapid change and modern capitalist-dominated social formations, provide the rationality for legitimating radical political action that opposes elite centres of power. Craig Calhoun, 'The radicalism of tradition: community strength or venerable disguise and borrowed language?' *American Journal of Sociology* 88 (1983), pp. 886–914. Calhoun's analysis helps explain the seeming paradoxical yet consistent link between 'conservative' religious congregations and the 'radical' politics of community organising.

11. Tocqueville, *Democracy in America*, IV.6.
12. Quoted from Thomas Schlereth, *The Cosmopolitan Ideal* (Notre Dame: University of Notre Dame, 1977), pp. xxiv–xxv.
13. Mrs Jellyby is a character in Charles Dickens' *Bleak House* who is a 'telescopic philanthropist' more concerned with an obscure African tribe than her duty of care to her family to the extent that she nearly destroys herself and them.
14. Arguably, this would chime with such initiatives as transition towns.

CHAPTER SIXTEEN

The Labour Family

Michael Merrick

INTRODUCTION

The family. Not something the contemporary left is terribly good at talking about, the family. Mere mention of the word can bring about fits of blushes in the more timid whilst raising the hackles of an energetic few just waiting to pounce on anything that smacks of judgement or prejudice. When, in the occasional burst of courage, the left does advance and broach the subject of the family, the words that come out of its mouth are often so vague and platitudinous as to verge on the meaningless. They do not say anything in particular, because they think not saying anything in particular is the safest thing to say. Or, worse, they believe that not saying anything in particular is the right thing to say.

The reasons for this are myriad, though one main problem is that there are so many people one can potentially upset, or at least presume to upset (which is not quite the same thing). So many identities and ideologies, so many lifestyles and life choices, all of which must be respected if we are to fulfil what has become the ultimate and overriding goal of the contemporary left: to be inclusive. The logic of this is circular, as we shall see, but for now suffice it to say that talk of the family can appear such a toxic issue because, save for the release of saccharine niceties laden with innumerable caveats so as to avoid all possible offence, it is just so hard to get right. Politicians, terrified of appearing moralistic before an electorate who know all too well the shortcomings of the political classes, instead choose silence for fear their appeal to accounts of the good might instead appear as diatribe delivered from upon high to those living on the truly sharp edge of such realities.

For those who disregard the taboos, who earnestly appeal to the values of the Labour Party they grew up with, the values of their parents and grandparents before them, who speak honestly and unambiguously about the family, its importance to society, its breakdown, the role of the state in its breakdown and the consequences of that breakdown – for those courageous souls the political collateral is significant. If their ideas are tolerated then their presence within positions of prominence with which to enact their delusions and/or prejudices most certainly is not. Such speakers are banished to the fringes, since in daring to say something particular they also sound exclusionary, thereby abandoning (their opponents would claim) those vulnerable people whom the aim of Labour it is to champion.

Yet it must be recognised that the left have not always placed themselves in this position. There was a time when they talked openly and freely on the subject of the family, primarily because they talked openly and freely about moral imperatives and the common good without the constraints of relativism and reticence that so besets the contemporary left. Which leads us to the single biggest reason why the contemporary left does not and often cannot talk effectively about the family: *it has embraced a creed that limits its ability to do so.*

This creed, the unchallengeable orthodoxy of a liberal activist core (which shall hereafter be referred to as the New Left), though not of many others, is a political and philosophical stumbling block. The contemporary left, dominated by their middle-class urban intelligentsia, have adopted an account of self and social more consistent with the free-marketeering logic they claim to despise than the mutualistic Labour tradition under whose banner they earnestly march. Ideas supposedly shunned in the economic sphere are the same ideas warmly embraced in the social. In the words of John Milbank, 'Politics has become a shadow play. In reality, economic and cultural liberalism go together and increase together. The left has won the cultural war, and the right has won the economic war. But of course, they are really both on the same side'.[1]

As such, the contemporary left has wandered down a logical and political blind-alley. Cognisant of ways in which liberalism in the economic markets has ravaged communities, it refuses to countenance ways in which liberalism in the social markets has produced.

the same. Able to give coherent accounts of how economic capital, or the lack of it, can corrode the roots of family life, it nonetheless stumbles and stutters when confronted with how social capital, or the lack of it, has proven every bit as insidious. The contemporary left will acknowledge that the family was the traditional bulwark against the acute poverty suffered by our forebears, though refuse to countenance ways in which the 'progress' championed by Labour Mum, to use Maurice Glasman's terms, has often come through jettisoning precisely those protective customs and conventions once upheld by (now-cowed) Labour Dad.[2]

In what follows I shall try to give an account of how these ideas inhibit the left's ability to talk meaningfully about the family, a dereliction that has harmed its core constituency more than any other. The evidential argument is not one that I seek to offer. The evidence pertaining to the broad superiority of the stable family for producing positive life outcomes for children is so overwhelming that it seems tedious to reproduce it here. Besides, such an argument is unlikely to convince those that have set their face against it, precisely because they have set their face against it primarily on non-evidential terms. The questions I shall attempt to address, then, are these: how has this situation come to pass? What form has it taken? And what can Blue Labour offer in response?

THE RISE OF THE REVOLUTIONARY NEW LEFT

To tell the tale of the revolutionary New Left is actually to tell the tale of the gradual triumph of radically right-wing accounts of the social sphere. Or, perhaps more accurately, it is to document the gradual triumph of a fundamentally asocial ideology able to manifest itself in the language and thought of both wings of the political spectrum. It is for this reason that the saga is not restricted to the political left, even whilst we can readily admit that the political left is where the culture and thought of which we speak originally found its most obliging host. Rather, documented here is the broad advance of an idea, a habit of thought, which gradually commanded loyalty across the political spectrum. The left's role as recounted here, therefore, was as much through contribution to the evolution of this doctrine as through the pursuit of particular legislation, be it their own or that of others.

The key word that frames the entire movement here described is 'liberty', the cherished goal that runs through the very DNA of the

New Left. However, the liberty of the revolution was not, to phrase it in Blue Labour terms, constructed within relational frameworks drawing upon notions of virtue to define civic and social freedoms, but was instead portrayed as the autonomous individual empowered to freely contract relationships of consensual exchange. Liberty so defined was predicated upon a rejection of the social: the founding principle was that agents should have freedom to enter the social marketplace as autonomous actors, liberated of unwarrantable restraints spread horizontally throughout the community and/or imposed vertically through the levers of the state.

Thus, the organic interweaving of *civitas* and *societas* that traditionally constructed the 'social conscience', within which the individual operated as one interconnecting link in a living social chain, was gradually decried as imposing upon the individual illegitimate restrictions to the reasonable pursuit of self-interest. Norman Dennis, speaking from within the tradition of English ethical socialism, commented on the similarities between free-market thinking and the post-1960s social and sexual revolution championed primarily by a middle-class intelligentsia. For him, the common feature was the primacy of self-interest over 'the irrational restrictions of socially inculcated "conscience" and rules of conduct regarded as being absolutely binding regardless of the wishes or welfare of the particular individual'.[3]

In other words, potentially restrictive claims of family, custom, community or tradition were out, and the pursuit of self-interest was in. In this sense, the social revolutionaries really were constitutionally anti-social, the ASBO generation of their time. They elevated 'I' over 'us', promoted the pursuit of individual goals over claims of communal interest, and used the reasoning they would later claim to eschew in order to achieve it. Laissez-faire liberalism was embraced in the personal sphere even whilst denounced, for a time at least, in the economic. Or, put more glibly, what the New Left claimed to reject in the boardroom they demanded in the bedroom.

The problem was, as Phillip Blond has argued, this deified not choice but rather the act of choosing, such that the left's accounts of autonomy no longer consisted in a particular vision of the good life, based upon distinctions between good and bad choices, but instead on an illusory 'neutrality' that offered only the guarantee of the freedom to choose.[4] The refusal to distinguish between successful and unsuccessful attempts at the art of living well left politicians using libertarian means to pursue libertine ends, such that fashionable political mantras focused exclusively on the noble ideal of giving people more power, without ever indulging discussion on what people ought properly to do with it. The role of the state was not to cajole citizens into making the kind of life choices that the chief custodians of relational politics, tradition and community had long decreed were best for both individual and society, but rather to remove potential impediments to self-fulfilment and secure the capacity of the individual to act as an autonomous agent within the social marketplace. Here, then, is the source of spittle-flecked disdain towards those heresies to the progressive creed, social and moral conservatism, that articulated fixed ideas on behavioural standards in satisfaction of the obligations one owes principally toward not oneself, but others.

As such, the advance of the New Left established the near-wholesale acceptance within the Labour Party, and more recently within the Tory Party too, of the language and logic of absolutised individual sovereignty: the belief that society, custom, convention, ritual, duty, responsibility, taboo and tradition held no legitimate transcending claim over individual action – that these were arbitrary, unreasonable and illegitimate, remnants of a romanticism that the new rationalism does not permit.[5] Individuals were competitors in the social markets, and so long as interactions were conducted upon lines of mutual consent then good government consisted in guaranteeing the freedom necessary for that exchange.

Whilst this constituted a departure from certain classical liberal thinkers, who upheld the importance of social restraints even if they could not adequately explain why, the triumph of coldly contractual accounts of the social revealed the Rousseauian ancestry from which it derived, such that the idea that commitments should pertain beyond the collapse of mutual consent was anathema. Liberal economic dogma was producing an army of free-marketeers on the political right who maintained that two independent agents should be allowed to enter freely into contracts of exchange without external interference; preceding it was an army of free-marketeers on the left using much the same arguments to break open the social markets.

Accordingly, the left became stultified by an attempt at neutrality that neutered its ability to articulate the moral instincts of the many, choosing instead to level down all life choices as equally valid and tarring those who challenged such accounts of freedom as moralistic, judgemental or prejudiced. In so doing, the left ceased to communicate what its tradition instinctively knew: that true and authentic freedom comes not through liberation of choice, but through the act of choosing wisely.

STATISM AND WELFARE

The lurch toward statism that had become a hallmark of post-war left-wing politics provided the intellectual infrastructure for a re-envisioning of a state that could police and underwrite these new accounts of freedom. For liberty to flourish the state had to remain neutral toward the conduct of those residing within it. It could dispense justice where contracts were unjustly breached, but the manner in which they were drawn, the manner in which they ended, and the manner in which they affected third parties and society as a whole remained outside the purview of the state. Yet it also needed vigorous protection and a legislative commitment to mitigate the fallout from such self-centred accounts of freedom. This put the state in direct competition with that supportive web of relationships that traditionally regulated individual behaviour as well as helped absorb fallout when required. In providing an alternative to these networks, in rendering associative, reciprocal, mutualistic society no longer at the core of individual progress and preservation, the state had begun to monopolise the space where society used to be. The result was corrosive to any sort of relational politics; a system with a focus on outcomes, as Ruth Porter explains, 'removes any connection between action and consequence. In doing so, it destroys the very reflex which encourages moral action. By consequence, this breeds a sense of entitlement. This undermines social bonds both in families and also communities more broadly'.[6]

Thus welfare became the vehicle that reflected and advanced the newly reconfigured social arena: if a key Blue Labour principle is 'no responsibility without power', then this becomes a rejection of the statist liberalism that had guaranteed power and eschewed respon-sibility.[7] The theoretical universalisms which informed accounts of individual freedom thus nudged welfare provision toward assessment of need, freed of important contextual detail.[8] The inherent relativism in the 'freedom' of the New Left produced a morally neutral welfare system offering assistance regardless of personal behaviour. On such terms the state alleviated only material deprivation, a morally neutral

scale that did not impinge upon the free agency of the individual. The
result was a system that increasingly bore the cost of family
breakdown rather than challenging it. Mitigation soon resembled
facilitation.[9]

Welfare, then, corroded those behavioural norms and expectations
that historically constituted the social conscience. Welfare was
rendered a 'right' distinct from any authentic notion of reciprocity,
precisely because the commonly held moral framework within which
reciprocity might have held meaning was denied by the relativism
inherent to the system. As such, welfare became disconnected from
the lived realities of its recipients, no longer reflecting situated
concepts of fairness or justice. Detached, distant, bureaucratic,
unreflective of the moral framework within which most people still
operated, at times even agitating against it: little wonder that public
faith in the system corroded.[10] Old networks underpinning
community and place, family and friendships, had fallen prey to
the flourishing doctrine of social isolationism among our newly
nihilistic elites. Putting right this wrong, through the resurrection of a
reciprocal, contributory approach toward welfare, has become a
touchstone issue for Blue Labour, an instinct that has received broad
support across the political spectrum.

The cumulative effect of these changes was a challenge to the
primacy of the family as the fundamental social (and socialising)
institution, the unit that had proved the most effective safety net and
ladder for the most vulnerable. In making neediness the criterion for
state help, so neediness itself was incentivised, implicitly encouraging
the abandonment of those relational bonds that could now actually
render one less eligible for state assistance. The state had, in effect,
bypassed lateral relations and set up a panopticonic relationship
between the individual agent and the central authority – what John
Milbank has termed the 'simple space'. The condition-free support of
the state provided an easy alternative that undermined family
authority and its capacity to influence behaviour. Obligations proper
to kith and kin, and the power of kith and kin to insist on them, had
been negated in the name of freedom.

INDIVIDUAL CHOICE AND THE MARKET

Far from being an unforeseen consequence, such a development was
the logical outcome of the marketisation of personal and social

relationships, since if the state was obliged to preserve freedom of contract then it also had to accept the freedom of individuals to break contract. In the family realm, this meant two individuals could legitimately separate simply because they no longer wished to be together, regardless of third-party commitments. Obligations beyond the pursuit of individual happiness, such as the presence of children in the family home, no longer had the moral gravity to trump the pursuit of self-interest of those adults that had entered into the original agreement. Divorce law began to reflect this change. Research bodies and charitable organisations, pockets full with government funding, celebrated new diverse family forms that began to take shape and disparaged the notion that the old model was best.[11] The state funded more and more schemes to advise, support and help pay for divorce and separation, through legal aid, whilst remaining strictly indifferent to whether divorce or separation was the desirable outcome. The idea that policy might be developed to actively build resilience and stability within the family, as outlined recently by Jon Cruddas,[12] was largely anathema.[13] Yet again, mitigation began to look like facilitation.

The extended family unit, appealed to as the saving grace by those seeking to stress the outmoded character of the nuclear model around which extended ties spread, became harder to establish since the strong and closely knit extended family grew around the stability of the founding unit, that being the mutual creation shared by mother and father of the child. The blood and guts realities of such freedoms, the significant statistical deterioration of potential life outcomes for children growing up in such circumstances, or the significant increase in the likelihood of child abuse in non-traditional family structures, was brushed aside through a mixture of what Norman Dennis has neatly referred to as Social Micawberism and the habit of treating genuinely heart-breaking exceptions to the rules as the normative policy by which to proceed.

Just as the pursuit of self-interest lay at the heart of this new philosophy, so it was no surprise that its adherents were unable to confront the consequences of the abandonment of relational accounts of the individual. Intellectually tidy accounts of freedom formulated by a class of upwardly mobile and privileged theorists displaced genuinely social accounts of how concepts such as freedom are actually lived out in the complex and messy world of relationships, with heretics denounced as prejudiced throwbacks to an uncivilised age. Yet, as Tristram Hunt noted when writing of the metropolitan left's hostility to marriage, opposition to sexism meant 'many on the metropolitan left embraced a Marxist hostility to marriage and the family as a political end in itself. As it did so, it aligned itself with an ethos of social hedonism with profoundly unprogressive consequences for the offspring of generations of unstable households'.[14]

Swathes of evidence mapping the significant statistical deterioration of life chances for those experiencing family breakdown, data illustrating the disastrous effects on the poorest communities, even the impassioned testimonies of those living on the sharp edge of such realities, were routinely rebuffed with manufactured ambiguities and smear: this was really just a right-wing attack on single mothers, or the outrageous imposition of the right-wing bigotry of a previous age, or the chauvinistic right-wing assumption that women need men in child-rearing. That the consequences most acutely affected the poorest allowed the professional left to convince themselves, in a neat non sequitur, that the sole enemy was poverty, even whilst its own tradition held that impoverishment could be caused by and expressed through more than just the material.[15]

At root, this was a clash of interests, in which the central dogma had to be protected because the relatively empowered New Left set that had dominated the landscape for so long were the very people who benefited most from the tilting of the social markets: as with economic free-marketeers, cries of 'freedom' rang most loudly from that already empowered bloc that had the most to gain from it. The poorest, increasingly without the networks that once sustained and propelled them, living the consequences of this new 'freedom', were simply less competitive in the markets. The words of Chesterton took on a prophetic air: 'Modern broad-mindedness benefits the rich; and benefits nobody else. It was meant to benefit the rich; and meant to benefit nobody else'.

As such, the wider cultural erosion of the family hastened the triumph of the free-marketeers, who asserted the natural right to independent action, an account of liberty more structured toward removing restraints on the powerful than enhancing the life chances of the vulnerable. The result, more often than not, was the same: the poorest, without the resources to absorb the consequences of this latest revolution, more reliant than their empowered comrades on those institutions and safety nets that the new philosophy corroded, became most entrapped by the pernicious consequences of it. The most vulnerable became more enchained by circumstance, all in the name of making them free.

Indeed, so complete was the triumph that Labour even pursued the dissolution of those charitable institutions that maintained the primacy of the traditional family unit as the framework within which to provide loving and stable family homes for vulnerable children. The traditional family unit was no longer a protected model, and had to be opened up to free-market competition. Any political move to suggest otherwise was fiercely rejected. Those who refused the move, who elevated one model over another, who practised market protectionism, soon found themselves on the wrong side of the law. Not because of any sense that harm might come to children helped by such agencies, but rather because the refusal to embrace neutralism collided with the dogmas of the new open-market morality. The language within which such action proceeded perhaps provides the best view of the phenomenon I am attempting to describe; Catholic adoption agencies were closed down, even whilst the pool of adoptive parents was (and has continued) in an alarming downward spiral, since it was deemed they contravened equality laws constructed to prevent discrimination in the provision of 'goods and services'. Whilst Catholic adoption agencies spoke of vulnerable orphans needing the love of mothers and fathers, Labour was theorising equality through access to markets, to 'goods and services'.

FREEDOM, FRAGMENTATION, FATHERHOOD

Whilst the social revolution of the 1960s can be linked to the economic revolution of the 1980s in many ways, one key theme around which both came to coalesce was the notion that financial independence, viewed in isolationist terms, was the guarantor of individual sovereignty. Not genuine independence, with individuals owning the means or fruits of their production, but relational independence, visualised as freedom from monetary reliance upon others within the immediate circle of relationships. To be free, the individual had to be able to be alone.

And this directly influenced welfare policy. Mothers were offered such freedom as financial independence from the father of their child, the state assuming the role of surrogate parent in the provision of resources, an incentive all the more potent the further one descended down the economic scale and the potential financial contribution of the father decreased. This constituted the rejection of interdependence in the family home and parenting, a corrosion of the dignity of fatherhood all the more powerful in the most vulnerable communities. Put simply, fathers were deemed less than necessary, both financially and developmentally.[16] In the words of Frank Field, responding to the testimony of a young father detailing from personal experience what the Centre for Social Justice have termed 'the couples' penalty', 'if you were devising a crazy system in which to mess up kids, you'd come up with the system we've got now, wouldn't you?'[17]

As such, fathers were increasingly redundant. Young men were made the beneficiaries of a philosophy that claimed to liberate females, dissolving as it did traditional accounts of obligation and duty, eradicating those civilising and socialising responsibilities traditionally bestowed by social rites of passage, chief among them being fatherhood. Whilst the financial implications of fatherhood could be met by the state, the idea gained momentum that children suffered no developmental or emotional impairment from the lack of a father-figure within the family home.[18] Thus mothers were convinced they need not rely upon men, whereupon more and more young males became the kind of men that women really could not rely upon.

Whilst the state could offer autonomy through welfare provision, for most financial sovereignty came through labouring for a wage. Or, put another way, by the new rules of the game people were most free when they worked, which for the vast majority meant when they worked for someone else. Such logic was untouched by older insights on the spiritual value of work, insights that informed a once widespread critique of capitalism, but focused instead on the capacity to labour for a wage in order to prevent dependence on others. Thus, in a neat irony, subjugation to capitalist interest was all of a sudden a legitimate means of securing autonomy, rather than the chief impediment against it. This distinctly anti-social autonomy was still, for the majority, framed in terms of reliance, only now reliance was spread outside of the immediate relationship circle and toward distant agencies, thus freeing the individual from dependence upon those within their vicinity.

This narrative proved most radical for women, traditionally financially dependent on their spouse, and was instructive of the creeds of a particular, privileged middle-class movement trading on the theories of a nineteenth-century factory owner that the domestic was the most intimate site of the exploitative capitalistic economy. All of a sudden, relying on the income of a spouse was an affront to authentic autonomy rather than a possible, if not only, enabler of it. Thus the progressive march set about removing all obstacles to entry into the workplace: the irony did not register that in so single-minded a pursuit one saw eliminated all those competing loyalties and commitments that might traditionally have preserved the freedom of women not to be co-opted into a lifetime on the factory floor.

With competing ties dissolved, accordingly the left began to treat mothers as absentees from the marketplace, a truancy that dovetailed with a coldly bureaucratic vision of mothers as independent economic units, not yet fulfilling their potential, to be re-entered into the markets as soon as the opportunity presented itself. Here, the value and importance of domestic work was downplayed, precisely because it did not conform to either market liberalism and GDP generation, or a new and highly particular form of feminism unwilling to value the significance of work done in the home. The positive freedom to choose stay-at-home parenting received limited support, seen as an unproductive lifestyle choice, less desirable than re-entry into the GDP-generating workplace. Government assistance here also combined with market forces to exert pressure on women to become GDP-generators once more, abrogating to the state responsibilities once undertaken within the family home, intertwining nudge welfare designed to bring new mothers back into the workplace.

The outcome was a left-wing politics that thought it best represented mothers by removing all obstacles, biological and familial, to their re-entry into the workplace. In reality, an already empowered group were raising to the status of universal progress that which best coalesced around their own interests, desires and priorities. The equality narrative took on a distinctly middle-class air, such that progress focused on the relative lack of females in the boardrooms of top companies and corporations and rarely addressed the changing economic landscape that, over the decades, had made stay-at-home motherhood, or indeed fatherhood, a privilege exclusive to the wealthy classes.[19] Clearly discernible was the latent prejudice which deemed domesticity unable to secure either empowerment or autonomy, so that those seeking independence must either forsake one or juggle both. The instinct stemmed from the liberal re-envisioning of relationships: 'family is often, after all, an impediment to freedom and autonomy, a constraining realm of obligation and duty'.[20] In the guise of freedom to work, Labour increasingly demanded that all did so: they fought the good fight for parents to have freedom from the family, but expended far less effort in guaranteeing the freedom to stay with the family. And rarely did the welfare claims of children feature in this negotiation of individual freedoms.

This same restraint toward the associative ties of the family was also evident in education policy. After all, if parents were to be coaxed back to work, then schools needed to pick up the slack. Schools thus took on more and more responsibility for child welfare, and on much broader criteria than the traditional responsibility for development of the intellect. Once deemed to exist in order to assist parents in the education of their children, for our political classes schools took on the role of parenting our children, too. Policy had long marched toward wrap-around child care, which both underpinned the freedom of parents to work whilst keeping the markets serviced with reliable labour. This reached a peak under Michael Gove, whose inability to draw the line between family and state became a defining characteristic of his liberal interventionism, speaking regularly of a vision in which schools were childcare units, complete with longer days, shorter holidays, summer camps and sleepovers.[21] Such a blurring of the lines was advanced amidst pious cries of ensuring children 'get a good start', or for helping families 'juggle family life and work commitments'. In the clash between the market, the family and individual empowerment, our political classes decided we best help the family by paying for parents to spend less time with it.[22]

This presumption of fracture is clearly visible in what has become the cause célèbre of education reformers: social mobility. Whilst academic attainment is almost universally desired by parents, the cold utilitarianism that has long underpinned the reformers' approach betrays an implicit distaste – educational achievement for the poorest is too often about ensuring poorer children are different from their parents. With the absence of any account of the value of rootedness and place, social mobility became little more than the ability to move away from those we know and love, a phenomenon that affected the regions more acutely since moving away was often the non-negotiable price for pursuing such accounts of success.[23] Thus, family and background was a potential drag, something to be left behind or at the very least overcome, Billy Elliot-like, rather than the very foundations of future achievement and flourishing. We may now be beginning to scratch our heads and wonder at isolation and social atomism, yet we must consider the impact of having spent a generation and more telling young people that the reason we educate ourselves is to be able to walk away from who we are, or at the very least where we are from.

The net result of all of the above was the emergence of a left-wing politics incapable of speaking in the language of the family. Consideration of child welfare was rarely broached: the new morality was about the liberty of consenting adults. The embrace and pursuit of the free-market social sphere dissolved historic obligations to protect the family over and above alternative models, and indeed impressed upon the revolutionaries every reason not to do so. The family, long buffeted by the economic markets, now also buffeted by the social markets, began to dissolve. And its dissolution has destabilised more than anyone else that very constituency that Labour historically fought the hardest to protect.

THE CONTEMPORARY CONTEXT AND THE CHALLENGE OF BLUE LABOUR

Looking round, it would seem the landscape is changing. The very emergence of Blue Labour testifies to that. Emboldened by opportunities presented by the political dislocation of recent years, more and more dare question the zeitgeist. Following decades of socio-economic flux, there has emerged, in Jonathan Rutherford's words, 'an appetite in the country to conserve, safeguard, protect, defend and improve the fundamental elements of social life which are relationships, a sense of belonging, the familiarity of place, social security, the valuing of tradition, history, the past which is the basis of contemporary culture and social meaningfulness'.[24] The revivification of mutualism and reciprocity in the Labour conversation has meant revolutionary orthodoxies are beginning to creak. People look at the society they have delivered and sense something is wrong. And the questions are fundamental: what has the breakdown of the family achieved? How has it happened? Who has it really set free? How do we make things better? As Andrea Westall has suggested, the implicit neo-liberalism of the New Labour years had a tendency to use the language and logic of the markets, even in those places where the market did not belong.[25] A Labour tradition capable of permitting the new conversation, let alone pursuing it, will find itself connecting with the innermost anxieties and concerns of those it wishes to represent. It will ditch its off-the-peg nihilism and once again find fluency in the language of life, of love, of liberty.

The left has within its tradition the tools to critique the external pressures placed on the family and the wider community by the advances of global capital systems. With this it offers something unique to the political milieu, allowing it to talk with clarity and wisdom on the pernicious outcomes delivered by the uncritical embrace of globalisation and economic liberalism, most explicit during Thatcher's reign though embraced further by the New Labour project. Labour also has within its tradition the tools to critique the pressures placed on family and community by the drastic draining of social capital from our communities. This also offers something unique to the political milieu, something genuinely ordered toward the protection of the most vulnerable. Each of these analyses need each other if they are to be truly holistic, truly penetrative in insight. The left seeks to offer the former, but fails in its articulation of the latter, unable to speak the gritty language of lived relationships, incapable of verbalising what most instinctively feel, of taking its insights on vertical systems and institutions and spreading them horizontally through communities and individuals.

But it really should. With a renewed critique of liberalism, the left will rediscover the tools with which to fight the unjust pressure being exerted upon those most susceptible to social and economic libertarianism. If, on the contrary, Labour remains speechless on the good, the virtuous, even (dare one say it) the moral, then lost is a narrative lens through which to articulate and determine such fuzzy concepts as 'social justice'. After all, if one eschews talk of moral and virtuous action, then one can no more deride the selfish pursuit of self-interest that breaks up economies than the selfish pursuit of self-interest that breaks up families – they share the same moral roots. In which case what frameworks, other than mere subjectivistic outrage, does the morally neutral left have available to call out such conduct? By critiquing liberalism, Labour will rediscover its voice, and rediscover its radicalism. Blue Labour can help our proud tradition re-articulate one of its most important insights: disempowerment comes through fracturing of relationships; we are weaker when we cease to live and stand together.

NOTES

1. John Milbank, 'Three questions on modern atheism: an interview by Ben Suriano', *The Other Journal*, 4 June 2008.
2. Maurice Glasman, Jonathan Rutherford, Marc Stears and Stuart White (eds), *The Labour Tradition and the Politics of Paradox*, The Oxford London Seminars 2010–11. Available at http://www.lwbooks.co.uk/journals/soundings/Labour_tradition_and_the_politics_of_paradox.pdf (accessed on 25 August 2014).
3. Norman Dennis, *Families Without Fatherhood* (London: IEA, 1992).
4. Phillip Blond, *Red Tory: How Left and Right Have Broken Britain and How We Can Fix It* (London: Faber and Faber, 2010).
5. This fracture is increasingly visible not between political parties, but within them, seen in the increasing friction on both sides between 'small c' conservatives and cosmopolitan liberalism. This sense of dislocation and conflict perhaps explains the interest generated by Jonathan Haidt in his book *The Righteous Mind* (London: Allen Lane, 2012) in trying to articulate the fundamental sociological and perhaps anthropological aspects of this fracture.
6. Ruth Porter, 'The case for connection', in N. Spencer (ed.), *The Future of Welfare* (London: Theos, 2014).
7. From Maurice Glasman's speech at the Tackling Poverty Conference 2013. Available at http://cuf.org.uk/blog/text-maurice-glasmans-speech-tackling-poverty-conference-2013 (accessed on 25 August 2014).
8. An issue explored by Geoff Dench, Kate Gavron and Michael Young, *The New East End: Kinship, Race and Conflict* (London: Profile Books, 2006).
9. See the influential report *Breakthrough Britain: Dynamic Benefits* (London: Centre for Social Justice, 2009).
10. In addition, the RSA paper 'What do people want, need and expect from public services' (March, 2010) usefully explores the concept of fairness in public service benefits, with popular notions of legitimate need being determined by both circumstance and, importantly, life choices. Similar considerations, and suggestions for reform, can be found throughout the collection of essays gathered together in Nick Spencer (ed.), *The Future of Welfare* (London: Theos, 2014).
11. Dr Katharine Rake caused controversy when, as the newly installed head of the Labour-established Family and Parenting Institute, she used her opening address to talk of the decline of the nuclear family and discouraged use of government to support a now outmoded 'traditional' family model.

12. Jon Cruddas, 'How Labour will strengthen family life and relationships', *The New Statesman*, March 2014.

13. For example, the responses of senior Labour figures to the proposed Marriage Tax Allowance, criticised for being 'expensive' and guilty of 'social engineering'. That the status quo was both expensive and served to socially engineer was an irony left largely unattended in Labour circles.

14. Tristram Hunt, 'Divorced from reality', *The Guardian*, 9 January 2010.

15. Reactions to the London riots were intriguing in this regard, since they demonstrated a tendency to explain the rioting by appeal to issues of poverty and/or the withdrawal of services and benefit entitlements. Wider concerns regarding family breakdown, loss of parental authority and fatherlessness received far less attention on the political left, though some did choose to assess the importance of these factors, such as David Lammy MP in his book *Out of the Ashes: Britain After the Riots* (London: Guardian Books, 2011).

16. The vote against a clause in the Human Fertilisation and Embryology Bill requiring those undergoing fertility treatment to take into account the need for a father-figure when considering the future welfare of their child is a good example of how fathers had become an optional extra, a motion which attracted the votes of even those politicians who have since rediscovered the importance of fatherhood.

17. *Panorama: Britain's Missing Dads*, BBC One, 17 January 2011.

18. Pamphlets such as *The Family Way*, co-authored by Harriet Harman, Patricia Hewitt and Anna Coote, were full of such prejudices, such that Erin Pizzey, founder of the first battered wives' refuge in 1971, could criticise the aforementioned as being part of an anti-male and anti-family politico-cultural agenda.

19. The Centre for Policy Studies published a booklet entitled *What Women Want* (2009) which would suggest the New Left narrative account of liberty does not align with the interests of a majority of women; its account of liberty is too narrow, often restricted to the freedom to go beyond the domestic, yet leaving untouched the freedom to choose the domestic and reject, even for a limited time, the workplace. This option is now available almost exclusively to the wealthy.

20. David Goodhart, 'A Postliberal Future?' *Demos Quarterly*, Issue 1, January 2014.

21. Department for Education, 'More affordable childcare', July 2013. Available at https://www.gov.uk/government/uploads/system/uploads/attachment_data/file/212671/More_Affordable_Childcare.pdf (accessed on 25 August 2014).

22. Stephen Twigg, former Shadow Secretary of State for Education, articulated this view in his speech at the 2013 Labour Party conference:

'This [the Primary Childcare Guarantee] will give all parents of primary school children the certainty that they can access childcare from 8 a.m.–6 p.m. through their school [...] A clear message to hard-working parents: Labour is on your side'. Unless, of course, those hard-working parents happen to wish they didn't have to work so long and so hard and miss their children growing up as a consequence, and who with this have even less of a case to make to an employer seeking extended hours and commitment.

23. For example, the child from Wembley seeking to pursue a career in the professions can conceivably do so whilst remaining geographically close to her family and social surroundings, limiting familial and social dislocation. This is quite often simply not the case in many parts of the country, without the same opportunities, institutions, networks and cultural infrastructure to allow such an option.

24. Jonathan Rutherford, 'Should the Left go blue?', an interview with Alan Finlayson. Available at https://www.opendemocracy.net/ourkingdom/alan-finlayson-john-rutherford/what-is-blue-labour-interview-with-jonathan-rutherford (accessed on 25 August 2014).

25. Andrea Westall, 'Transforming Common Sense', in Glasman *et al.* (eds), *The Labour Tradition and the Politics of Paradox* (London: Oxford London Seminars, 2011).

CONCLUSION

Blue Labour – Principles, Policy Ideas and Prospects

Adrian Pabst

BLUE LABOUR PRINCIPLES

Blue Labour reclaims a rich political and cultural inheritance that was exiled but never vanquished – radical traditions of a British Romantic modernity of virtue and sensibility of which William Morris was the most articulate advocate. Quoting from Raymond Williams' classic *Culture and Society*, Jon Cruddas writes:

> Starting with John Ruskin, he [Williams] focuses on his resistance to laissez-faire society through artistic criticism where 'the art of any country is the exponent of its social and political virtues [...] the exponent of its ethical life'. What we value in life is taken out of the realm of political economy – of supply and demand, and calculus – and instead relates to the virtue of the labour itself – seen as the 'joyful and right exertion of perfect life in man'.
>
> Within Ruskin, the notion of wealth and value, and indeed labour, are used to attack nineteenth-century liberalism for its cold utilitarianism, and instead promote a society governed by 'what is good for men, raising them and making them happy'. To live a virtuous life; to become wiser, compassionate, righteous, creative. What it is to become a 'freeborn Englishman'.
>
> What is of value is not the notion of 'exchange value'. It amounts to a radical critique of political economy; of economic

transactions. It is the source of a distinctly English, radical transformative politics. One that is sometimes identifiable within the Labour Party.[1]

Blue Labour recovers and extends these traditions of English and equally British radical politics. They are vital at a time when the Union is deeply divided and England's place within it remains unresolved. Following the Scottish referendum, Britain needs a new constitutional settlement – as the pledge to introduce home rule for Scotland has intensified long-standing resentment about the under-representation of England within the UK. Blue Labour calls for the self-government of towns, cities and regions that will promote popular participation in decision-making far more effectively than the concentration of powers in the capitals of the four home nations. Self-government at the lowest appropriate level in accordance with the principle of subsidiarity is also the best way of addressing the anti-Westminster mood that is fuelling support for the radical right – along with legitimate concerns about immigration and the wide-spread sense that the EU has never been more remote from the needs and interests of Europe's citizens. Blue Labour's paradoxical blending of honest contribution with realistic generosity can also speak to the growing number of disaffected workers who are socially conservative and turning to UKIP.[2] Key to Blue Labour is its emphasis on virtue, value and vocation. The practice of virtue serves the flourishing of the person, both individually and in relation to others. By contrast with utility or private happiness, flourishing requires a recognition of mutual needs and common interests, as nobody can fulfil their potential in isolation. Beyond the abstract wealth so beloved by liberals, Blue Labour argues for the creation of real, shared value that can provide stability, hope and energy. Vocation is vital because it acknowledges our unique talents and the importance of nurturing interpersonal relationships that can provide educative guidance.

Essentially, Blue Labour seeks to renew the Labour Party's commitment to solidarity amongst labourers. It views all humans as workers because it is work that most of all reveals the *personal* origin of all of human society and culture – one of the constituent elements of Catholic Social Teaching, as several contributors remind us. Work links people to other people and to particular places. Work also involves time: it requires learning from the past, embracing inherited lineages of good craft and accepting leadership by others if one is eventually to lead in one's turn, to echo John Milbank. In her contribution Ruth Yeoman shows how the centrality of work as a virtuous practice can overcome the meaninglessness of commodified labour and open up new spaces for meaningful, creative activity.

Moreover, Blue Labour's appeal to perennial principles of reciprocity and the common good is connected with a commitment to the flourishing of persons, communities and the country as a whole. Only reciprocal arrangements can bind together rights with responsibilities and certain individual entitlements with mutual obligations. Without this 'radical balance', Britain's society will not be able to overcome the many divisions that have characterised its national life for so long. In both the public and the private sector, Blue Labour therefore seeks to strengthen subsidiarity, solidarity and status – i.e. self-government at the most appropriate level, mutual assistance for those in need and the honouring of contribution. This has profound implications for both work and welfare, as Maurice Glasman, Frank Field and Tom Watson argue in different ways – including corporate governance reform (such as workers' representation on company boards), regional and local banks as well as contributory welfare in the national insurance system.

Blue Labour also aspires to move British politics away from abstract liberal ideals of freedom of choice and absolute equality in the direction of a post-liberal pursuit of substantive individual and shared flourishing. That means valuing virtuous leadership and rewarding virtuous behaviour – whether through a new system of public awards or even some form of material reward such as tax breaks. In this manner, it seeks to transform both democracy and the market economy in line with the common good – not ideology or sectional interest. Transformation marks a radical alternative to timid reform and reckless revolution – neither of which can do justice to formative traditions and the importance of place and habit that are so central to the authentic British tradition. Crucially, Blue Labour's emphasis on the common good moves the debate away from utility and/or happiness to the question of shared ends and substantive goods that support human realisation.

Thus Blue Labour's post-liberalism is neither nostalgic nor reactionary. It appeals to rooted principles of the common good, participation and association. The task is to renew such notions and to build institutions that can translate into transformative practices of reciprocal giving, mutual assistance and cooperation across society –

in particular all the intermediary, democratically self-governing bodies that constitute the 'complex space' (John Milbank) between the individual, on the one hand, and the institutions of state and market on the other hand.

BLUE LABOUR POLICY IDEAS

From the outset, Blue Labour thinkers have stressed the link between principles and practices precisely because the notion of virtue involves both. As the 16 essays demonstrate, there is a plethora of fresh policy ideas which can be divided into four broad groups: (1) the Labour Party; (2) the state; (3) the market; (4) society. The aim of the main policies is to pluralise all institutions by enhancing civic participation and to direct activities to the common good in which all should have a stake.

In this light, the goal of Labour Party reform should be not merely to build another election-winning machine (as with New Labour). Instead, the purpose is to reconnect the party to the people and thereby to reconnect the electorate to politics. While Old Labour was too dominated by trade union bosses, New Labour relied excessively on the support of big, corporate money. Thus the alternative to either is to break this double dependence in favour of individual members, communities and new forms of association that have emerged in the digital age – as David Lammy argues. Key to this process of transformation is the tradition of community organising – an approach that privileges encounters between individuals and in small groups as well as the brokering of relationships rather than formal procedure and a top-down politics that is determined by party HQ – as the chapter by Arnie Graf so powerfully demonstrates. Community organising as part of London Citizens (now Citizens UK) has brought together faith groups and communities to use their power in order to improve the lives of their members and those living around them. New civic institutions are central to such a renewal, including the representations of different professions and faiths in the governance of cities, counties and the Union as a whole. Tom Watson's plea for new forms of partnership between companies and the trade unions also reflects Blue Labour's uniquely sensible position of being both pro-business and pro-worker.

This vision has been taken forward by Arnie Graf and Iain McNicol, the party's current general secretary. Both have sought to make Labour once again a broad popular force, working alongside grassroots civic organisations and local communities. Community organising is not simply compatible with technology but can deploy it positively by connecting more people with each other and enabling their participation. As McNicol writes,

> We're changing from a party that floods voters with leaflets delivered by a handful of volunteers; to being a movement, having hundreds of thousands of conversations with people. Our organisers are using both high-tech big data targeting techniques, digital campaigning and old-fashioned community organising to win voters to Labour. As we saw in May's elections, there's a real link between where Labour has already picked its 2015 parliamentary candidates, recruited organisers and where we won council seats. We have put our faith in community organising and we will soon have 110 organisers across our 106 battleground parliamentary seats. People coming together to oppose loan sharks and sky-high interest rates, to protect their post offices, fire stations and hospitals. It reminds us that the Labour Party was founded as a party of action, taking on local landlords, bosses and racketeers, long before there were Labour governments.[3]

In short, Blue Labour is promoting a relational politics that focuses on work, families and home – with a specific emphasis on higher pay, lower prices and more targeted help in order to address the twin crisis of inequality and identity that affects Britain. All this helped to shape the Labour Party's policy review led by Jon Cruddas.

As with its approach to party reform, Blue Labour argues for the pluralisation of the state and greater civic participation in both policy and decision-making. The key transformation is to rebalance the relations between government, parliament, the courts and the administration away from the dominance of the executive and the technocrats. This dominance betrays the spirit of Britain's 'mixed constitution', which differs sharply from the US and continental European separation of powers in which either one branch of government always ends up ruling over the others (the executive or the judiciary) or there is permanent paralysis (US gridlock over the budget and fundamental reforms such as immigration). Linked to this is the need to honour the ethos and integrity of institutions such as the civil service, which has had to endure the corrosive effects of the permanent bureaucratic-managerialist revolution imposed by successive governments.

Another vital transformation consists in introducing self-government to regional, local and communal levels as well as pooling some sovereign power at the European and global level. This should occur in accordance with the principle of subsidiarity which stipulates action at the most appropriate level in order to safeguard human dignity and the flourishing of the person. For example, new forms of financial regulation or a serious crackdown on tax evasion require action by the EU or the G20. The same is true for the fight against organised crime and against global warming. However, for a vast array of areas – from welfare via education to housing – self-government at the level of county, city or even parish councils would be preferable compared with existing arrangements. That is because it would help ensure that the provision of services is more personal, local and holistic than the homogenised standards and uniform targets imposed by central government and the global market.

Moreover, Blue Labour argues that all the mediating institutions of civil society (professional associations, universities, manufacturing and trading guilds, etc.), which are democratically self-governed, should be associated to public policy and decision-making. Concretely, this would involve a greater role for local assemblies and professional associations in order to counterbalance the writ of the executive, political parties and the managerial bureaucracy of the central state.

In relation to welfare reform, Blue Labour argues that the social security system has tended to function as a substitute for high employment, decent jobs and widespread asset ownership – the statist model effectively (and ironically) propping up the free-market one. In its place, Blue Labour defends the contributory principle that breaks with the culture of 'something for nothing', as Frank Field outlines in his contribution. Recently, the Labour Party has begun to move in this direction with the commitment to pay a higher level of Jobseeker's Allowance for a short period to those who have contributed more. More widely this implies 'responsible reciprocity', a mutualised welfare settlement that is personal, local and participatory. This would involve a renewal and extension of Attlee's original idea of a unified insurance-based social security system alongside a 'preferential option for the poor', moving away from means-testing, and developing locally based welfare schemes that embed people in meaningful relationships.

More specifically, in Britain's low-wage and low-growth economy state welfare is currently compensating for the failure of finance capitalism, and perpetuates a system wherein the governing elites do not abide by the standards of transparent virtue they purportedly demand of everyone else. By contrast, a mutualised social security model would fuse greater economic justice with an updated form of social conservatism that honours people's deep desire to earn respect and a place in society through family, community, locality, profession and faith. Mutualising social security would involve a number of reforms and policies. First, moving from means-testing to an expanded insurance-based system. This would include creating a new healthcare insurance system and transforming the NHS from a bureaucratic-managerialist machine into a mutual trust – run independently of central government and accountable to its members. Second, making work pay by expanding the 'living wage' and linking wage rise to labour productivity growth. Third, supporting the creation of locally based welfare schemes that are personal and participatory and that treat persons with dignity by making them members rather than passive benefit-recipients or clients of for-profit private service providers.

Fourth, promoting fair prices by enabling councils, communities and housing associations to negotiate not just energy and water prices but also rent on behalf of tenants. Fifth, creating an alternative social market in housing through innovative measures such as the 'mutual listing' of council houses. Finally, incentivising the expansion of wages in the direction of profit-sharing to reduce the welfare dependency of the poor and the 'squeezed middle' and also to break the vicious circle of debt and demoralisation. Welfare provision should include health, employment and education policy because it is ultimately a joined-up reality – reflecting the true needs of the whole human person.

In terms of the economy, the Blue Labour focus on pluralisation aims to mutualise the market and to strengthen both representation and participation in business. The mutualisation of markets would help shift the emphasis from short-term profits and pure price competition towards longer-term, sustainable profitability and competition centred on quality and wider social impact (including the so-called environmental 'externalities'). Connected with this are principles and practices of cooperation beyond pure self-interest, involving especially the distribution of assets (e.g. asset-based welfare, employee ownership and cooperatives, including in the public sector).

Crucially, mutualising markets involves abandoning the current separation of profit and risk between investors and lenders on the one hand, and customers and employees on the other, in favour of alternative arrangements whereby some debt is converted into equity and both profit and risk are shared more fairly rather than being artificially and coercively divorced from one another. Examples include mortgages with long-term, fixed interest rates; debt equitisation schemes for over-leveraged banks and corporations; the introduction of growth warrants in addition to ordinary national or corporate bonds.

In the short to medium term, debt can only be brought under control by capping usurious interest rates and providing fresh sources of lending, including credit unions, building societies and initiatives such as the nascent Bank of Salford and similar local arrangements – with a requirement for banking structures to lend within certain areas (cities or counties) and within specific sectors.

In terms of growing inequality and the plight of hard-working families, Blue Labour has long championed a combination of breaking up monopolies (in retail, energy, banking, etc.) and promoting the introduction of the 'living wage'. It is therefore vital to raise pay in line with labour productivity, which in turn requires a policy of innovation, including targeted investment in R&D, greater sharing of research outcomes and large-scale projects that the private sector cannot shoulder alone. Crucially, it needs a new policy of boosting vocational training and offering more hybrid forms that combine some academic skills with vocational skills (as for law, medicine and banking).

Constitutionally, Blue Labour's version of post-liberalism promotes the active participation of citizens – individually and in groups – in the governance of the public realm. Here the guiding principle is the ancient and medieval notion of 'mixed government' where the rule of the 'one' (the monarchy representing the nation), 'the few' (virtuous elites in all professions and sections of society) and 'the many' (the populace) are blended in mutually balancing and augmenting ways. Whether Edmund Burke's 'little platoons', or G. D. H. Cole's guilds, 'the few' could mediate between families, households, communities, localities on the one hand, and national states and transnational markets on the other. So configured, 'the few' would have a constitutional role that helps secure the autonomy of the mediating institutions that constitute civil society.

A renewed form of guilds and professional associations would help develop and protect standards of excellence and honourable practices – if necessary by means of revoking licences to trade, for example in the case of banks that have behaved criminally. Blue Labour's emphasis on ethos shifts the focus away from a 'compliance culture' towards a moral economy in which duties beget rights and there are incentives for virtue, not vice, and rewards for contributing to the common good – not merely attempts to regulate bad behaviour. In the past when craft-guilds were frequently organised as confraternities, they participated in the life of the polity based on their own distinct 'legal personality'. Some of the most successful economies in Europe – including Germany and Northern Italy – are based on strong intermediary institutions and new forms of guild-like professional associations that foster strong economic growth based on innovation and productivity.

So if the left truly believes in worker self-organisation, it must encourage the introduction of a constitutional status for professional and other associations, as Blue Labour has suggested. This, coupled with a pluralised state and mutualised markets, can help build a new covenant that blends proper political representation with greater civic participation.

BLUE LABOUR: FUTURE AVENUES

Blue Labour is a movement that seeks to transform British politics – forging a new settlement by drawing on resources and traditions that have been exiled for too long. It combines a critique of liberalism with an alternative vision – the fight for greater economic justice yoked to a renewed emphasis on interpersonal relationships, social bonds and civic ties. The task for Blue Labour is to develop both this narrative and a number of concrete ideas that translate the vision into transformative, practicable policies.

More specifically, the overriding task is to repeat again and again the point that economic liberalism has largely benefited the few and ended in a catastrophic financial crash which has left the country not just saddled with personal debt and public deficits but has also plunged it into a state of political demoralisation and self-defeatist decline. Meanwhile, periodic inner-city riots across parts of the country since the early 2000s have discredited social liberalism, highlighting the simultaneous atomisation and interdependence in a climate of fear, mutual distrust and lack of cooperation.

Another key task is to show that a majority of the British population is in fact post-liberal. Most people are attached to the principles of liberality (justice, generosity and integrity) but they are increasingly sceptical about the capacity of both economic and social liberalism to deliver freedom, equality and security. The challenge is to show that post-liberal principles and practices respect and reflect the views and interests of this often obscured majority. This means that the honouring of work, home, family and faith is absolutely vital.

Concretely, such a perspective promotes policies that link rights to responsibilities and entitlements to obligations, e.g. community work in exchange for welfare benefits for people who are capable of working. Similarly, it means policies of 'tough love' for inner-city children – coupled with concrete opportunities to escape from a life of exclusion, deprivation and gang crime. It also means strict limits on low-skilled immigration (as advocated by both Frank Field and David Goodhart) – combined with genuine efforts to integrate migrants in a spirit of hospitality and the common good. Finally, it also involves transforming globalisation where it accelerates and amplifies a race to the bottom, including some limits on the power of what Karl Polanyi called 'high finance' – the predators who eschew long-term shared prosperity in favour of their own short-term self-interest.

Perhaps most fundamentally of all, it involves valuing work through higher pay and better (vocational) training. More meaning and status (and more income) for the routine jobs means that Blue Labour will always champion apprenticeships more than an ever-expanding number of university students. Against the divisive language of shirkers vs strivers, Blue Labour advocates the introduction of incentives and rewards for virtuous behaviour. That is a surer path towards individual flourishing and the common good than the bizarre idea that private vice somehow leads to public benefits – an idea that has pervaded much of economics since Bernard de Mandeville.

Crucially, Blue Labour needs to demonstrate that its critique of liberalism is not a mere cry of anguish and anxiety against the inexorable advance of liberal modernity. It must rather show how post-liberalism defends and promotes the interests and values of a 'hidden' majority and how novel institutions can be built using new alliances of different groups in society who are not used to cooperating – for example the Labour Party, faith communities and trade unions on usurious interest rates and alternative forms of banking.

Ultimately, only a universal vision will do. In the words of Frank Field, 'the appeal to country, loyalty to old friends, the belief that duties beget rights, are all sentiments that appeal across classes. It is on this universalism of Blue Labour's common good that Labour should begin rebuilding that wider coalition of voters which is so crucial to general election successes'.

If Blue Labour continues to tell a story of national renewal based on character and ethical principle, then it can help inspire a popular movement that really could transform the country.

NOTES

1. Jon Cruddas, 'George Lansbury memorial lecture', Queen Mary, University of London, 7 November 2013. Available at http://www.newstatesman.com/politics/2013/11/jon-cruddass-george-lansbury-memorial-lecture-full-text (accessed on 25 August 2014).
2. Robert Ford and Matthew J. Goodwin, *Revolt on the Right: Explaining Support for the Radical Right in Britain* (London: Routledge, 2014), pp. 183–219.
3. Iain McNicol, 'Labour's faith in community organising will lead it to victory', *New Statesman*, 21 September 2013. Available at http://www.newstatesman.com/politics/2013/09/labours-faith-community-organis-ing-will-lead-it-victory (accessed on 25 August 2014).

POSTSCRIPT TO THE NEW EDITION

Blue Labour and Common Good Politics

Maurice Glasman

Muhammad Ali said that you never get knocked out by a punch you see coming. The Labour Party did not expect to be defeated on 7 May 2015 to the extent and scale that we were.

Scotland embraced a progressive position against austerity and that is one thing. In England UKIP have replaced the Liberal Democrats as the third force and are in second place in 120 seats with nearly four million votes, and that is quite another. Indeed, UKIP polled much higher than the Greens and Liberal Democrats combined. There is no progressive majority to be found in England.

The Conservative Government moved quickly to reassert their ownership of 'One Nation' by bringing in a 'national living wage' in which the private sector would raise the minimum wage by forty pence every six months over the course of the Parliament in order to improve the pay of those worse off. It is a significant state interference in the market, paid entirely by employers, and intensifies the estrangement between low-paid private sector employees and the Labour Party, which was one of the phenomena of the last election. The Conservatives have also introduced a levy on private companies to pay for apprenticeships and vocational training. A coalition between the rich, middle class and working poor is thus pursued which is not fictitious or abstract, but one that will kick in throughout the next Parliament. In marketing terms it is known as detoxifying the brand but in political terms it is hegemonic, building a cross-class coalition around a state that supports work within a market economy that provides jobs that pay enough to live. Combined with the redistribution of political power to the north of England, with the support of Labour councils, it marginalises Labour as a constructive force in the political life of the nation.

Under these circumstances, a rational analysis should surely proceed as to how Labour contests the partiality of the Conservative move and how it could renew its relationship with the mainstream of English society.

This is not, however, what happened. From the soft left to the Blairite right, from Compass through the Fabians to Progress, a hollow, calculating impotence emerged, which could express neither humility in relation to what went before, nor confidence in what should follow. Whether it was Burnham, Kendall or Cooper, an incomprehension of the desertion that people felt, the powerlessness of their experience and their sense of rage at the abandonment of the Labour tradition and its values in the face of finance capital and its instruments of global governance was manifest.

The decline of the Parliamentary Labour Party, and of Parliament itself, was played out through the development of a leadership election in which a vote for leader was given a price of three pounds. Rarely in human history has a birth right been sold so cheaply.

With European Social Democracy in a desultory state of marginalisation, with the EU itself in the grip of a monetarist orthodoxy outside all political or democratic control, with the dissolution of the officer class in Parliament and their arrogant march to defeat, the unlikely but profound figure of Jeremy Corbyn appeared as both anti-hero and saviour. With four minutes to spare he secured the necessary 35 nominations required from the PLP to be a candidate and the regrets expressed within days were to no avail.

New Labour may have led the Party to three general election victories but there seemed to be no reckoning with its bitter fruit – from the Iraq war to the financial crash, from welfare reform to a quiescence to corporate capitalism. Over the five years of Ed Miliband's leadership there seemed to be no more than an uneasy holding operation and no real reckoning with the record. There was no expression of rage at a world which rewarded the already rich and then could not develop a constructive alternative to a Conservative government that explicitly modelled itself on New Labour. Labour lost in Scotland to the SNP. It lost across the south of England to the Conservatives. It was hounded in the north-east by UKIP and barely held across the Midlands.

The answer was not to be found in more of the same and so it was that a conscientious constituency MP and rebel, who represented the part of Islington that Tony and Gordon did not meet in to carve out their rule at the now-closed Granita restaurant, became a unifying candidate for the disaffection and humiliation of those who expected more from Labour.

Corbyn has none of the oratory or writing talent of Michael Foot, none of his intimacy with the great and the good of left and right, but he has built a coalition of real interests who were humiliated and excluded by New Labour. Public sector unions who had real and ideological problems with the acceptance of austerity, anti-war campaigners who saw the emergence of ISIS not only as the result of internal forces within the Islamic world but also as the direct result of a misconceived and bungled external intervention that has made things worse. A genuine post-colonial story could be told of Britain's future, which included the children of immigrants actively participating as part of that different narrative. It opened up the possibility of a politics which stopped blaming the poor, in our country and the world, for its problems but instead championed their cause.

In terms of the economy the withdrawal of the state from production was seen as an entirely unnecessary and ideological defeat by a neo-liberalism that could not distinguish between a commodity produced for sale in the market and that which was necessary for survival. Water, heat and housing are not optional extras in life, they are necessities and the state has a role in subordinating profit to need.

These are not concerns that animate only a sectarian form of left-wing politics. They provide the basis of a real and democratic political renewal of the nation. A humble man who served his constituency well and did not abandon his beliefs in socialism, in the poor leading a dignified life, in the rich not owning the world, became a figurehead for what is wrong with a narrow political class, in hock to the financial interest dominating our economy.

The problem is that having spent so long in a marginalised and besieged space, Corbyn has appeal to the student union left and public sector unions but does not yet have a relationship with the mainstream of the nation who do not want an over-mighty state, who support our armed forces, who believe that work and not welfare is the right way to organise society, who are as angry with neglect in hospitals as they are with abuse by the bankers. People who are concerned as to how we earn a living in the world as well as how it is distributed. People who view their faith not as a patriarchal oppression but as a source of goodness and of hope.

In short, beyond a coalition of the already political and ideological it is not a politics of the common good: a politics that reconciles the relationships between estranged interests so that it can take its place in a national politics which is not polarising and denunciatory but as gentle as it is stubborn, as forgiving as it is determined. Pope Francis, for example, pursues a politics of the common good that gives a priority to the poor by bringing different interests with him for the conversation and the engagement.

A common good politics that would have a national renewal at its centre is hard to craft without the active engagement of the Church, of environmental groups, of small business and without a politics that looks to greater agency by citizens in a more decentralised polity. Greater centralisation and administration will not generate the necessary coalition. Labour needs to rediscover its relationships with people around interests as well as ideology, and a constructive alternative to finance capital and the centralised state that puts vocation and productivity at the centre of its concerns.

Where there is clear common ground between Blue Labour and Corbyn's politics is on the organising agenda, to develop leaders from working-class and immigrant backgrounds who are showing the way within their workplaces and congregations. The essays by Arnie Graf and by Tom Watson are worth revisiting for that reason. It is also seen in the need to develop an economic policy in which human beings and nature are not viewed as commodities. That means exploring different forms of corporate governance, which involve the participation of workers and local groups. It involves building a common life and a common good that resists the domination of any one group or interest by another. It also, as Luke Bretherton develops in his essay, involves beginning with where people are. Blue Labour will continue to organise and develop leadership from excluded and marginalised groups within Labour for whom a commitment to family, place and work are central motivations in their life.

It is essential to develop a foreign policy that is not only pro-worker and gives a priority to free and democratic trade unions but also combines patriotism and internationalism in new ways. The European Union is an answer to a problem that Britain never had. We did not turn either fascist or communist, we were not invaded and while the EU requires centralisation and moves to 'ever-closer political union', this would not be an acceptable outcome for the English in particular who do not wish to be ruled by either Germany or France. It is time to think creatively about the possibility of confederation in which free trade with Europe does not involve the free movement of labour and in which the Ancient Constitution can form the basis of a new Constitutional settlement, not only between the nations of the United Kingdom but within them. Self-governing cities and counties must be a part of that conversation. It is vital that in both the EU referendum and in terms of the Constitution, Labour develops a position that is an alternative to the status quo and honours its commitments to democracy and internationalism.

There is something indecent about a form of capitalism that rewards those who already own and discards those who don't. A generous politics is required now that does not give a voice to the voiceless, but allows them to speak for themselves and brings them together with others for the common good. We are working in the ruins of broken dreams and failed ideologies.

It would be in keeping with the paradoxical nature of Blue Labour to say that it is a time for courage and humility, faithfulness and transgression as we participate in crafting a new politics that can redistribute rather than centralise power. Blue Labour is a central force in rebuilding the Labour Party as a broad-based movement that can call on the affections and loyalty of people, and in order to do that it must work within their experience and traditions.

INDEX

I. Key Names

Alinsky, Saul 71, 78
Aquinas, Thomas 34, 35
Aristotle 33, 34, 35, 95, 223
Attlee, Clement 3, 69, 258
Augustine 34, 219

Benedict XVI (Pope) 103, 110,
    116n3, 118n25, 176n41
Benn, Tony 41
Bentham, Jeremy 33, 230
Blair, Tony 8, 63, 155, 156, 166,
    169, 175n35, 176n37, 204, 206
Blatchford, Robert 5
Blond, Phillip 7, 206, 209, 214n5,
    238, 250n4
Bretherton, Luke 174n4, 217–33
Brown, Gordon 9, 207
Bruni, Luigino 38, 47n11, 47n12,
    48n25, 48n27, 49n33, 116n3,
    118n22
Buber, Martin 73
Burke, Edmund 15, 23, 28, 171,
    260

Cameron, David 67, 80, 170, 196,
    209, 212
Carlyle, Thomas 3, 4
Chesterton, G. K. 206, 243
Churchill, Winston 150
Cicero 229
Clare, John 147, 148, 149, 154n3
Cobbett, William 4
Cole, G. D. H. 4, 260

Crouch, Colin 117n8
Cruddas, Jon 2, 3, 4, 7, 10n1, 33,
    47n13, 68, 87–95, 150, 166,
    176n38, 200, 207, 211, 214n6,
    242, 251n12, 253, 257, 263n1

Darwin, Charles 144, 145
Davis, Rowenna 5, 10n6, 195–201
Davis, Ruth 7, 143–54
Dickens, Charles 3, 233n13
Disraeli, Benjamin 3, 35

Engels, Friedrich 166, 191n6

Field, Frank 6, 7, 51–60, 245, 255,
    258, 262, 263
Foucault, Michel 88, 166, 219
Francis (Pope) 25, 103, 117n13
Fraser, Nancy 47n9

Gaskell, Elizabeth 3
Genovesi, Antonio 114, 119n30
Geuss, Raymond 47n8
Glasman, Maurice 4, 7, 9, 10n3,
    10n8, 13–26, 27, 35, 42, 46n3,
    47n18, 48n24, 63, 71, 81, 82,
    100, 106, 114, 116n6, 118n19,
    209, 231, 237, 250n2, 250n7,
    252n25, 255
Goodhart, David 7, 27, 30, 43,
    46n2, 47n7, 121–40, 177n58,
    251n20, 262
Gove, Michael 87, 247

Graf, Arnie 8, 71–8, 81, 256
Gray, John 160, 161, 174n10,
    174n13, 174n16, 174n17,
    175n19, 175n20, 175n22,
    175n23, 175n27, 175n28,
    176n44, 177n61
Grotius, Hugo 29

Hardie, Keir 3, 196, 204
Hitchens, Peter 210, 214n11
Hobbes, Thomas 29, 35
Hutton, Will 48n29, 113, 119n29

John-Paul II (Pope) 22
Johnson, Lyndon 95

Kant, Immanuel 107, 230
Kennedy, Robert (Bobby) 88, 90,
    95
Ketteler, Wilhelm Emmanuel
    Freiherr von (Cardinal) 22

Lamennais, Hugues Felicité Robert
    de 19
Lammy, David 7, 63–70, 251n15,
    256
Landrum, Dave 4, 155–78
Lansbury, George 3, 4, 10n1, 196,
    263n1
Leo XIII (Pope) 21, 22, 103, 110
Liddle, Rod 203, 213n1
Locke, John 29, 35, 164, 175n34

MacDonald, Ramsey 3
McLellan, David 156, 174n2
Malthus, Thomas 40
Mandelson, Peter 156, 203, 204
Marquand, David 4, 5, 10n4
Marx, Karl 19, 34, 40, 47n8, 99,
    163, 191n6, 207, 219, 232n10
Merrick, Michael 7, 235–52

Michéa, Jean-Claude 46n4
Milbank, John 4, 27–50, 46n4,
    46n5, 48n19, 48n28, 48n31, 90,
    114, 117n12, 118n21, 119n32,
    236, 241, 250n1, 255, 256
Miliband, David 128, 140n3
Miliband, Ed 10n3, 32, 69, 71, 75,
    89, 195, 197, 198, 199, 200
Mill, John Stuart 173
Morris, William 3, 4, 182, 190,
    191n4, 191n9, 192n34, 253

Nelson, Fraser 136, 140n10

Orwell, George 31, 47n10, 123,
    161, 209

Pabst, Adrian 1–10, 46n5, 48n28,
    48n31, 97–119, 116n3, 117n12,
    118n21, 119n30, 119n32, 253–
    64
Piketty, Thomas 103, 117n12,
    117n15
Plato 33
Polanyi, Karl 5, 10n5, 47n9, 97,
    116n2, 118n23, 262
Pugh, Martin 4, 10n4

Ricardo, David 40
Röpke, Wilhelm 106, 118n18
Rousseau, Jean-Jacques 29, 30, 35,
    47n6
Ruskin, John 3, 4, 253

Salter, Alfred 196
Sandbrook, Dominic 4, 10n2
Schmitt, Carl 43, 49n34
Scott, Walter 4
Scruton, Roger 176n50, 204, 213n2
Skidelsky, Edward 35, 48n21
Skidelsky, Robert 35, 48n21

Smith, Adam 29, 34, 46n5, 99, 114, 116n4, 163, 175n25, 191n5

Tawney, R. H. 4, 55
Thatcher, Margaret 6, 102, 205, 249
Thompson, E. P. 116n1
Tocqueville, Alexis de 35, 223, 226, 233n11
Turner, Adair 36, 48n22, 132, 140n4

Watson, Tom 8, 79–84, 255, 256

Welby, Justin 26
West, Ed 5, 203–14
Williams, Bernard 191n22
Williams, Raymond 253
Williams, Rowan ix–xi
Wordsworth, William 147, 150, 154n2, 155
Yeoman, Ruth 7, 179–92, 255

Zamagni, Stefano 38, 48n26, 48n27, 116n3, 117n16

II. Key Subjects

abstraction 36, 90, 109, 230
accumulation 99, 100, 109, 146
agency 116, 150, 190n1, 220, 241
affiliation 79, 80, 81
alienation 56, 144, 147, 149, 152
anger 57, 78, 93, 195
Anglican/-ism 5, 8, 211
anthropology/-ical/-ist 21, 158, 205, 250n5
antiquity 90
apprenticeship 25, 42, 110, 136, 198, 219, 262
asset 19, 80, 101, 102, 103, 104, 111, 113, 258, 260
association 7, 9, 16, 21, 22, 23, 30, 31, 35, 36, 37, 39, 41, 42, 43, 48n30, 92, 93, 94, 108, 110, 111, 114, 255, 256, 258, 259, 260, 261
atomised/-ation 7, 87, 89, 98, 262
austerity 4, 87, 89, 94, 95, 98, 105, 112, 113, 170, 198
award 115, 116, 255

bank/-er/-ing 15, 16, 19, 20, 24, 26, 42, 117n14, 137, 197, 198, 199, 205, 201, 255, 260, 261
Bank of Salford 26, 81, 83, 260
belonging 7, 19, 47n14, 79, 146, 188, 189, 248
benefit 1, 38, 42, 59, 64, 76, 77, 82, 91, 92, 94, 98, 99, 100, 102, 103, 105, 107, 108, 109, 115, 116, 127, 129, 130, 135, 136 137, 138, 139, 152, 155, 196, 197, 198, 199, 204, 205, 219, 225, 243, 250n9, 250n10, 251n15, 259, 262
Big Business 67, 100, 102, 126, 210
Big Government 67, 100
Big Society 16, 17, 18, 23, 67, 95
bonds 30, 46, 55, 90, 148, 163, 171, 172, 179, 190, 240, 241, 260, 261
Britain 1, 2, 4, 5, 6, 7, 8, 9, 10n4, 19, 43, 58, 59, 63, 64, 65, 67, 87, 89, 92, 95, 97, 98, 101–6, 108, 117n11, 119n28, 121, 124,

126–9, 131–9, 140n9, 148, 175n35, 198, 203, 207, 208, 211–13, 214n5, 250n4, 251n15, 254, 255, 257, 259, 263n2

bureaucracy/-tic 3, 27, 32, 41, 93, 101, 106–8, 128, 139, 200, 217, 218, 222, 225, 226, 241, 246, 258, 259

capability 189

capital 15, 17, 19–23, 36, 37, 38, 39, 42, 83, 92, 95, 99, 100, 104, 105, 109, 111, 117n12, 117n15, 118n21, 122, 129, 137, 149, 172, 191n6, 198, 211, 212, 221, 237, 249

capitalist/-ism 5, 6, 9, 18, 19, 21, 22, 32, 36, 38, 40, 42, 43, 44, 48n26, 69, 80, 97, 99, 102–10, 113, 116, 116n3, 117n12, 118n23, 125, 163, 191n12, 198, 208–10, 220, 227, 229, 232n10, 245, 246, 259

care 17, 23, 31, 48n31, 64, 65, 93, 95, 134, 135, 136, 138, 139, 186, 187–9, 192n25, 192n31, 212, 222, 225, 229, 233n13, 247, 251n21, 252n22

Catholic/-ism 5, 13, 14, 19, 21, 22, 34, 48n26, 74, 114, 174n2, 211, 212, 224, 244

Catholic Social Thought (CST)/ Catholic Social Teaching 8, 13–26, 48n26, 78, 98, 103, 106, 108, 110, 116n3, 119n27, 254

centralisation 15, 17, 89, 101, 224

character 3, 7, 16, 29, 33, 37, 44, 46, 146, 180, 187, 191n22, 242, 263

child/-hood/-ren 25, 38, 48n31, 59, 64, 65, 67, 74, 75, 88, 103, 125, 143, 146, 148, 153, 159, 208, 212, 213, 237, 242–5, 247, 248, 251n16, 251n21, 252n22, 262

child poverty 59

Christian/-ity 18, 37, 40, 43, 60, 70, 81–3, 87, 90, 134, 145, 160–2, 171, 172, 175n34, 177n60, 210, 225

Christian Democracy 18

Christian Socialism 172

church 6, 8, 16, 24, 26, 65, 74, 76, 81, 83, 118n27, 199, 200, 204, 208, 211, 212, 219

citizenship 14, 23, 24, 78, 126, 128, 137, 181, 190, 226–9, 231n1

City of London 13, 15, 21, 24, 68, 134, 204; *see also* finance

civic x, 1, 7, 8, 13, 24–6, 71, 77, 80, 81, 83, 104, 109, 171, 196, 197, 199, 211, 224, 227, 229, 230, 238, 256, 257, 261

civil economy 37–40, 42, 48n26, 48n27, 97–119

civil society 35, 48n31, 68, 69, 118n26, 163, 171–3, 196, 258, 260

class 15, 19, 51, 54, 55, 56, 60, 79, 103, 124, 128, 138, 156, 160, 164, 171, 204, 207–9, 235–6, 238, 242, 245, 246, 247, 263; *see also* working class

co-determination 35, 82, 106, 108

collectivisation 18, 19, 110

commodification 1, 15, 18, 19, 109, 110, 189, 222, 223, 228

commodity/-ies x, 15, 19, 33, 67, 99, 148, 163, 205, 207

common good 1, 6–8, 13–21, 23, 25, 26, 34, 36, 38, 45, 46, 51, 54, 57, 58, 60, 66, 83, 87–95, 99, 100, 104, 106, 108, 115,

151, 173, 217, 219, 221, 222, 226, 229, 236, 255, 256, 261–3
Commonwealth 14, 42–4, 94, 100, 132, 230
communism/-ist 6, 40, 80, 161, 163, 203
community x, xi, 26, 34, 38, 43, 44, 59, 65, 70–8, 91, 93, 95, 125, 128, 129, 130, 131, 144, 146, 152, 156, 165, 172, 179, 180, 195, 199, 200, 207, 211, 214n12, 221, 224, 226, 229, 230, 232n10, 238, 239, 249, 259, 262
community organising 8, 71–8, 256, 257, 263n3
compassion/-ate 64, 88, 196, 208, 253
concentration 15, 30, 89, 101, 109, 151, 228, 254
conservative/-ism 5, 8, 13–16, 29, 32, 45, 52, 53, 105, 108, 126, 164, 170, 173, 176n46, 195–201, 203–14
constitution/-al 6, 22, 37, 41–3, 79, 93, 111, 190n1, 232n9, 238, 254, 257, 260, 261
contribution/-ive 4, 5, 8, 9, 14, 17, 39, 48n31, 57, 90, 115, 132, 179, 188, 191n18, 197, 223, 224, 237, 244, 254, 255, 258, 261
conversation 63, 66, 67, 74, 88, 248, 249, 257
cooperative 4, 5, 8, 9, 37, 40, 41, 44, 45, 68, 91, 93, 108, 109, 188, 189, 225, 227, 260
core vote 51, 55, 56, 58, 60
corporate governance 1, 7, 21, 22, 25, 82, 113, 255

corporation/-ism/-ist 21, 37, 42, 111, 232n10
courage 5, 6, 9, 42, 88, 97, 149, 235
covenant/-al 90–5, 173, 261
creation 145, 146, 151, 242
credit xi, 26, 59, 68, 100, 101, 104, 110, 113, 155, 170, 197, 209, 213, 260
Crown 24, 92
custom/-ary 19, 116n1, 165, 218, 230, 237, 238, 239

debt x, 16, 17, 20, 23, 25, 36, 42, 46n5, 67, 89, 93, 98, 100, 101, 102, 104, 107, 112, 113, 156, 209, 259–61
decency/-t 13, 31, 57, 60, 63, 94, 132, 149, 181, 197, 258
decentralisation 14, 17, 18, 25, 254; *see also* devolution; self-government
deficit 17, 113, 261
democracy 3, 14, 16, 17, 18, 28, 41, 43, 52, 80, 100, 105, 114, 123, 124, 159, 180, 181, 183, 186, 189, 190, 203, 223, 224, 227, 231n1, 233n11, 255
demoralisation 15, 17, 100, 102, 259, 261
demos 123, 228, 229
devolution 124, 254, 258; *see also* decentralisation; self-government
dignity 18, 31, 59, 64, 75, 88, 92, 110, 172, 199, 245, 258, 259
disembedding 97
disengagement 51, 53, 55, 57, 80
dispossession 19, 109
diversity 17, 58, 136, 137, 145, 146, 151, 206–8

earning 7, 23, 47n14, 57, 67, 76

ecology 159, 170

economics 4, 6, 32, 33, 40, 47n11, 48n22, 88, 89, 105, 108, 112, 118n22, 121, 134, 137, 139, 140n4, 150, 160, 163, 191n7, 206, 225, 262

economy xi, 2, 4, 6, 7, 9, 13, 16–20, 22, 23, 32, 36–40, 42, 46n5, 48n2648n27, 51, 57, 59, 60, 82, 83, 90–2, 97–9, 101–16, 116n1, 116n2, 116n3, 118n20, 118n23, 119n28, 119n30, 119n32, 119n33, 127, 137, 143, 145, 151, 163, 170, 173, 189, 190, 197, 200, 203, 213, 225, 246, 253, 255, 259, 261

egalitarian 104, 125, 207, 212

electorate 51–4, 56, 58, 235, 256

embedding 97

employee 37, 39, 66, 76, 92, 112–14, 138, 189, 191n3, 200, 260

employer 14, 39, 66, 67, 113–15, 130, 131, 133, 135–8, 252n22

enclosure 9, 19, 147–9

England 3, 15, 17, 45, 101, 131, 138, 147, 148, 156, 212, 214n6, 231, 254

English Defence League (EDL) 69, 176n48

Enlightenment 36, 37, 147, 151, 160, 161, 164, 165

environment/-al/-alist x, 15, 70, 83, 98, 143, 145, 147, 149, 151, 152, 155, 159, 161, 163, 192n30, 210, 218, 220, 229, 259

esteem 75, 119n33

estrangement estrangement

ethical/-ics 2, 3, 7, 18, 22, 25, 35, 37, 39, 46, 56, 60, 63–5, 67, 91,

93, 97, 98, 100, 103, 105, 106, 107, 108, 112, 113, 115, 119n31, 128, 154n6, 157, 164, 167, 173, 186–8, 192n27, 238, 253, 263

ethos 2, 27, 35, 39, 42, 44, 48n25, 91, 98, 104, 105, 108, 110, 114–16, 117n14, 243, 257, 258, 261

eudaimonia 33; *see also* flourishing

Europe/-an 2, 41, 44–6, 49n36, 55, 93, 106, 107, 112, 118n23, 121, 123, 124, 126–9, 130, 132, 135–9, 140n3, 204, 257, 258, 261

eurozone 107, 124

evangelical 5, 13, 172, 224

excellence 39, 98, 105, 113–16, 146, 261

Fabian 40, 70, 156

fair trade 42, 110

faith/-ful/-fulness 2, 6, 8, 10n2, 14, 16, 20, 22, 23, 45, 67, 74, 81, 83, 87, 90, 145, 151, 157, 160, 161, 163, 172, 174n2, 176n52, 177n59, 199, 200, 209, 228, 229, 231n1, 241, 256, 257, 259, 262, 263, 263n3

fall 2, 22

family 7, 10n2, 17, 23, 25, 33, 57–9, 64–7, 70, 73, 75, 76, 106, 124, 126, 144, 156, 157, 168, 169, 172, 173, 179, 196, 210–14, 225, 229, 235–52, 259, 262

festivity 32, 46

finance ix, 20, 36, 43, 89, 100, 102, 104, 110, 112–14, 117n14, 122, 210, 259, 262; *see also* City of London

fishing 145, 148, 149, 152, 153

flag 10n2, 56, 229

flourishing xi, 1, 2, 4, 6, 17, 28, 33, 35, 36, 39, 46, 82, 87, 89, 98, 106, 107, 109, 162, 179, 190, 224, 226, 229, 230, 241, 248, 254, 255, 258, 262; *see also eudaimonia*

food 37, 60, 74, 98, 102, 147, 149

forbearance 90, 97

fraternity 41, 65, 67, 110

free trade 42

freedom 1, 4, 28, 33, 34, 36, 37, 43, 65, 66, 93, 98, 100, 109, 111, 146, 148, 155, 156, 159, 160, 162, 167, 168, 180, 184–7, 190, 210, 211, 221, 225, 238, 239–47, 251n19, 255, 262

friendship 27, 33, 196, 230, 241

generosity x, 154, 245, 262

German/-y 16, 37, 42, 44, 82, 92, 98, 106, 107, 111, 118n20, 123–4, 198, 230, 261

gift/-exchange 20, 27, 32, 36, 46, 46n1, 72, 110, 112, 116, 119n33, 153, 160

globalisation 7, 21, 69, 88, 89, 99, 113, 121, 122, 125–6, 166, 221, 249, 262

good/-ness ix, x, 1, 2, 6–8, 13–26, 27–9, 31, 33–8, 42, 43, 45, 46, 48n21, 48n30, 51, 54, 57, 58, 60, 63, 65–8, 71, 73, 77, 83, 87–95, 98–101, 103–6, 108, 110–12, 114–15, 124, 134, 135, 137, 138, 145, 147, 151, 153, 155, 157, 160, 163, 166, 168, 170, 173, 174n3, 175n36, 179, 180, 183, 184, 186–90, 197, 199, 205, 217, 219–31, 235, 236, 238, 239, 244, 247, 249, 251n16, 253–5, 261–3

government 3, 16, 25, 28, 30, 32, 33, 35, 41, 42, 59, 64, 67–9, 76, 80, 92, 100–2, 108, 115–16, 122, 128, 132–3, 148, 150, 155, 156, 158, 159, 163, 168, 169, 192n33, 197, 205, 210–12, 219, 222, 223, 225, 227, 231, 239, 242, 246, 250n11, 257–60.

grace/-ful x, 21, 44, 132, 242

grassroots 69, 171, 196, 257

gratuitous/-ness 32, 110

Great Depression 1, 101, 102

greed/-y 1, 16, 21, 29, 36, 64, 89, 91, 92, 97, 101, 104, 206

hierarchy/-ical 31, 47n9, 69, 125, 180, 189

honest/-y 16, 59, 104, 161, 196, 198, 210, 236, 254

honour/-able/-ing 2, 5–8, 17, 19, 27, 31, 39, 41, 75, 98, 99, 104, 108, 115, 196–9, 227, 257, 261

hope/-ful xi, 3, 7, 89, 115, 144, 145, 150, 152, 153, 154n6, 161, 162, 166, 169, 171, 176n50, 177n58, 181, 196, 213, 228, 254

housing 57, 59, 60, 98, 130, 131, 133, 138, 158, 209, 212, 213, 258, 259

identity ix, 2, 7, 45, 58, 59, 87, 89, 90, 91, 123, 126, 128, 130, 144, 146, 149, 165, 166, 168, 171, 173, 174n3, 184, 186, 189n1, 192n25, 195, 221, 224, 226, 229, 230, 257

ideology/-ical 1, 6, 8, 9, 29, 33, 78, 99, 108, 122, 126, 152, 157–60, 163–6, 170, 173, 175n30, 203, 210, 221, 235, 237, 255 immigrant 58, 83, 102, 122, 126, 127, 129–36

immigration 30, 46n2, 56, 58, 63, 66, 67, 121, 126, 127, 129–39, 140n1, 140n5, 140n6, 140n7, 140n8, 140n11, 195, 206, 207, 209, 214n7, 254, 257, 262

imperial 43, 44, 126, 163

impersonal/-ism 6, 27, 30, 32, 36, 89, 118n22

incentive 13, 15, 16, 17, 21, 22, 33, 82, 97, 98, 101, 111, 113–15, 127, 138, 244, 261, 262

individual/-ism/-ist ix, x, 2, 6, 7, 16–18, 20, 21, 27, 29–36, 38, 63–6, 69, 70, 71, 73–7, 90, 92, 94, 97–9, 105, 109, 110, 115, 123, 128, 131, 135, 139, 144, 156, 167, 169, 170, 179, 182, 186, 189, 210–12, 220–2, 226, 228, 238, 240–2, 244–5, 247, 249, 254–6, 260, 262

industry 38, 104, 115, 136, 148, 150, 152, 154n5

Industrial Areas Foundation (IAF) 71, 73, 74

inequality 2, 23, 36, 87, 89, 90, 101–3, 106, 117n7, 117n12, 125, 134, 164, 205, 209, 211–13, 257, 260

interdependence 98, 123, 180, 245, 262

interest/-ed/-s 1, 2, 8, 13–26, 29, 30, 36, 38–40, 44, 57, 58, 63, 73, 74, 77, 80, 82, 83, 87, 89, 92–4, 98, 100, 104, 105, 107, 109, 110, 113–16, 122, 123, 124, 129, 130, 150, 166, 168, 173, 179, 184, 190, 206, 209, 211, 212, 217, 219–28, 230, 232n8, 238, 240, 242, 243, 245, 246, 249, 250n5, 251n19, 254, 255, 257, 259–63

intermediary institutions 115, 261

interpersonal 2, 88, 89, 93, 95, 100, 105, 106, 108, 118n22, 254, 261

'invisible hand' 34, 89

Italy/-ian 37, 38, 40, 42, 111, 112, 261

Jerusalem 57, 177n60

justice 5, 15, 18–20, 23, 27, 32, 39, 66, 69, 87, 90, 91, 93–5, 100, 106, 114, 118n22, 118n27, 119n31, 126, 155, 156, 162, 168, 169, 176n46, 181, 187, 188, 191n18, 211, 212, 240, 241, 245, 249, 255, 259, 261, 262

Keynesian/-ism 20, 98, 104, 105, 112, 117n8, 163

Laborem Exercens 22

laissez-faire 5, 9, 105, 163, 238, 253

language ix, 24, 65, 66, 88, 122, 148, 158, 161, 175n35, 228, 229, 232n10, 237, 239, 244, 248, 249, 262

leadership 9, 26, 27, 42, 43, 47n8, 51, 57–9, 72, 81, 156, 197, 200, 254–5

left (political stance) 4, 6, 7, 30–5, 47n8, 47n9, 47n13, 51, 55, 60, 64, 70, 78, 89, 90, 97, 101, 103, 124–6, 128, 140n3, 155, 157, 165, 166, 168, 169–73, 175n24, 177n56, 177n57, 177n58, 196, 199, 203–13, 213n1, 214n5, 214n8, 229, 232n10, 235–40, 243, 246, 248, 249, 250n4,

251n13, 251n15, 251n19, 252n24, 261

legitimacy 1, 15, 80, 93, 123, 124, 157, 161, 186, 208, 209, 223

liberalisation 1, 36, 102, 125, 168, 205

liberal/-ism 2, 4, 5–7, 10n7, 13, 17, 27–38, 42, 45, 46n4, 47n13, 48n20, 48n28, 48n31, 63, 65, 69, 70, 80, 82, 83, 87–92, 95, 97–9, 102, 104, 105–8, 111–13, 118n22, 119n32, 122, 124, 125–8, 131, 146, 150, 156, 157, 160, 161, 166–73, 174n3, 175n24, 176n46, 176n49, 177n57, 180, 183, 195, 196, 203, 205, 206, 208–12, 219, 223–7, 230, 232n8, 236, 238, 239, 240, 246–9, 250n5, 251n20, 253–5, 260–2

Liberal Democrat 52, 53

Liberty 14, 30, 36, 65, 168, 195, 219, 237, 238, 240, 243, 248, 249, 251n19; *see also* freedom

'living wage' 22, 23, 68, 75–7, 113–14, 119n31, 198, 259, 260

local/-ity x, xi, 2, 8, 16, 19, 21, 24–6, 30, 41–5, 48n31, 65, 68–72, 78, 83, 87, 88, 91, 93, 95, 111, 114, 124, 130, 133–6, 138, 149, 171, 172, 196–200, 207, 210, 218, 225, 228–30, 255, 257–60

London Citizens/CitizensUK 22, 171, 197, 199, 200, 224, 231n1, 256

loyal/-ty 9, 16, 43, 55–7, 60, 79, 123, 217, 222, 226–8, 230, 237, 246, 263

Magna Carta 4, 14

managerial/-ism 20, 93, 146, 195, 258, 259

manufacturing 41, 60, 101, 106, 114, 191n12, 197, 258

marginal/-ist/-ism 32–4, 36, 105, 219

Marxism/-ist 19, 40, 57, 106, 166, 175n26, 206, 243

materialism/-ist 3, 29, 95, 146, 151

meaningful/-fulness 7, 18, 123, 128, 145, 150, 153, 165, 179–92, 200, 221, 224, 226, 237, 248, 255, 259

meaningless/-ness 161, 174n6, 179, 180, 235, 255

means-testing 39, 59, 258, 259

mediation 17, 20

metropolitan 5, 7, 169, 212, 243

minimum wage 76, 77, 135, 155, 198

'mixed constitution' 6, 257

mobilise(r) 72, 79, 123

monarchy 6

monetarist/-ism 105, 112

monopoly 102, 110, 114, 191n12, 219

moral/-ity x, 2, 3, 4, 6, 18, 28, 33, 34, 51, 59, 60, 91, 95, 97–102, 104, 106, 107, 109, 112, 116n1, 125, 126, 144–7, 152, 158, 164, 167, 168, 171, 174n3, 174n5, 175n33, 182, 185, 187, 190, 191n22, 204, 205, 209–12, 219, 226, 229, 231, 235, 236, 239–42, 244, 248, 249, 259, 261

mortgage 20, 39, 100, 113, 260

multicultural/-ism 31, 168, 206, 224, 226

multinational 126

mutual/-ism/-ity 1, 4–7, 9, 15, 18, 20, 21, 23, 25, 28, 31, 32, 34,

39, 41, 42, 44, 48n31, 63–6, 81,
83, 87, 91–4, 98, 99, 101, 105,
109, 110, 112, 115, 118n22,
170, 180, 189, 196, 210, 219,
222, 223, 228–30, 236, 239,
240, 242, 248, 254, 255, 258–
62
myth ix, x, 108, 131, 146, 157, 158,
160, 170

narrative 2, 90, 92, 94, 99, 118n21,
125, 144, 160–3, 167, 170, 171,
181, 226, 245, 246, 249,
251n19, 261
nation state 43, 44, 89, 121–9, 224,
228
neighbour/-hood 38, 63–70, 77, 90,
97, 109, 124, 130, 229, 230
neighbourliness 94, 196
neoclassical 20, 47n17, 87, 88, 105
neo-liberal/-ism 31, 42, 82, 87, 88,
92, 98, 104–6, 111, 113, 146,
150, 156, 161, 166, 168, 173,
176n46, 180, 226
New Labour 7, 8, 16, 55, 56, 69,
83, 164, 166, 169, 175n35,
175n37, 176n53, 206, 211, 212,
248, 249, 256
New Left 30, 205, 206, 236–40,
243, 251n19
NHS 64, 65, 259
nostalgia/-ic 6, 7, 70, 165, 213, 255

obligation 5, 6, 73, 95, 99, 100, 105,
125, 126, 128, 171, 192n31,
199, 200, 204, 229, 239, 241–2,
245, 247–8, 255, 262
Office of National Statistics (ONS)
129
Old Labour 8, 171, 256
oligarchic/-y 4, 44, 223

One Nation 3, 27, 35, 41, 43, 69,
89, 99
ordo-liberalism 98, 106–8
organise(r) 18, 21, 22, 31, 34, 72–5,
76, 80, 81, 93, 146, 180–5, 188,
219, 222, 227, 229, 257, 258,
261

paradox/-ical ix, 4, 10n3, 14, 18,
26, 27, 35, 45, 99, 102, 108,
116, 167, 168, 205, 206, 212,
213, 219, 224, 232n10, 250n2,
252n25, 254, 256
Parliament/-ary 6, 24, 42, 60, 80,
92, 114, 123, 196, 200, 231,
254, 257
participation xi, 7, 14, 16, 26, 37,
78, 79, 93, 95, 108, 111, 182,
184, 224, 254–7, 259–61
participatory 32, 94, 258–9
pessimism/-istic 6, 30, 94, 176n50
phronesis 28, 218
pietas 229–30
place 2, 3, 5, 8, 17, 19, 21, 23, 24,
29, 41, 74, 81, 110, 122, 127,
130, 134, 135, 137, 144, 145,
149–52, 155, 179, 196, 208,
218, 221, 222, 224–30, 236,
241, 247–8, 254, 255, 258, 259
political economy 13, 23, 38, 40,
46n5, 82, 83, 97, 106, 112,
116n3, 119n30, 151, 170, 173,
189, 190, 253
polity 2, 14, 17, 93, 100, 108, 114,
261
post-liberal/-ism 6, 27, 28, 48n28,
48n31, 69, 83, 112, 119n32,
255, 260, 262
poverty 16, 59, 67, 68, 76, 88, 158,
180, 199, 211, 237, 243, 250n7,
251n15

power 2, 3, 8, 13–19, 21–4, 30–2, 34, 36, 37, 42, 45, 49n37, 68, 69, 73, 75, 77, 78, 81, 82, 87, 89, 92, 93, 97, 98, 101, 104, 105, 111, 121–5, 131, 137, 138, 145–7, 151, 153, 154, 157, 161, 162, 166, 168, 175n18, 180, 181, 183, 184, 186, 188–90, 196–7, 199, 209, 218–20, 227–9, 231, 232n8, 232n10, 239–41, 254–8, 262

practice 5, 7, 8, 14, 17–19, 21, 23, 25, 31–3, 39, 40, 42, 46, 48n30, 67, 90, 91, 98, 110, 111, 115, 183–8, 217–22, 224, 227–30, 254–6, 259, 261, 262

precariat 102

pre-distribution 32

pride 31, 34, 39, 41, 57, 91, 171

principle 2, 7, 17, 27, 38, 66, 82, 90, 91, 94, 97, 98, 108, 110, 125, 139, 160, 164, 218, 238, 240, 253–63

privatisation 2, 77, 102, 115, 148, 149, 210

progress/-ive 4, 6, 9, 13, 18, 47n14, 51, 70, 80, 105, 124, 155–77, 195, 197, 206, 212, 213, 224, 237, 239, 240, 243, 246

prosperity 2, 7, 18, 20, 59, 92, 100, 113, 115, 117n14, 131, 160, 163, 262

prudence 93, 198

public good ix, 28, 101, 189; *see also* common good

public service(s) ix, 41, 57, 94, 116, 130, 155, 170, 197, 207, 250n10

purpose 7, 30, 35, 39, 41, 46, 79, 81, 88, 93, 95, 98, 104, 107, 111–12, 114, 117n14, 143, 150, 152, 167, 169–70, 173, 180, 182, 183, 185, 189, 192n32, 207, 227, 256

radical/-ism 4–6, 16, 18, 32, 73, 83, 103, 108, 116, 117n11, 125, 127, 150, 153, 154n6, 155, 165–6, 170, 173, 176n37, 184, 195–6, 201, 208, 218–19, 232n4, 232n10, 237, 245, 249, 253–5, 263n2

rationalist/-ism 2, 3, 9, 14, 20, 21, 34, 40, 97, 107, 160, 239

reactionary 6, 7, 13, 176n48, 218, 255

reciprocity 2, 16–19, 21, 23, 27, 31, 39, 40, 46, 91, 97, 98, 100, 108, 118n22, 170, 222, 226, 241, 248, 255, 258

recognition 2, 5–7, 13, 25, 27, 31, 39, 91, 98, 104, 110, 115, 116, 128, 184–6, 190, 217, 224, 228, 254

reconciliation 13, 143, 150, 152

redemption 2, 13, 21

redistribution 16, 17, 32, 41, 104, 123, 207

Reformation 14

region/-al 15, 16, 19, 41, 42, 44, 78, 82, 83, 94, 106, 113, 114, 123, 124, 133, 198, 247, 254–5, 258

relational/-ity 2, 21, 31–3, 81–2, 90–1, 93, 109, 111, 113, 115, 200, 220–1, 226, 228, 238–42, 244, 257

relativism 166–8, 170, 173, 236, 240–1

religion 30, 46, 90, 91, 139, 143–5, 157, 160, 162–3, 169, 171, 173,

174n10, 175n18, 175n33, 179, 227–9

renewal 4, 5, 7, 8, 9, 14, 17, 41, 63, 80, 82, 83, 171, 173, 256, 258, 263

representation 66, 68, 99, 106, 189, 196, 198, 219, 255, 256, 259, 261

Rerum Novarum 21, 22, 103, 110

responsibility ix, 2, 14, 16–19, 21, 23, 24, 47n8, 63, 64, 66, 78, 81, 83, 91, 93, 94, 100, 110, 145, 156, 167, 172, 186–8, 192n31, 196, 199, 200, 219, 225, 239, 240, 247

reward 2, 47n14, 54, 56, 59, 91, 92, 94, 97–9, 102, 104, 106–8, 111, 115–16, 125, 127, 129, 204, 255, 261, 262

Rhineland model 92

right (political stance) 4, 6, 31, 32–4, 66, 69, 78, 101, 117n11, 168, 176n46, 199, 203, 206, 209, 210, 213, 236, 243, 263n2

riots 6, 63, 64, 174n4, 151n15, 261

risk 2, 21, 32, 39, 82, 91, 92, 94, 98, 102, 104, 112, 113, 115, 117n9, 152, 180, 198, 260

Romantic/-ism 2–5, 29, 44, 144, 166, 239, 253

root/-edness 87, 89, 90, 121, 129, 165, 181, 197, 247, 255

sacrifice 24, 30, 82, 123, 146, 164, 167, 176n43, 206

Scottish National Party (SNP) 2, 45, 52

secular/-isation/-ism 29, 43, 46, 60, 83, 157, 160, 161, 163, 165, 171, 172, 227, 228

self-government 254, 255, 258

self-interest 1, 36, 38, 73, 74, 77, 105, 109, 115, 116, 173, 211, 226, 232n8, 238, 242, 249

self-organisation 47n8, 196, 261

shame 83, 205, 210

skill 16, 17, 19–21, 25, 33, 41, 53–5, 82, 83, 102, 129–30, 132–6, 138, 149, 151, 152, 180, 198, 200, 207, 218, 260, 262

small- and medium-sized Enterprise (SME) 105, 106

social democracy/-tic 2, 3, 16, 137, 203, 112, 226

socialist/-ism 5, 6, 31, 34, 35, 37, 39–41, 47n13, 47n15, 47n16, 47n32, 64, 70, 82, 139, 156, 172, 174n2, 191n9, 192n34, 203, 206, 207, 238, 241, 245

'social animal' 35

social care 136

social market economy 106, 107, 118n20

social mobility 134, 247

social security 48n31, 59, 248, 258–9

solidarity x, 2, 6, 14, 17, 18, 19, 24, 26, 27, 28, 30, 40, 46n3, 66, 68, 81, 92, 11, 112, 118n19, 122, 124, 157, 169–72, 176n47, 179, 180, 230, 254–5

'something-for-nothing' 258

soul 10n6, 200, 236

soulless 95, 105

sovereign/-ty 6, 18, 42, 92, 107, 121, 123, 150, 224, 226, 239, 244, 245

stakeholder 91, 113, 114

statism/-ist 18, 32–4, 37–8, 44, 111, 211, 217, 240, 242, 258 status 8, 17–19, 24–6, 37, 55, 111, 116, 128, 138, 156, 163, 186, 197, 207, 225, 228, 232n10, 246, 251n13, 255, 261–2

subsidiarity 16, 18–20, 24, 42, 78, 82, 94, 111, 171, 254–5, 258

sympathy 97

Tory/-ism 4, 5, 29, 35, 41, 53, 59, 60, 64, 176n46, 206, 209–12, 214n5, 239, 250n4

trade union 8, 65, 58, 70, 72, 79–83, 114, 115, 230, 256, 263

tradition/-al 1–9, 10n3, 13–19, 21, 23–5, 27–8, 30, 37, 41, 45, 47n14, 58, 59, 69, 70, 82, 87, 88, 90–2, 98–100, 103, 106, 108, 109–12, 116, 116n1, 116n3, 143, 145, 146, 149, 151–3, 158, 160, 162–3, 165–8, 170–3, 179, 195–7, 199–201, 206, 210, 213, 218, 224, 225, 229, 232n4, 232n10, 236–40, 242–9, 250n2, 250n11, 252n25, 253–6, 261

transaction(al) 2, 4–6, 8, 32, 36, 39, 91, 97, 222, 254

transformation/-ive 2–5, 7–9, 10n5, 13, 22, 25, 79, 83, 88, 99, 112–13, 116, 116n2, 118n23, 169, 254–8, 261

Treasury 100, 132, 135, 204

trust x, 9, 14, 17, 19, 21, 24, 30, 31, 36, 37, 39, 63, 64, 66, 68, 72, 74, 78, 99, 100, 110, 113, 150, 152, 157, 179, 199, 210–12, 217, 221–4, 226, 228, 259, 262

Tudor 14

tyranny 14, 45, 146, 151, 161, 165, 167, 168, 223

underclass 156, 164, 174n3

United Kingdom Independence Party (UKIP) 2, 45, 51, 55, 83, 93, 103, 254

usury 22, 25, 110, 111

utilitarian/-ism 2, 4, 6, 22, 34, 38, 40, 97, 105, 107, 247, 253

utopia/-ian 6, 8, 18, 47n18, 98, 99, 160, 161, 162, 165, 174n10, 175n36, 176n40, 176n42, 176n45, 212

vice 1, 13, 15–17, 20, 23, 29, 97, 99, 101, 261, 262

Victorian/-ism 4, 174n5

virtue/virtuous 1–7, 9, 13–18, 21, 22, 27–9, 35, 39, 41, 45, 48n28, 92, 97, 99, 104, 107, 111–16, 117n14, 119n30, 119n32, 145, 146, 149, 151, 167, 174n5, 176n49, 190, 211–12, 217, 222, 226, 229, 231, 238, 249, 253–6, 259, 260–2

vocation/-al 2–4, 9, 13–14, 16–19, 21, 23–5, 39, 41, 82, 87, 91, 100, 106, 110, 113, 114, 197, 198, 200, 227, 231, 254, 260, 262

volunteering 16

wage 16, 17, 22, 23, 34, 39, 40, 67, 68, 75–7, 91, 98, 101, 102–4, 106, 110–14, 119n31, 130, 131, 133–8, 140n8, 140n9, 155, 1998, 207, 213, 245, 259, 260

welfare 7, 13, 17, 19, 20, 23, 27, 33, 39, 48n31, 54, 56, 59, 64, 69, 101, 107, 117n10, 122, 124, 132, 133, 135, 137, 157, 175n35, 185, 187, 192n32, 196, 199, 200, 238, 240–1, 244–8,

250n6, 250n10, 255, 258–9, 262

Westminster 13, 14, 93, 195, 209, 231, 254

Whitehall 69, 138, 184

workforce 23, 25, 64, 66, 82, 83, 91, 132, 135

working class 3–5, 51, 53, 55, 56–9, 83, 165, 169, 171, 174n3, 206, 208–10, 212, 214n6